MIDNIGHT ASSASSIN

Anaïs Bocher

"I never lose"
Either I win or
I learn"

Mandela

A BUR OAK BOOK

Patricia L. Bryan & Thomas Wolf

MIDNIGHT ASSASSIN

A MURDER IN AMERICA'S HEARTLAND

☾

UNIVERSITY OF IOWA PRESS, IOWA CITY

University of Iowa Press, Iowa City 52242
www.uiowapress.org

Originally published in hardback by Algonquin Books of Chapel Hill

Printed in the United States of America
Design by Rebecca Giménez

The University of Iowa Press is a member of Green Press Initiative and is committed to preserving natural resources.
Printed on acid-free paper

Library of Congress Cataloging-in-Publication Data
Bryan, Patricia L., 1951–
Midnight assassin: a murder in America's heartland /
by Patricia L. Bryan and Thomas Wolf.—1st paperback edition.
p. cm.
Originally published: Chapel Hill, N.C.: Algonquin Books, 2005.
Includes bibliographical references.
ISBN-13: 978-1-58729-605-5 (paper)
ISBN-10: 1-58729-605-5 (paper)
1. Hossack, Margaret, 1843–1916. 2. Murder—Iowa. 3. Trials (Murder)—Iowa. 4. Murder—Press coverage—Iowa. 5. Glaspell, Susan, 1876–1948. I. Wolf, Thomas, 1947–. II. Title.
HV6533.I8B79 2007
364.152'3092—dc22 2007008284

Dedicated to

DORIS P. BRYAN

JOHN K. BRYAN

JEANNETTE H. WOLF

And in Memory of

IRVIN S. WOLF

(1914–2002)

TO THE READER

In writing this book, we have been scrupulous in staying true to the historical facts. None of the characters are invented. All of the scenes are based on primary sources—newspaper reports, legal records, transcripts of legal proceedings, local histories, interviews, memoirs—and we have quoted from these materials throughout the text.

When accounts of specific incidents differed, we presented both versions or the one that seemed most plausible based on the available facts. In quoted passages, we have occasionally made minor changes in spelling, punctuation, or wording for the sake of consistency or readability, which do not affect the original meaning of the text.

To the extent possible, we have tried to keep our authorial perspective in the background. The reader will find information about our sources in the Notes. ☾

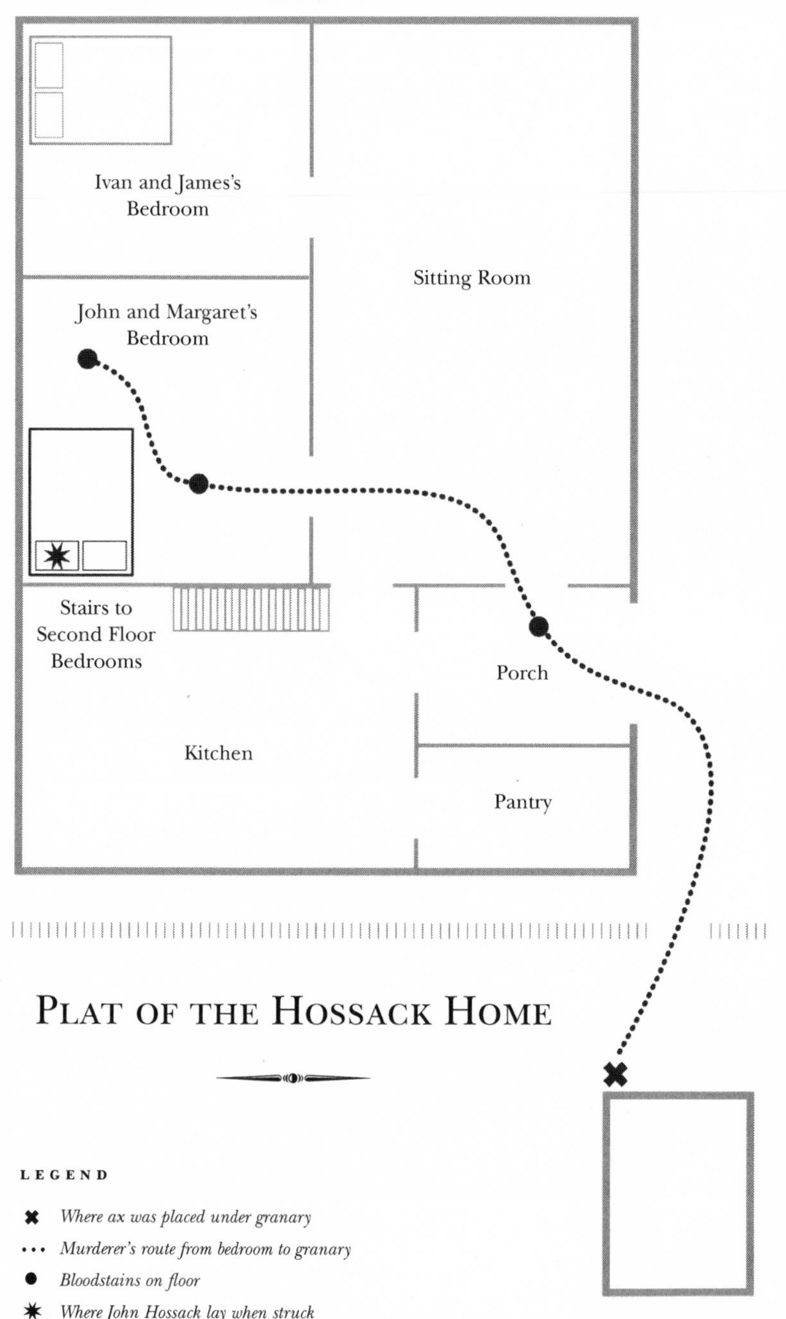
Ivan and James's
Bedroom
Sitting Room
John and Margaret's
Bedroom
Stairs to
Second Floor
Bedrooms
Porch
Kitchen
Pantry
PLAT OF THE HOSSACK HOME
LEGEND
✖ Where ax was placed under granary
• • • Murderer's route from bedroom to granary
● Bloodstains on floor
✷ Where John Hossack lay when struck

INTRODUCTION

AROUND MIDNIGHT ON A moonlit night in early December 1900, a prosperous and well-respected Iowa farmer named John Hossack was attacked and mortally wounded as he slept in his bed. The assailant struck the victim in the head with either an ax or a hatchet. Hossack lived through the night, partly conscious but unable to speak clearly. He died the next morning, about ten hours after the attack. Hossack was fifty-nine years old.

Hossack and his wife, Margaret, had nine children, including five, ranging in age from thirteen to twenty-six, who were in the house at the time of the assault. Margaret Hossack told investigators that she had been asleep beside her husband when an unidentified intruder struck the fatal blows. But reports soon surfaced that Hossack had abused and threatened his family, and for years his wife had gone to the neighbors to complain of his behavior. Warren County legal authorities quickly decided that Hossack's alleged mistreatment of his family constituted a motive for murder and fixed their attention on the victim's wife. Four days after the murder, as she was leaving her husband's burial, Margaret Hossack was arrested and charged with the crime.

In fact, other suspects abounded. Evidence that the family dog had been drugged on the night of the crime suggested premeditation on the part of an outsider. All of the Hossack children had reason to fear and resent their father. Several neighbors had intervened in the family disputes, and at least two of them had discussed the possibility of having Hossack committed to an insane asylum. A neighbor on an adjacent farm had a history of quarrels with Hossack. Rumors hinted at the possibility that Hossack might have had improper relations with another woman. A mysterious horseman was seen riding away from the Hossack property shortly after the attacks.

At the coroner's inquest, most of the Hossacks and their neighbors were tight-lipped about their knowledge of the turbulent family history. In 1900, communities largely ignored or tolerated domestic abuse, and no significant public discourse on the issue existed. A code of discreet silence prevailed. Conflict between a man and his family was deemed a private matter, something best forgotten and not spoken about, even under oath. As one witness testified, "I do not tax my memory with family quarrels."

Like the Lizzie Borden case in Fall River, Massachusetts, in 1892, the tragedy and subsequent legal proceedings against Margaret Hossack divided, horrified, and mesmerized the community. The family hired William H. Berry, a distinguished lawyer and former state senator, to defend the accused. Berry's adversary was George Clammer, a young and ambitious county attorney, who asked that Margaret Hossack be convicted of first-degree murder and sentenced to death. Overflowing crowds packed the courthouse to watch the legal drama.

Because of the sensational nature of the crime and the prominence of the victim, the murder of John Hossack attracted widespread attention in the press. More than a dozen newspapers, including some from as far away as Chicago, covered the story. One of the first journalists on the scene was Susan Glaspell, a twenty-four-year-old reporter for the *Des Moines Daily News*. From December 1900 until April 1901, she wrote more than twenty articles on the case. Although Glaspell had little exposure to criminal law, she initially approached the case like a detective; she personally investigated the murder, visiting the Hossack farmhouse, interviewing the attorneys, and studying the inquest testimony. Then her focus shifted to the woman accused of the crime. As Glaspell struggled to understand and describe Margaret Hossack, her accounts alternated between those that portrayed

Margaret Hossack as maternal and frail—anxious to see her family; tired and worn by the course of events—and those that depicted her as lacking in the typical emotional and feminine traits—not hysterical, but emotionless and dry-eyed; not weak, but determined and willful; not soft-featured, but square-jawed and hard.

The case made an indelible impression on Glaspell. More than fifteen years later, writing in a room that faced the ocean on the tip of Cape Cod, the haunting image of Margaret Hossack's kitchen came rushing back to Glaspell. In a span of ten days, Glaspell composed a one-act play, *Trifles,* the story of an inquiry into the murder of a taciturn and penurious Midwestern farmer, whose wife is charged with killing him in his sleep. A year later, Glaspell reworked the material into a short story titled "A Jury of Her Peers." Both works have found a place in the canon of twentieth-century American literature.

OUR INVESTIGATION BEGAN in a musty storage room in the Madison County courthouse in Winterset, Iowa, the same building where Margaret Hossack's legal trials had officially ended. A clerk showed us a metal drawer with a pink label on it. The only word on the label was HOSSACK. In the drawer, tied in a red ribbon, was a sheaf of brittle papers, yellowed and dried, and more than ninety years old. Included in the bundle were the typed transcript of the coroner's inquest into the death of John Hossack and the original handwritten summaries of testimony before the Warren County Grand Jury. In all, there were hundreds of pages of legal documents, including verbatim statements from the witnesses.

That discovery became the backbone of our inquiry. Like Glaspell, at first we thought we might, with patient sleuthing, solve the mystery of who killed John Hossack. We followed the footprints of the story along a crooked trail, searching the archives of county courthouses, visiting libraries and historical societies, reading articles about the case on microfilm, talking to descendants of people who were involved in the case, and interviewing contemporary lawyers and residents of the county. We found local histories, plat maps, probate records, marriage and death certificates. We turned the pages of old newspapers that threatened to crumble to dust on our fingertips.

A confluence of stories emerged. As we learned more, our interest shifted. We recognized that we were writing about a pivotal moment in the history of the Midwest. It was a time when notions about justice, law, and the roles of men and women in society were in transition. Each hypothesis we developed about the murder became a tantalizing path to follow with our imaginations, but the more compelling aspect of the case was how the story had been told and understood through time—in the press, in the courtroom, and in the community. We realized that stories of the Hossack murder continue to ripple through Warren County as generations pass down what they know about the case to their descendants—contemporary tales pieced together by conjecture, secrets, rumor, old feuds, and odd facts.

In 1998 we ran an advertisement in the *Record-Herald and Indianola Tribune* with a bold headline—WHO KILLED JOHN HOSSACK?—asking for information about the murder. We visited Warren County, a patchwork quilt of orderly farm fields, land sectioned today just as it was in 1849 when the county was first surveyed. Other than Indianola, a bucolic and peaceful town of 12,000 citizens and simple two-story clapboard houses on tree-lined streets, there are no towns of significant size in the county. Farmhouses dot the countryside, about a mile apart, not unlike the way the population was dispersed in 1900. Except for improved roads, power lines, modern vehicles, and an occasional satellite dish, the rural landscape looks just about the same as it did a century ago.

Most of the respondents to our advertisement indicated a willingness to share their recollections and theories, believing as the late Robert Moore, a retired auctioneer, stated, "that the truth should come out." But not everyone was pleased with our curiosity. One woman asked if we were "trying to clear somebody's name," fearful that our investigation might point a finger of guilt at a person whose descendants still lived in the area. Some residents expressed reluctance to talk about their memories, suggesting that old ghosts should not be disturbed.

We interviewed a local attorney named Stephen Hall, whose offices were located just a half block east from the courthouse in a one-story redbrick building. Tall and stooped, Hall greeted us in the waiting room and led us to his small office. He warned us that we might be in physical danger if we pursued our investigation and edged too close to the truth. Hall claimed to know a story with direct bearing on Margaret Hossack's guilt or innocence, a tale that had never been told. But he cited the lawyer's obligation not to reveal the substance of private conversations with clients or other attorneys. What he had been told about the Hossack murder was "lawyer to lawyer," as he put it. Hall, like the witnesses at the coroner's inquest into the death of John Hossack almost a century before, was unwilling to divulge all he knew. He said he didn't want to reopen the wounds of old cases. Before we left his office, he leaned across his desk and smiled impishly. His eyes twinkled behind large glasses. In a low, conspiratorial voice, he said, "I can't stop you from finding out anything you can find out. I just can't help you." ☾

WE CREATED OUR narrative from the recollections and voices of the men and women who confronted the issues of this case over a century ago. As we wrote about the Hossack family, we inevitably found ourselves thinking about broader topics: the ways that stories are told in communities and courtrooms and by the media; the assumptions about behavior and social roles that affect not only these stories but also the decisions that are made under the law; the interactions among neighbors and their obligations to one another; and the complexity of emotions, motivations, and loyalties that play into family relationships, often making them impossible for an outsider to reconstruct or ever fully comprehend.

Ultimately, the purpose of our inquiry was not to solve the murder of John Hossack. Our goal was to write a book that allows readers to form their own opinions about the crime and its consequences.

This is a true story, consistent with all the known facts. ☾

MIDNIGHT ASSASSIN

☾

PROLOGUE

ON A BRIGHT FALL day in October 1867, a young man of Scottish ancestry stood on the crest of a small Iowa hill. To the west and north, the land rolled like a calm earthen sea all the way to the horizon. Clumps of black walnut, elm, and white hickory punctuated the landscape, red and gold leaves clinging fiercely to their branches. A rough dirt road bordered the property on the east, and beyond the road a farmer's open field lay covered with thick-rooted prairie grasses that grew as high as a horse's back and swished gently in the breeze. To the south, the land dipped steeply toward the alluvial soil of the creek bottom, where cottonwoods sagged protectively over the stream.

The young man's name was John Hossack. This land would soon be his. He had made an agreement with John and Indiana Hollis, the owners, to purchase 120 acres for the price of $480. As he crouched to touch the rich black dirt—deposited by glaciers, groomed by time and weather—he felt in his fingertips the tangible proof of his good fortune.

He would build a sturdy house on this very spot, the highest point on his land. He would take a wife and raise a large family, including sons who could help him on the farm and take over its responsibilities as he aged. Around the house he would build a barn, a granary, a chicken house. In springtime he would watch with pleasure as his fields turned green and golden with crops of corn and wheat. He would own pigs and cows and horses. He would earn the respect of his neighbors and a place in the community.

Hossack was a man of modest height, about five feet eight inches tall. He was strong across the shoulders, powerfully built, proud and industrious. As he stood and let his gaze roam from one corner of the land to another, he let out a deep exhalation, taking comfort in the great emptiness of his surroundings. He would build his life on this spot. ☾

1.

PROMINENT FARMER ROBBED AND KILLED.

SUPPOSED THE BURGLARS ASSAULTED FARMER HOSSACK—CORONER HOLDING AN INVESTIGATION TODAY.

INDIANOLA, DEC. 3.—(Special.)—A foul murder was committed Saturday night near Medford, fifteen miles southwest of Indianola. A farmer named Hossack was struck over the head and killed by unknown parties, at his home a few miles out from Medford.

The assault was probably committed by burglars, though of this the officers are not yet sure. Sheriff Lew Hodson and Dr. Harry Dale, coroner, went to the place Sunday, and subpoenaed a jury which was called to meet this morning for an inquest. Mr. Hossack was an early settler, a prominent farmer, highly respected. He was about 60 years of age and leaves a wife and large family.—SUSAN GLASPELL, in the *Des Moines Daily News*, December 3, 1900, two days after the attack on John Hossack

ON THE LAST day of his life, John Hossack rose before daybreak and woke his youngest son, Ivan. The boy pushed back his quilt and rubbed the sleep from his eyes. Hossack urged him to hurry. He wanted Ivan to come with him to the coal bank, an exposed vein of soft coal located a few miles to the east of their family farm.

The two ate breakfast in the kitchen. When they finished, they put on heavy coats and went outside to get the wagon ready. It was just about 8 A.M.

No longer the robust young man he had been in 1867 when he purchased his farm in Warren County, Iowa, Hossack was now fifty-nine years old. He had his share of ailments—heart trouble, stomach problems, and what some called "nerves"—but he was a solid 160 pounds and physically fit for his age, still capable of handling livestock and working alongside his sons in the fields. Years of strenuous labor had claimed some of his stamina, but he had never stopped believing that hard work had its rewards. He raised corn, longhorn cattle, and red hogs, devoting most of his time and physical energy to the crops and animals. He kept a close eye on his fences, buildings, and tools, which required constant attention and frequent repair. As Hossack knew, the farmer who abused his property or animals, whether through neglect or incompetence, lost not only the potential profit from his labor but also the respect of his peers.

Hossack nurtured a deep love for his land, prime Iowa farmland that he had tended for more than three decades, and he was proud of his reputation in the community as a conscientious landowner and smart businessman. Known for being outspoken, Hossack held firm convictions, and as a long-time subscriber to the local newspapers, he was well informed on the issues of the day. In the summer of 1898 he was persuaded to run for the Republican Party nomination for county treasurer. He came within two votes of securing the post at the county convention, losing to the candidate who went on to victory in the general election. Hossack took the loss in stride, remarking to a friend that his opponent was a good man, and adding, "I've got two hundred acres of good land out here in the county, so I don't see but what it's all right."

It was Saturday, the first of December, just two days after Thanksgiving. That morning Hossack wasn't feeling well, and he feared a storm might be approaching. The weather had turned cold and gray, with the temperature hovering near freezing. It wouldn't be long before the full force of winter pressed down on the farm like a heavy weight. Already the days had shortened to the point where most of the evening chores were done in the dark. The last of the leaves had blown off the trees, and the fields had long since turned brown. From a distance the barn and buildings and animals appeared ghostly in the gray-white light of early winter. Soon snow would come—a foot deep at first, then two feet and more—and the prairie winds would whip across the frozen land like a punishment. The cold and snow would last for months, keeping the family mostly inside, crowded around the coal stove in the sitting room.

Hossack looked up at the sky. He snapped the reins and the wagon rattled down the road. ☾

IVAN HAD JUST turned thirteen. As the youngest in a family of nine children, he tended to be a silent observer who kept his thoughts to himself. The crucial dynamics of family interaction had been established long before his birth.

He didn't want to disturb his father's peace of mind. His father had been in good spirits recently, but Ivan knew how quickly his mood could change. There was a long history of conflict in the family. His father was prone to sudden and unpredictable bursts of rage, when a deep, black anger boiled out of him. His bad temper was easily triggered by Ivan's mother and older siblings, especially Johnnie; his eyes would turn wild, with a strange and detached look that served as a warning.

One of the worst quarrels had occurred almost exactly a year before, on Thanksgiving Day, 1899. Furious, John Hossack had ordered his wife to go upstairs and stay out of his sight. She later secretly left the house on foot, walking to a neighbor's house in the rain, and came home the next evening in a buggy with Ivan's oldest sister, Annie, and her husband, Ev Henry. John Hossack was incensed that his wife had spent the night with the Henrys, and he shook his fist at his son-in-law, shouting to get off his property and never return. Henry drove away, leaving the women at the house. A few minutes later, two of Ivan's father's friends, Mr. Johnston and Mr. Keller, appeared at the house and gathered everyone in the sitting room. Johnston and Keller knew what had happened, and they urged the family to try to live together more peaceably. Then the men took the children into the kitchen and spoke to them separately, instructing them to be more respectful of their father and to obey his wishes. Before leaving, both Johnston and Keller told the children and their mother that they must stop talking to the neighbors about their troubles. Domestic disputes were private matters and should be settled without help from outsiders.

The visit from the neighbors brought a calm to the household, and the past year had been more peaceful. John Hossack, regretting his harsh words to Ev Henry, repaired his relationship with his son-in-law. In the spring, two of Ivan's siblings moved away from home. Johnnie—at twenty-two the oldest of the boys at home—went to live a few miles away at Alger Truitt's farm, working there as a hired hand. For Johnnie, who had often chafed under the supervision of his father, it was a welcome change, though he still visited his family on weekends. In late March, Ivan's sister Louie married Alger Truitt's stepson, Joe Kemp, in a fancy wedding held at the Hossack farm. Kemp wore a formal black suit, and Louie was attired in a white cassimere dress trimmed in silk. More than sixty people from the neighborhood attended the ceremony and the reception that followed.

With Johnnie gone that spring, Ivan, Will, and Jimmie, who were still living at home, had more to do. They tended the animals in the barn, feeding them and shoveling manure. When the spring rains let up the boys helped with the planting. By July the corn was taller than Ivan. In mid-August a fierce hailstorm dumped nearly five inches of rain on the county, ruining the crops at many farms. Luckily, the Hossack fields escaped much of the damage, though the winds had been violent and the barn lot had turned into a muddy pond.

The family had celebrated their good harvest with a Thanksgiving party. Will slaughtered the turkey on Wednesday night, and the smell of the roasting bird greeted guests the next day. More than two dozen friends and family members, including the Truitts, the Henrys, the Kemps (Louie now eight months pregnant), and Johnnie and his new girlfriend, had crowded into the house for the feast. John Hossack was in an unusually good mood during the festivities.

Ev Henry would later call it "a good old-fashioned Thanksgiving turkey dinner," and Ivan and his siblings would tell the authorities that the two days after the party had passed free of acrimony. ☾

AT THE COAL BANK, Hossack stopped the horses and he and Ivan set to work. The chunks of coal weren't heavy. Father and son worked steadily, tossing the pieces into the back of the wagon, and the coal plunked softly off its wood floor. Sometimes a lump bounced out; Ivan picked up the stray pieces, throwing them back into the growing pile. It was good coal for their stove, the kind that burned easily. As they worked, a light breeze blew across the prairie. The horses shifted, turning their heads to catch the scent of the wind, leaning forward to munch on the prairie grass.

When Hossack was satisfied that they had a full load, they climbed back into the wagon and turned toward Medora. He wanted to pick up the mail and newspapers at the general store before returning home. ☾

THAT MORNING, AFTER his father and Ivan left, Will Hossack put on his warm coat and headed to the woodpile to split logs for firewood. Will was eighteen years old, muscular and broad-shouldered, hardened by farm work. He was now the oldest boy in the household, and he wanted to be sure that the family had enough wood for the fire to last through the weekend. The ax was an old one, with a dent in the handle and a distinctive nick in the blade; he had used it just days before to kill the turkey for the holiday. Now, as he picked it up, his older sisters, Cassie and May, walked past him on their way to the barn to milk the cows. His mother was churning butter in the kitchen.

Will placed a log on the chopping block, steadied it for a moment, and swung the ax. The log cracked open, and the vibration of the blade rippled back through his hands. One after another, he set logs up and split them. As a pile of splintered wood gathered at his feet, Will began to sweat and took off his coat, laying it across the grinding machine. He chopped for a while longer, and then sixteen-year-old Jimmie took over.

Late in the afternoon, at about the time her husband was reaching the Medora general store, Margaret Hossack walked across the road to the Nicholson farm, a half mile away. Harvey Nicholson had died just ten days earlier, at the age of forty-five, after a long battle with typhoid fever. Mary Nicholson was alone now with her three children and the burdens of running the farm.

Margaret had loaned Mary Nicholson a wash boiler, and she wanted it back in time to do laundry early the next week. Margaret knocked on the door and chatted with her neighbor for a few minutes. Then Mary remembered some sheets she had borrowed from the Hossacks. They were clean and she was ready to return them, Mary said, but she wanted to iron them first. Don't worry about the ironing, Margaret cheerfully told her neighbor. She would do it herself. Margaret took the wash boiler and the sheets and headed home. When Mary later thought back to the visit, she remarked that Margaret seemed to be in a good humor. ☾

AFTER THE STOP at the general store, John Hossack and his son traveled the dirt roads home. As farmers and mariners had done for centuries, Hossack appraised the darkening sky. He still feared that the weather was about to change for the worse.

They arrived at the house around 4 P.M., the wagon filled with coal. Hossack and Ivan had missed their regular meal in the middle of the day, and their stomachs were growling, but first they unloaded the coal and stored it in the granary.

Margaret prepared dinner for her husband and son, and they ate at the kitchen table as family members drifted in and out of the house. Margaret and May walked to the barn to do the evening milking. Dusk was falling and the air was growing colder.

Finished with his chores, Will came into the kitchen to wash up. When Ivan got up to leave the room, heading for the privy in the yard, Will remembered he had left his coat outside. He told Ivan to retrieve it.

John Hossack had finished his supper, but he continued to sit at the kitchen table reading the newspapers he had picked up in Medora. When he heard Will mention the woodpile, he asked whether the boys had put the ax away that afternoon when they finished chopping the wood. The air felt heavy to him, like a snowfall was possible that night, and he didn't want the ax covered up and difficult to find the next day.

Will stepped out on the porch and called to Ivan. "Pa thinks it will snow tonight. Get the ax at the woodpile and put it away."

After he finished in the privy, Ivan trudged across the yard to the woodpile. He put the ax away and carried Will's coat with him back to the house. With eight older siblings, Ivan was used to obeying orders.

As evening fell Cassie and May helped their mother prepare supper for themselves and the two older boys. The five of them ate in the kitchen, where their father still sat with the newspapers spread out before him.

That night John Hossack seemed to be in a better mood as he talked to his family about the stories in the newspapers. The featured article on the front page of the November 29, 1900, edition of the *Indianola Herald* was titled "The Holiday's Dinner" and described table decorations for Thanksgiving dinner. Inside were several humorous pieces: an illustrated poem entitled "A Thanksgiving Dream" and another entitled "Two People and a Parrot." There was a report of the death and funeral of the Hossacks' neighbor, Harvey Nicholson, and an account of a political banquet in Indianola, with speeches by County Attorney George Clammer and Senator William Berry, to celebrate recent Republican victories in the county. An advertisement promoted the upcoming performance of the Chicago Symphony Orchestra in Indianola.

Eventually Hossack put down the paper and played a game with Ivan, waving a whip back and forth on the floor so that Ivan could jump over it. Hossack laughed and joked as he watched his son. Will and Jimmie joined in the game, and then the three boys moved to the sitting room, where the stove was burning, to throw a cushion back and forth. Their father followed them and took up his newspapers again.

Cassie and May helped their mother clean up, and then the three went to sit with the others. The girls worked on sewing projects while Margaret mended clothes. Later, May recalled that the evening had been "harmonious" and that her "father and mother were in unusual good spirits."

Will was the first to retire, climbing the stairs sometime between 7 and 8 P.M. to his room directly over the kitchen. Shortly thereafter John Hossack declared that he was ready for bed. It was early for him, but he was tired from his long day at the coal bank. He undressed and lay down in the bedroom he and Margaret shared, one of two that opened onto the sitting room.

Ivan and Jimmie continued playing, wrestling on the floor until their mother told them to stop. They were making too much noise, she said, and their father was trying to sleep. The two boys gave up the game and climbed into the double bed in their downstairs room. A few minutes later Cassie went upstairs.

Before climbing the stairs to join Cassie in their bedroom, May said good night to her mother, who was still sewing in her chair. Outside it was quiet and peaceful and the sky had cleared. The stars were out. The moon was nearly full, casting its light across the yard.

As was her habit before going to bed, May wound the clock. It was just after 9 P.M. ☾

Testimony of Margaret Hossack in Warren County District Court, April 8, 1901

AFTER THE GIRLS and the children had all gone to bed, I took the lamp and went out to the pantry and rolled some butter I had churned that forenoon. When I came back in the sitting room, he was standing by the stove pulling his pants on, and I says, what are you up for? He says, I waked up and I can't lay in bed awake.

So he lit his pipe and went to smoking and was reading a while, and after a little he quit reading, and he says, well, I thought I would have the boys all start to school Monday, but he didn't think he could. He says, I wonder if Will would care if I kept him home next week. He says, we want to take them hogs away and get some lumber to put a new platform on the wells; said he would like to get a hog butchered. I told him Will wasn't counting on going to school next week, and he wanted to know why. I says because . . . when he started he didn't want to stop. . . . He wanted to go steady.

Then he said that he felt lots better than he did this

morning, and he hoped it would be a nice day tomorrow, for he wanted to go to hear Mr. Hopkins preach. That was the last that he said.

I think it must have been half past nine when I got in from the kitchen. After the children had gone to bed, I heard the dog that night. He was barking and fussing around an awful sight. . . . Often one of the neighbor's stock would come and bother around, and the dog wouldn't let them be until he would get them away. I thought if they was around, I was going to go out and shut the lot gate so they couldn't get in and I went out but couldn't see anything. The dog was down in the road barking or fussing as if he had seen something, but I couldn't see anything. . . .

It was pretty well on to 10 o'clock when I went to bed. I went first. I knew of Mr. Hossack's coming to bed. I was at the front side of the bed, lying on my right side, with my face to the east. There was nothing said between us when he got in bed. As to which went to sleep first, I thought he was asleep from the way he was breathing, that was the only way I could tell. He was lying on his left side. I went to sleep.

At various legal proceedings over the course of the next few months, the five children in the Hossack household answered many questions about that Saturday evening and the hours immediately following the attack on their father. The stories they told were consistent with one another's, and with their mother's, in every important respect.

According to their reports it was shortly after midnight when Margaret Hossack called up the stairs to her three older children.

"Cassie," she called out, "did you hear a noise?"

Startled out of sleep by her mother's voice, Cassie called back. "No, Ma, I didn't hear anything. Go back to bed."

But Margaret Hossack, standing in the kitchen at the foot of the stairs, called again. "I think somebody is in the house," she said, "and something is the matter with Pa. Come down quick."

This time May, lying in bed next to Cassie, also heard her mother's plea, uttered with a strange tremor in her voice, as if she were afraid. Both girls quickly rose and rushed out of their bedroom. Their brother Willie, dressed in pants but barefoot, was just ahead of them, descending the dark staircase to the kitchen. Cassie heard the striking of a match and then another sound, a kind of groaning or choking sound, coming from somewhere downstairs.

Margaret Hossack was clothed only in the chemise and drawers she usually wore to bed, and she was holding a small oil lamp that illuminated the kitchen. She was crying but she didn't speak as she led them to the door of the bedroom, where she handed Willie the lamp. In the flickering yellow light, the boy saw his father lying in bed, his head a bloody mass, an open wound above his right ear.

Willie turned to Cassie and said, "Run for the Nicholsons." Without a word, Cassie left the house and raced barefoot across the field to the neighbors' farm.

May woke Jimmie and Ivan. They quickly dressed and followed her to where John Hossack lay on his left side, facing the wall. His head looked disfigured, his right eye bluish and swollen shut; the bedclothes were soaked in blood and gore. Ivan began to sob, and the sound filled the small room.

"Why is he crying?" John Hossack asked faintly.

Willie managed to respond. "It's because you are hurt, Pa."

"No," said Hossack. "I am not hurt. I am only sick."

"Who hurt you, Pa?" Willie asked.

"Nobody hurt me," Hossack repeated.

Moments later, Cassie returned with their nineteen-year-old neighbor, John Nicholson. The young man entered the bedroom and looked down at John Hossack.

"Where did you find him?" Nicholson asked Margaret Hossack, who stood next to her husband's bed. She didn't speak but motioned toward her husband.

A few minutes later, without asking any more questions, Nicholson left. He would get a horse, he told the Hossacks, and ride to Liberty to take the news to the Henrys and Kemps.

Once Nicholson was gone, Margaret Hossack got dressed, pulling on the blue dress she'd worn during the day.

May and Jimmie left to seek help from Will and Rinda Haines, whose farm was a half mile to the north. The moon was bright, illuminating the road and the edge of the fields. They hurried, afraid that the intruder their mother had heard in the house might be watching as they made their way. They mounted the Haineses' porch steps, and May knocked loudly on the door and called out. In a moment Haines, fully dressed, came to the door. Excitedly, May told him that her family needed help; her father had been attacked and was badly hurt. Haines peered south into the dark fields that separated his land from his neighbors'. Perhaps he could see the yellow lights burning in the Hossack farmhouse.

Haines refused to come with them. He told them that he'd heard a noise a short time earlier, about 11 P.M. He had lit a lamp and seen a strange man standing on the porch just where they were now. It seemed that the man had gone away, he said, but he couldn't be sure.

Unable to persuade Haines, May and Jimmie hurriedly retraced their steps to where their father lay dying. ☾

MEANWHILE WILL STOOD watch over his father with his mother and Ivan. The blows to Hossack's head had left him paralyzed along the left side of his body, but he was able to move his right arm. Now he reached out weakly and said he was cold. Will realized that the fire in the sitting-room stove had gone out. The temperature outside had dropped below freezing, and the house was chilly.

Will knew he should go to the granary for a bucket of coal, but he was reluctant to go outside by himself, fearful of walking even that short distance in the dark. He wanted the dog, Shep, to accompany him. As Will later told the story,

> I started after a bucket of coal and wanted him to come along, because I was afraid. The coal was in the granary. I went out at the south kitchen door, but didn't see him there. I went around to the east porch, found the dog and told him to come on. He didn't do anything, didn't move, didn't pay any attention to me. I then said, Shep; he didn't move, then I went up on the porch and told him to come on, he just looked up at me and I started on, and then he didn't come, I talked to him a little sharp, then he didn't come and I went on. I didn't take hold of him at all. He didn't get up at all. Other times when I would be going out of nights, he would come with me.

Will hurried to fill the bucket with coal, then returned to the house.

Shortly after May and Jimmie returned, neighbors began to congregate at the Hossack farmhouse. Cassie went back across the fields and brought Mary Nicholson home with her, and at 2 A.M. Neil Morrison arrived. When Margaret Hossack told Morrison what had happened, he followed her to the bedroom to see the wounded man, now lying in the middle of the bed with his face turned to the ceiling. The vicious wound on the right side of his head was evident in the light of the lantern, and blood continued to run onto the bedclothes. Hossack was breathing hard. Morrison assumed that he was unconscious, but then he saw Hossack slightly raise his right hand and move his fingers. Morrison watched as Margaret Hossack, silently weeping, wiped the blood off her husband's face with a cloth. She moistened his lips with water from a spoon she held up to his face. When

Morrison saw her open a bottle of camphor, a medicine used externally to relieve pain, he intervened, saying that he didn't think that Hossack could stand having the liquid applied directly to the open wounds.

Within an hour, Will Conrad, another neighbor, appeared. He stood with Morrison in the bedroom doorway, and Margaret Hossack, sitting at her husband's side, spoke.

"Be quiet," she said to the men. "He's just coming to."

Just then Hossack moved slightly on the bed and made a choking sound, as if he were having trouble breathing. In tears, Margaret Hossack turned to Morrison and Conrad and said, "Ain't this awful?"

Gradually, throughout the early morning hours on Sunday, families in the vicinity were awakened and told that John Hossack had been attacked and lay close to death. The Nicholson boys rode south and west to notify family members and fetch the nearest doctor. John Burrell, a hired hand at the Nicholsons', saddled a horse and traveled around the neighborhood, shouting out a report of the tragedy as he rode from farm to farm.

An observer from above could have clearly seen the path of the news: the darkness of the night broken in a slowly expanding circle around the Hossack farm as lamps were lit and houses illuminated. Neighbors rose out of their beds, dressed, hitched horses to their buggies, and rode to the Hossack home. A few of the closest neighbors came on foot, guided by moonlight or lanterns they carried.

About two hours after the attack, John Nicholson arrived at the Henry farm to tell Annie and Ev that Annie's father was badly hurt and seemed close to death. Annie and Ev woke and dressed their five young children and bundled them into the buggy. The Henrys went to the Hossack farm as quickly as they could, covering the five-mile distance in about an hour. They found the house full of light and crowded with people. On their way inside, both of them noticed that Shep, the family dog, was lying quietly on the front porch. His behavior seemed strange to them; despite the many visitors and the commotion, Shep seemed passive and uninterested, not like his usual self.

May met Annie and Ev and their children at the kitchen door.

"Be as quiet as you possibly can," May softly told her sister and brother-in-law.

"Is he killed?" asked Annie.

"No," said May, "he's not dead yet."

2.

"I went to the Hossack residence, I endeavored to disabuse my mind of all bias or prejudice. I attempted to conduct the inquiry with a fixed determination not to formulate any theory and try to adjust the fact to it, but rather to allow the facts to develop the theory."—*Des Moines Daily Leader*, December 7, 1900, quoting GEORGE CLAMMER, county attorney for Warren County, speaking to a representative from the newspaper

DR. WILLIAM DEAN, a graduate of the medical school at Vanderbilt University, was thirty-nine years old in 1900 and had lived and practiced in New Virginia, Iowa, for six years. He was proud of having a telephone, one of the few in Squaw Township, although it didn't ring in the early-morning hours of Sunday, December 2, 1900. Instead he was awakened shortly after 2 A.M. by Charlie Nicholson, who had ridden seven miles on horseback to tell the doctor in person that John Hossack needed help. Dean had been the Hossacks' family doctor for the past several years, and he understood from Nicholson that the situation was urgent. But it took time to prepare to leave his home, and then an hour to make the trip by buggy to the Hossack farm. When he arrived at 4:30, John Hossack had been lying wounded in his bed for more than four hours.

Dr. Dean reached the farm at the same time as Lew Braucht, a forty-two-year-old blacksmith who also lived in New Virginia. Braucht and Dean were met outside the house by Neil Morrison and Will Hossack. Will held a lighted lantern by his side.

Dean asked what the trouble was, and Morrison was quick to respond. "It's a bad case, doctor," he said. "A murder." Turning back to the house, Morrison led the doctor inside and pointed to the bedroom door.

Dr. Dean went quickly to the wounded man, whose head was now covered with cloths and supported by several pillows. Mrs. Hossack was standing at the bedside, and Dr. Dean could tell right away that she was very anxious.

Dr. Dean unwound the wrappings to examine Hossack's injured skull. Wiping away the blood, he saw that the right side of the head, several inches above the ear, had been both deeply cut and severely crushed. It seemed that Hossack had been hit twice, his head first struck with a sharp blade and his skull then fractured by a blow from a blunt instrument. Brain matter had spilled out of the open wounds, making the right side of Hossack's head appear to be greatly enlarged. His right eye was swollen shut and the flesh around it had a bluish tint. The pillows and bedclothes were soaked with blood, and Dr. Dean noted that blood was oozing from the wounds.

As a result of the injury to his brain, Hossack was totally paralyzed on the left side of his body and appeared to be unconscious. His breathing was shallow and irregular, and his pulse was rapid and weak. His body was covered with a cold and clammy sweat. Aside from keeping him as comfortable as possible, there was nothing Dr. Dean could do for this patient.

As the doctor examined her husband, Margaret Hossack spoke.

"Is there any hope for him?"

Dr. Dean shook his head. "No," he said, "there is no hope."

Later, Dr. Dean described Margaret Hossack's reaction:

> She turned around and sat down on a chair . . . and cried a little while. . . . She sobbed audibly, though I could not see

her face; it was turned from me. And presently she got up from that and came out into the sitting room and sat down by the stove on a chair. Sat there a little while and got up and came back. She was in the bedroom most of the time until he died. And had hold of his hand considerable of the time. He kept one hand out like, and she had hold of his hand, and was by him most of the time. . . .

After I had seen the man and found the condition he was in, then I waited probably ten or fifteen minutes, and I called Mrs. Hossack into this room . . . and asked her if she knew anything about how it occurred. . . .

She said she didn't know, only that she heard a sharp sound like the striking of two boards together, or something like that, something similar, and jumped up and came into this room, and after she came into the room she heard a noise as of that door shutting, and saw a light flashing on this wall here, just a passing light. She went to that door and found it was not shut, and then turned, whether she shut the door or not, she didn't say, and then went to the stair door and called the children from upstairs. . . . She told them there was somebody in the house, but they told her she was mistaken, and then she came back to this room and called him three or four times but got no answer. By that time the older boy . . . came down, and they . . . went to the bedroom door. They seen him laying there with his face turned toward the wall, and the gash in his head. ☾

George McIntosh, a twenty-five-year-old neighbor of the Hossacks' who lived a half mile east, rode on horseback to notify Johnnie Hossack of the attack on his father. The Truitt house, where Johnnie boarded, was dark when McIntosh arrived, and there was no response to his knock. He shouted several times, calling out the young man's name, and finally Johnnie himself came to the door. McIntosh quickly told him the news.

Johnnie seemed shocked and surprised. He asked how his father had been attacked—what weapon had been used—but McIntosh told him he didn't know anything more. Johnnie asked him to wait, saying he would ride back with him. He told McIntosh that he couldn't believe that such a thing had happened.

Like many of the neighbors, McIntosh knew that Johnnie Hossack had frequently quarreled with his father and had moved off the family farm less than a year earlier. So, when the two men hurried to the barn to saddle a horse, McIntosh noted that Johnnie's horse, a light bay, was cool to the touch. It didn't seem to him that she had been ridden within the past hour.

Alger Truitt had been awakened by his wife, Nancy, when she heard Johnnie talking to someone on the porch. He overheard McIntosh deliver the news that John Hossack had been attacked. Earlier that day Johnnie had driven Truitt's wife and son, Harold, to Indianola, using his own horse and one of Truitt's grays as the team. Truitt knew they'd stopped at the farm of Alonzo Odell and returned for dinner around 6 P.M. Johnnie played cards in the Truitts' sitting room that evening, and then, so Truitt thought, the Hossack boy had gone to bed. Truitt was the last one to retire that evening, going to his bedroom on the first floor shortly after 10 P.M. Now it occurred to him that Johnnie might have crept out of the house later, with time enough to ride to the Hossack farm and back.

After McIntosh and Johnnie left, Truitt walked to the barn. As McIntosh had done only moments before, Truitt checked the horses in the barn. None of them were sweaty or seemed as if they had been ridden during the night. ☾

WHEN JOHNNIE REACHED the farm, he went straight to his father's bedside. Dr. Dean, still attending to his patient, watched the young man enter the room and stand looking down at his dying father, and then, without saying a word, walk out.

Will approached Johnnie and asked if he had seen Shep on the porch, saying that he thought there was something the matter with the dog and describing Shep's refusal to come with him to the granary for coal a few hours earlier. Johnnie went to the porch and called the dog by name. Shep's eyes were open, but his body was limp. Johnnie reached down and took hold of Shep's head, pulled him to a standing position, and shook him, talking to him all the while. Shep fell back to the floor. The dog seemed to be sick.

During the next few hours others noted Shep's lethargy. Will Conrad thought that the dog seemed "whipped or cowed . . . and in an unnatural state." Neil Morrison noticed the dog's peculiar behavior and even tested him, trying to startle him by going out and coming up suddenly, but Shep continued to lie in a motionless stupor.

People began talking about the possibility that the dog had been drugged by the same person who had attacked John Hossack in his bed. If Shep had been drugged, with chloroform perhaps, his passivity could be explained. It would also explain why the dog had not raised an alarm when the intruder, whom Margaret said she had heard leaving the house, first opened the door. Despite Shep's well-known habit of barking at strangers, none of the children remembered hearing him bark before they were awakened by their mother.

As the darkness of the winter night was broken by the first rays of the sun on the morning of Sunday, December 2, neighbors and family continued to assemble at the Hossack farmhouse. Will Haines walked down from his house to join the other men outside. Soon Louie, the fourth Hossack daughter, arrived with her husband, Joe Kemp. While Louie spoke quietly to her sisters, Joe entered the bedroom where John Hossack lay.

Margaret once again broke into tears as she described to her son-in-law her first sight of her husband in bed, so badly hurt. Hossack, now with a bloody froth around his mouth, was close to death. He was making low choking noises in his throat, and Joe heard him call for "Ma" and ask for water. Joe took up his father-in-law's hand and grasped it in the traditional Masonic grip. He thought he felt the dying man respond to his handshake.

A few minutes later, Frank Keller arrived. A tall, long-limbed sixty-nine-year-old with a shock of unruly white hair and a puckered mouth, known to most in the county as "Uncle Frank," Keller was one of the county's original pioneers and John Hossack's oldest friend. The two men had known each other for more than thirty years, since the spring of 1868.

Keller had been at the Hossacks' just a few days earlier, on Thanksgiving afternoon, when he'd stopped by to return a meat grinder late in the day. Keller's wife was sick, and he had spent the day at home, butchering. He was in dirty work clothes and hadn't planned to stay, but Hossack, in a jovial mood, insisted that his old friend come into the house and join the party.

When Keller was notified of the attack early Sunday morning, his wife and daughter were badly frightened by the news, and they begged him not to leave them alone in the dark. So Keller waited until dawn to go to his friend. Upon reaching the farm, he went straight to the bedroom. Hossack's eyes were closed, and he was almost motionless; Keller could tell that he was alive only by the slight rise and fall of his chest. Keller took Hossack's hand in his and clasped it in one of the secret Masonic grips, just as Kemp had done moments before. He spoke softly to the dying man, asking whether he could hear him or knew who he was. Keller thought that he heard Hossack faintly call his name: "Frank."

Keller bent down, moving his head close to Hossack's. "Put your trust in the Lord," he told his friend.

Hossack drifted in and out of consciousness for the next few hours. Neighbors and family members heard him speak several times, asking for a fire, his eyeglasses, water. He called repeatedly for his wife—"Ma"—as well as for several of his children. Margaret Hossack had stayed next to him throughout the night and into the morning. She continued to hold his hand, wipe his forehead, and moisten his lips. To those who saw her, it seemed that she did everything she could to ease her husband's pain and to make him more comfortable in the last hours of his life.

But there was nothing that Margaret Hossack, or anyone else, could do to keep John Hossack alive. At 9:45 A.M. on Sunday, December 2, 1900, nearly ten hours after the brutal attack, he died. ☾

EARLIER THAT MORNING, Johnnie had searched for the murder weapon. Finding nothing close to the house, he walked to the woodpile to look for the family ax. When he couldn't find it there, he asked his brothers if they knew where it was. Ivan, remembering that Will had told him to put the ax away where it wouldn't be covered up if it snowed, told him to look inside the granary.

Lew Braucht accompanied Johnnie on the short walk. As they approached the granary, they could see a wooden handle protruding from the dirt underneath the shed. Yanking it out, Johnnie immediately recognized the nicked blade. Braucht thought he saw stains of blood on the handle and hairs stuck to the metal blade, and he was quick to conclude that they had found the murder weapon.

"That's the thing that done the deed," Braucht announced. Johnnie was not so sure. The blood, he told Braucht, could be from the turkey Will had slaughtered for Thanksgiving dinner just three days before. And sometimes the younger boys simply threw the ax underneath the granary instead of opening the door and placing it inside. Johnnie threw the ax back in the dirt and returned to the house with Braucht.

Ivan was in the yard, and Johnnie told him that he was mistaken about putting the ax inside the granary; the two men had just found it lying underneath. But, as Braucht later recollected, Ivan insisted that he had done as he said. The top part of the granary door had been open, and he had reached in and set the ax against a barrel. The implication was obvious: If Ivan had put the ax inside, then someone—quite possibly the murderer—had moved it during the night.

Braucht was convinced that the ax was an essential piece of evidence. He found Neil Morrison and asked him to come to the granary, where Braucht retrieved the ax and the two men examined it together. Then Morrison noticed Frank Keller walking away from the house, and he called him to join them. Keller took the ax in his hands. As Keller was to recollect,

> I looked at the ax. I can see as good as some people and thought I saw blood on the blade, and I thought I saw more blood on the back, on the pole of the ax than there was on the blade. Getting old, I can see anything that glistens or is bright—anything dark I cannot see so well. Held the ax in my hand that way. Says I, there you see one of poor John's old gray hairs. Somebody says, well they have been killing turkeys with this ax. Well, says I, that is not turkey feathers. . . .

Keller touched the blood on the ax handle; it felt wet, and a bit adhered to his finger. Just then Dr. Dean stepped out of the house. Keller called to the doctor that they had found the murder weapon.

Dr. Dean joined the group of men standing near the granary. Taking the ax in his hands, he, like the others, noticed blood spots on the handle and several hairs on the blade. Dean also realized that the constant handling of the ax was compromising its value as evidence. Giving it back to Lew Braucht, Dean told him to return the ax to its original location and to make sure that no one else touched it. Braucht shoved the ax under the granary.

Around noon Warren County Sheriff Lewis Hodson, accompanied by his deputy, Grant Kimer, arrived at the Hossack farm. Hodson guided his buggy into the side yard and reined his horses to a stop. The two men stepped down.

Hodson and Kimer noted the crowd of men clustered near the granary and walked toward them. Side by side, the sheriff and his deputy looked mismatched. Hodson was a short, barrel-chested, heavyset man; Kimer was tall and loose limbed, as lean as a rail. Both men were recently elected to their posts, and neither had ever investigated a murder.

Lew Braucht stepped forward to explain that he was standing guard over the ax, which he and many of the neighbor men thought might be the murder weapon.

Sheriff Hodson pulled the ax from under the granary and examined it closely. He noted spots that looked like blood on the wooden handle and three hairs on the blade. He removed the hairs and put them in his pocketbook for safekeeping. Then he wrapped the ax in newspaper and handed it to Deputy Kimer, instructing him to keep it in his possession. He told Kimer to go into the house and sit with the corpse in the bedroom.

Hodson spoke briefly to the neighbor men, some of whom had been at the farm since the middle of the night. Frank Keller led the sheriff across the small yard to the front porch, where he pointed out drops of blood on the steps. Then the two men went into the house and proceeded to the bedroom where the murder had occurred. Hodson saw the body of John Hossack lying on its back in the middle of a narrow bed, leaving little room on either side. An ugly gash creased the right side of the victim's head, just above his ear.

Hodson turned away and went back outside. One of the neighbors approached the sheriff and suggested that perhaps bloodhounds should be put on the trail of the assailant. Hodson was quick to squelch the idea:

"We don't want a pack of dogs yelping around the corpse." ☾

SHORTLY AFTER SHERIFF Hodson's inspection of the bedroom, George Clammer, the county attorney, arrived. Clammer was the son of a Methodist minister, and unlike most of those who were gathered at the Hossacks', he was not a farmer. He had lived his adult life in Indianola, where he attended Simpson College and won acclaim as a student, orator, and football player. He had also served as editor in chief of the school newspaper. After graduation, he pursued a career in law. He was a handsome young man, slender and well dressed, with thick brown hair that he combed back in a high wave above his thin face. He had a studious look, which was accented by gold wire-frame glasses balanced on his prominent nose.

Ambitious and self-confident, Clammer, at twenty-seven years of age, had recently been elected to his second term as county attorney. He listened as the sheriff told him what he knew so far, and then the two men climbed onto the porch. Clammer noticed a half-dozen dark spots that looked like dried blood on the floor. A barrel of rainwater sat to one side of the porch. The door, opening into the kitchen, had a broken pane of glass.

The kitchen looked typical for a farmhouse. It had a clock on one wall, a table and chairs in the center, and a cook stove against the west wall. The pantry was on the east side of the room; a second door on the south side led to the yard, and a staircase led to the bedrooms upstairs. Clammer looked down at the wooden floorboards, noting that that they were clean and showed no evidence of blood.

The county attorney passed through the kitchen and entered

the sitting room, which was modestly furnished with a few pieces of furniture pushed against the walls. A coal stove stood in the center, with a small table and chair pulled up close to it. Two curtained windows were on the north wall. On the east wall hung a crayon portrait of John Hossack, depicting him with a fashionable bushy beard.

Turning west, Clammer faced two bedroom doors. He glanced into the north bedroom and saw a bed, a three-drawer chest wedged into a corner, and an oval mirror hanging above the chest. The bed was covered with a brightly colored patchwork quilt; a single word, IVAN, stood out in neat stitches near the bottom.

Then Clammer stood in the doorway of the other bedroom, looking into the room shared by the victim and his wife. The bed was against the walls of the southwest corner. The body lay in the middle of the mattress, surrounded by bloody bedclothes. The two pillows that supported the victim's head were also soaked with blood. Clammer noticed a window at the foot of the bed; neither the sash nor the pane seemed disturbed. A sewing machine rested next to a dresser. A piece of carpet lay on the floor beside the bed, marked with a small triangular stain that looked like blood. A Winchester rifle leaned against the wall.

Sheriff Hodson told Clammer that when Margaret Hossack was awakened—and before she knew her husband was hurt—she left the bedroom and went to the kitchen to call to her children upstairs. Clammer was puzzled by the story. If a woman were startled and frightened in the night, wouldn't her first thought, her natural instinct, be to call upon her husband for help? ☾

LATE IN THE AFTERNOON, another county official, Dr. Harry Dale, the thirty-three-year-old coroner, arrived. After discussing what they knew so far, Clammer and Dale decided that they would question Margaret Hossack together. They asked Dr. Dean, the physician who had attended John Hossack in the hours before his death, to be present. Perhaps in an attempt to make Mrs. Hossack feel more comfortable, they also asked a woman, Sue Himstreet, a neighbor who'd arrived a few hours earlier, to be in the room during the interrogation.

That evening, the group climbed the stairs to the upstairs bedroom where Margaret Hossack was waiting. She was a big woman, about Clammer's own height or an inch taller, sturdy and large boned. Clammer judged that she must have weighed around 160 pounds. She was in her late fifties and had high cheekbones and a weathered face; her small, deep-set, blue eyes were reddened from crying. Wrinkles furrowed her brow, and her thick, steel-gray hair was pinned in a tight bun on top of her head. She wore a blue dress.

When Clammer asked Margaret Hossack what had happened, she told the same story she'd already given many times over the past sixteen hours. According to Mrs. Himstreet, she answered Clammer's questions without complaint or hesitation, seeming to be "perfectly free" with her responses.

Clammer inquired whether her husband had any enemies. No, Margaret Hossack said; she didn't think so.

Did she know, Clammer asked, where the ax had been stored the night before? Margaret Hossack responded that she had heard Willie tell Ivan to put it in the granary late on Saturday afternoon. But, she said, Ivan was gone such a short time that she thought he'd probably thrown it underneath, as the boys sometimes did, rather than taking the time to put it inside.

Did she know that the ax had in fact been found underneath the granary that morning? Did she know that the handle had blood spots on it, and that it was suspected to be the murder weapon? No, Margaret Hossack answered calmly; she didn't know those things.

Then Clammer asked about troubles in the family. Did she fight with her husband, or with the children?

Over the past decade, Margaret Hossack had told many of her neighbors that she was afraid of her husband and that he'd frequently threatened her and her children. Surely she knew that these conversations would be reported to the authorities. But she did not admit her fears to Clammer, just as she would not admit them to other questioners who interrogated her at later stages of the investigation. No, she replied to Clammer. There was no trouble.

Clammer asked whether she had been hurt when her husband was attacked. Had she felt any part of the weapon come in contact with her? No, she responded, she had not been hit. She had been awakened by a sound, not a touch.

At the end of the interview, he asked about her clothes: What had she worn to bed that night? She had slept in a chemise and drawers, she told him, the same ones she was wearing now, beneath her dress.

Then Clammer made a bold request: Could she remove her dress?

At that point, according to Sue Himstreet, Margaret Hossack hesitated for the first time. Clammer repeated that he wanted her to take off her dress so that the three men could examine the clothes underneath for blood spots.

Mrs. Himstreet later recalled the moment: "Mrs. Hossack made no objection to removing her clothing, only she said she hated to do it in the presence of the men, and because she hadn't changed her clothes for the week, she hated to have them see her."

Clammer was not to be deterred. It was essential, he explained, that her underclothes be inspected at this point. But he would be willing to leave the room and let the doctors conduct the examination.

Once Clammer was gone, Margaret Hossack stood and slipped the dress over her head as Dr. Dean and Dr. Dale watched. According to Mrs. Himstreet, she showed no hesitation or fear as she exhibited the garments she wore underneath. In turn, the doctors scrutinized her clothing and then left the room to report their findings to George Clammer.

The two women were left alone. Margaret Hossack, clad only in her underclothes, asked Mrs. Himstreet to look at her clothes, just as the doctors had. Was there blood?

Mrs. Himstreet studied the garments, noting a sprinkle of blood on the right shoulder of the chemise. She saw more spots on the back: at the bottom and at the center, near the top. She saw no blood on the front.

When Mrs. Himstreet described what she had found, Margaret expressed surprise. She hadn't thought to look at her clothes, Margaret said, and she didn't know that there was any blood on her at all.

Testimony of Margaret Hossack, in Warren County District Court, April 8, 1901

> I think it was about one o'clock when I heard the noise . . . as though you would hit two boards together, or something broke. . . . I just jumped out of bed and was going to go and see. When I got outside the bedroom door, I heard him breathing as though he was kind of choking, but I thought he was, by the noise, disturbed in his sleep. I went out a little further, and I seen a light shining on the wall, and then I heard the door pulled to, and went on and found out it wasn't clear shut.
>
> He still kept making that noise, only louder, so I went and called the children and told them there had been someone in the house and I thought Pa was hurt. Cassie said, No, you are only scared; you go back to bed. I could hear him still making a noise and I went back to the room, called him, he didn't answer, so I went back again and told

them that I knowed he was hurt, and they came downstairs then. Will come first, the girls soon after. I lit a lamp. Will carried the lamp into the bedroom. Will ahead, I just behind him. All that I had on was my chemise and drawers, just as I had dressed when I went to bed that night. . . .

When we went in, Will kind of put the pillow down from his head with his hands. Pa said, What are you doing? Will answered, We are looking at you, you are hurt; he answered, No, I am not hurt, I am sick. Cassie and May were in the bedroom by that time. . . . May asked if I had wakened Jimmie and Ivan, and I said, no. She wakened them up and Ivan was at the door, crying. Pa wanted to know what was the matter with Ivan. Will says, He is crying because you are hurt; he says, I am not hurt, I am sick. Cassie went over to the Nicholsons. I remained in the room with Mr. Hossack. ☾

DARKNESS FELL. Of the nine Hossack children, eight spent the night at the farm, including the three who lived on nearby farms. Alex, the eldest son, was absent, but he had been notified of his father's death and would arrive the next day.

Still, the family was not alone. Neighbors continued to drift in and out of the house, and most of the authorities in charge of the investigation remained throughout the night.

County Attorney Clammer had asked his wife's cousin, E. A. Osborne, a druggist and amateur photographer, to come to the Hossack farm that Sunday to take pictures of the dead man. Osborne arrived after midnight with a friend, H. H. Hartman, a local attorney and amateur photographer. They took four flashlight pictures of the body while Clammer and Dale watched. When they were finished, Deputy Kimer escorted them to their buggy and gave the ax, still wrapped in newspaper, to Hartman. Hartman had been asked by Clammer to take possession of the ax and send it for examination to Dr. Eli Grimes in Des Moines.

Around 4 A.M., the undertaker, George Moore, was ready to perform his duties. Moore had been at the house since midafternoon, and he now entered the bedroom for the first time and went to work. He found a small piece of carpet on the floor, doubled it over, and placed it under the dead man's head. The undertaker wiped the blood from the wounds, cleaned the body, and prepared it for the next day's official medical examination. Then he stuffed the scrap of carpet in a bucket of water, which also contained some bloody rags, opened the window at the foot of the bed, and placed the bucket on the ground outside.

By the time Moore completed his work, it was dawn.

3.

How do we tell the truth in a small town? . . . The truth, the whole truth, tends to be complex, its contentments and joys wrestled out of doubt, pain, and change. How to tell the truth in a small town, where, if a discouraging word is heard, it is not for public consumption?—KATHLEEN NORRIS, in *Dakota: A Spiritual Geography*

"We have found that you as a family done the right thing in trying to keep your quarrels to yourselves, and yet we have found out a good deal about the contentions in the family, and there is no reason why you should not speak with entire frankness."—QUESTIONER at the coroner's inquest on December 4, 1900, addressing Annie Henry

THE DAY AFTER John Hossack's death, Coroner Harry Dale selected three men to serve as the inquest jury. T. W. Passwater was an Indianola resident with experience in law enforcement; he had served as a deputy warden at the state penitentiary at Anamosa and as deputy sheriff for the county. The other two men, C. D. Johnson and Fred Johnston, were farmers who knew the victim and lived near the Hossack farm.

Fred Johnston was an especially important choice. He was fifty-nine, well respected as a leader in the community, and had been a close friend of the Hossack family for more than two decades. Johnston and Hossack had served together as trustees for Warren County and as elders in their church, and Johnston knew firsthand about the domestic troubles that had plagued the Hossacks over the years. In fact, the previous year, he had visited the family to discuss the conflicts and urge reconciliation. As it turned out, he would be asked to describe that meeting under oath at the inquest.

County Attorney Clammer and Dr. Dale joined the three members of the jury at the proceeding. In addition, there was a sixth man in the room: W. A. Olive, a stenographer regularly employed by the Indianola law firm of Henderson and Berry, had been hired to transcribe the questions and answers during the two days of the inquiry.

Robbery was no longer a suspected motive. The Hossack family confirmed that nothing of value was missing from the household. Owing to the history of domestic troubles, however, family members were under suspicion, and Dale took measures to make sure that they were not alerted to specific lines of questioning and did not discuss answers among themselves. Once the inquest began, on Monday afternoon, the dead man's wife and nine children were kept under guard in a single upstairs bedroom. They were instructed not to speak to one another about the crime or the investigation. After testifying, they were sent to another room, separate from those who had not yet been questioned. Exceptions were made for Margaret Hossack's two sons-in-law, Ev Henry and Joe Kemp, who were allowed to leave the house and return to their own farms to do their chores.

Dr. Dale escorted the jurors into the small downstairs bedroom where the murder had occurred. The corpse was just as the undertaker had left it, covered with a cloth and lying on a cooling board on the small double bed. Dale pulled back the cloth, exposing the victim's head and displaying the wounds. Then he pointed out the blood spots on the bedclothes and the walls, noting the splatters in the southwest corner, a few feet from John Hossack's head at the time of the attack, and a spray of blood on the wall at the foot of the bed, more than eight feet away. There was also some blood nearly nine feet away from Hossack's body, on the east wall and doorjamb, the area behind where the assailant must have stood. The amount of blood on the walls, and the fact that the blood appeared to spray in four directions at once, indicated the force of the blows.

The blood splatters may have suggested something else as well to the jurors: The assailant, who wielded the ax just a few feet from Hossack's head, must have been sprayed with blood; the murderer's body partially blocked the path of the spray to the east wall.

As a final piece of evidence, Dr. Dale held up the chemise that Margaret Hossack said she'd been wearing the night of the murder, and he indicated blood spots on the right sleeve and on the back. Johnson and Passwater both remembered—and later testified—that there was no blood on the front of the chemise.

Dale finished with his exhibits, pulled the sheet back over the body, and left the bedroom, followed by Clammer, Johnson, and Passwater. Fred Johnston stayed behind, holding the chemise in his hands and noting the absence of blood on its front. To Johnston, almost all of the blood spots on the back looked as if they had been splattered against the cloth. Only one spot, a mark at the lower end of the right side, looked different to Johnston, more like a smear, as if the cloth had rubbed against something.

Clammer called to Johnston from the adjacent room, saying they were ready to proceed with the witnesses. Johnston dropped the chemise onto the sheet covering John Hossack's body and left the room to join the other jurors. None of the authorities remembered seeing the chemise again until it was found a few days later in the bottom of a bucket of bloody water, saturated and destroyed as evidence. ☾

THE TESTIMONY AT any legal proceeding with multiple witnesses inevitably becomes a kind of narrative, with overlapping and sometimes contradictory tales. For George Clammer, the testimony at the coroner's inquest would provide much of the evidence that would help him to create a single chronology of the events that culminated in the death of John Hossack.

From his investigation of the crime scene and his informal discussions with neighbors at the Hossack farm on Sunday, Clammer had already formulated a theory about the murder, and he strongly suspected that Hossack's wife was guilty. Her story about sleeping through the attack didn't make sense to him, especially given the small size of the bed she shared with her husband. If she had been lying there, as she claimed, surely she would have been hit by the handle of the ax, or at least awakened by the presence of the intruder, who would have been standing only inches away from her face. And why would an intruder have used the Hossacks' ax as his weapon?

Margaret Hossack also appeared to have a motive to kill her husband. Apparently, she had said many times that she feared him and even that she wished he were dead. There was talk in the neighborhood that the couple had reconciled; some people said that the family had lived in peace for the last twelve months. But, after decades of hostility, at least as Clammer saw it, a one-year truce was hardly to be trusted. If the neighbors were willing to testify about what she had told them in the past—and they would be under oath and sworn to tell the truth—their statements could be persuasive.

The suspicion that Margaret Hossack had killed her husband was obvious throughout the inquest proceeding, starting with the questioning of Drs. L. H. Surber and Emmett Porterfield. Both were middle-aged physicians who practiced in Indianola. They had performed the autopsy together and were among the first witnesses to testify. Porterfield had previously served as Warren County coroner.

According to the doctors, who were questioned separately, the first blow resulted in a wound five inches long, just above and in front of the right ear. The blow was powerful enough to drive the weapon, either a hatchet or an ax, about four and a half inches into Hossack's head. The second one, struck about an inch below the first and resulting in a wound slightly more than three inches long, was also delivered with a good deal of strength and splintered bones of his skull so that they were forced into the floor of the brain cavity. The doctors had examined the rest of Hossack's body and, finding no other unusual signs or marks of violence, had concluded that Hossack was alive when he was struck. Although they couldn't be sure how much time had elapsed between the two blows, the doctors speculated that they came close together.

In addition to the details of the wound, each doctor was also asked for an opinion about whether the victim would have lost consciousness after the attack and, if so, when he would have regained the ability to speak. The jury knew that the victim's wife claimed to have called the children only moments after being awakened by the assault on her husband and that the children said that John Hossack spoke to them just moments after they entered his bedroom. Would speech have been possible just minutes after such a violent attack on the brain?

Dr. Surber hedged, first saying that the blows would produce immediate unconsciousness, then adding that it was also possible that Hossack could have spoken some words right away. Dr. Porterfield was also uncertain: "I think it would take a while. It might not take very long."

Then each was asked whether he thought that the blows were struck by a right-handed person or a left-handed person. Both answered with assurance: Given the position of the body in the bed and the nature of the blows, it appeared that the attacker was left-handed.

Margaret Hossack was right-handed. Perhaps Clammer had shared that information with the jury members, who challenged the doctors' conclusion with a series of pointed questions.

Dr. Surber was asked whether a right-handed person could have inflicted the wounds. He replied that it did not seem possible to him. When it was Dr. Porterfield's turn, Passwater, the ex-deputy sheriff on the jury, asked him to elaborate. Wouldn't his conclusion depend on the number of pillows supporting the head at the time the blows were struck and how close to the foot of the bed the attacker had stood? Dr. Porterfield refused to change his mind: "My answer [is] that I thought they were left-handed blows."

It was a critical point. Still not satisfied, the jurors asked for a demonstration. Passwater lay down on the sitting-room floor, acting the role of John Hossack, and stuck two pillows under his head. He requested that the doctor stand next to him, indicating how the blows might have been hit from that position. Playing the part of the attacker, Porterfield demonstrated how the ax was swung, in a left-handed fashion, to cause the wounds that he had observed.

The jurors continued to press the point. Wasn't it conceivable, given the possible position of the assailant and the angle of Hossack's head at the exact moment he was struck, that the blows had been delivered with a right-handed stroke? Eventually, after having testified repeatedly that the murderer was surely left-handed, Porterfield conceded that yes, it was possible that a right-handed person was the attacker.

It was later established that the only left-handed member of the household present on the night of the murder was Will Hossack. ☾

TWELVE NEIGHBORS WERE called to testify at the inquest: eight men and four women. All of them had been acquainted with John Hossack for many years, more than two decades in several cases, and they knew him as a fellow farmer, a respected leader in the community, and a friend. Yet almost all of them also knew a different side of John Hossack, one that had been revealed to them over the years through their conversations with his wife. Those conversations were of significant interest to the questioners at the inquest.

The neighbors were typically asked first about the night of the attack: when they had been alerted to the news and what they had seen and heard at the farmhouse. Inevitably, though, the questions shifted to what they knew about the Hossack family troubles. What had Margaret Hossack told them about her husband?

Many of them were reluctant to talk. Neil Morrison repeatedly said that he couldn't remember his conversations with Margaret Hossack, explaining that "I do not tax my memory with family quarrels," and William Haines justified his poor recollection by saying "I never know anything more about anybody's business than I can help." Fred Johnston admitted that he knew about the turmoil, but that all had been "hushed up" over the years. Ev Henry, John and Margaret Hossack's son-in-law, reported that he had always understood that the family tried to keep their conflicts secret. Clammer told them the time for secrecy was over; the inquest was serious business, and now that a crime had been committed, the neighbors had a responsibility to tell the jury everything they knew.

It turned out that they knew a great deal. Within minutes of entering the sitting room, Neil Morrison admitted that he'd heard from Margaret Hossack about the troubles in her family for more than fifteen years. He initially thought the arguments were between father and children; Margaret said that her husband was too severe with them and that she was afraid he'd hurt them or drive them away. Morrison tried to placate her: "I told her I thought he would never do them any harm," but he heard the same kind of complaints from her "quite a number of times over the years."

Eventually Morrison had learned that there were also conflicts between husband and wife. Margaret Hossack told him that her life was a "misery," that her husband "abused her," and that she was "afraid for her life, afraid he would do something to her or the children." On one occasion, Morrison told the jury, she had stopped him on the road and asked him to come to her house, saying that her husband was "acting like a crazy man" and she feared for the safety of her family. Morrison tried to calm her, but she persisted, and he finally agreed to come. He visited the following day, but by then the trouble had passed.

Other neighbors confirmed that they'd also heard Margaret Hossack speak of her husband's frequent threats to hurt her or the children and that he often wielded a knife or a loaded gun. They told of Margaret Hossack coming to their farms or running out to them in the road in a desperate state, crying and saying that he was "wild" and that she was afraid he would kill one of them as he declared he would do. In fact, they knew of few specific acts of violence, although several neighbors had heard reports that Hossack slapped and whipped his children, hit his wife with his fists, and once threw a stove lid at her. Almost all who testified said that the threat of violence from her husband had been a constant source of fear for Mrs. Hossack.

Some of the most detailed testimony came from Frank Keller, a neighbor who'd known the family for more than three decades. It was eight or ten years ago, he reported, when Mrs. Hossack first came to talk to him about her fear of her husband, and she'd talked to him many times after that. Sometimes, at her request, Keller had gone to her house, inventing some pretense to explain his visit to her husband. But she had implored him not to tell her husband that she was talking about him, and Keller hadn't known how to help her.

Keller described one particular incident:

> At a certain time about five years ago, I was working in my garden—this is not the first complaint I have ever heard—and my attention was called to the north part of the garden. I looked and there stood Mrs. Hossack, she had slipped through my fence. How she knew I was in the garden I do not know. She came to me crying, and said Mr. Hossack was wild; he had threatened to kill her and the children, and she would like for me to come out and do something.
>
> I says, sister Hossack, what could I do? These things she would always tell me was secret, everything was secret and I must tell nobody about this. That if Hossack knew of this he would kill the whole family.
>
> At that time she told me he had bundled up his clothes . . . and said he was going to leave, and . . . she wished to the Lord he had done it. . . . There was no peace in this family nor never would be as long as he lived. She bursted out with a kind of screaming and she says, why is it that the Lord don't remove him out of the way?

Will Conrad, another neighbor, testified that the conversations with Margaret Hossack had been "more frequent than we wanted them." He described an occasion, six years earlier, when one of the Hossack girls had come running to his house to ask for help, reporting that Hossack had ordered Johnnie to leave the place:

> I understood that Hossack got up and went to kick Annie, and Johnnie jumped up and grabbed him. . . . Mr. Hossack told him to let him alone, and Johnnie told him he would not do it unless he let her alone, and they said that Hossack says, If you don't I will cut your guts out. He went out and so they thought he was hunting a knife when May came for me.

Hossack was calmer by the time Conrad arrived, although he was distressed and seemed "very much broken down." It was the only time that Conrad talked to John Hossack about his family situation, and Hossack told him that he felt that they were all against him and that he was very "unfortunately situated." He was considering the possibility of dividing his property and giving his wife and children a portion for their own; he would live separately from them. Conrad told the jury his reply: "I told him he had always been a friend to me, but that I could not give him any advice in a question of this kind."

According to Conrad, Margaret Hossack continued to talk to him about her fears. She was afraid to go to sleep, she told him, and sometimes "there would be weeks at a time when she would not take her clothes off." As Conrad testified,

> It seems as though things were always in a pitiable state of affairs and seemed as though she was always imposed upon . . . and this state of affairs had been running for some time back and she did not know what she would do nor how it would end. She always seemed afraid that he would kill some of them.

Just as Morrison had done, Conrad told Margaret not to worry: "I tried to pay very little attention to these talks and just tried to quiet her." Privately, though, Conrad feared that eventually somebody might get hurt: "I rather expected that in some kind of a family row that someone would strike a harder blow than was intended."

Conrad wasn't alone in his concern. Others noted Hossack's strange behavior, especially when he'd just left his family. They could tell by the wild look in his eyes when he was in a "spell." Fred Johnston saw that Hossack could get "worked up over something so that he didn't seem to know what he was doing."

Ev Henry had talked to Conrad about the possibility that Mr. Hossack be arrested so he wouldn't harm his family, and Conrad wondered whether that "might be the only way out of it." Fred Johnston had discussed with others whether Hossack should be committed to an insane asylum. But the men, all friends of John Hossack's, were reluctant to intervene, and nothing was done in either regard.

Like other neighbors, Conrad had heard Margaret Hossack say that she wished her husband were dead, and both he and Keller testified that she'd even asked William Haines to kill her husband.

William and Rinda Haines were in their midthirties, the same generation as the older Hossack children, and they lived just half a mile from the Hossack farm. On the night of the attack, Haines had told the Hossack children that he'd seen a strange man on his porch, but he wasn't asked about that at the inquest. The inquiries to both Haines and his wife focused primarily on their knowledge of strife in the Hossack family.

According to William and Rinda Haines, they'd known for years that John Hossack had a "pretty high temper." Many times, they'd come to visit the Hossacks and, according to Mrs. Haines, they could tell that the family had been quarreling: "Mr. Hossack would not talk, and you could see he was awful mad, and we just judged from his looks [that] they had been in trouble." She had often heard Margaret say that it would be better for the family if her husband were dead and that "it would be a God's blessing if he were taken."

But Mr. Haines denied that Margaret Hossack had asked him to kill her husband. On one occasion, he admitted, she had been "in a passion" and had told Haines that he and the other neighbors should come and "fix" her husband and "attend" to him. Haines hadn't thought, though, that she was suggesting murder, only that her husband deserved a good beating for the way he treated his family, "one he would remember and make him afraid to do these things any more." Haines told her that he would never do such a thing. He didn't want to "get into trouble by laying hands on my neighbors."

Rinda Haines remembered the conversation differently. She'd been in the buggy with her husband when Margaret had run out of her house and into the road to stop them:

> She wanted us to go down that night, that Mr. Hossack was on his tantrum; she always said he was on his tantrum. She was crying and she said she was afraid he would kill them. And Will says, there is a law for such as that. She went on talking, and she wanted him to bring another neighbor or two, just the same as to say, to mob him. At first she asked us to go. She wanted him to bring another man or two along. Will said it was not for him to hurt any of the family, that there was a law for such. Then she said, if you touch him, finish him. Don't touch him without you finish him. Well, that was just awful to Will and I, we couldn't hardly bear it. . . . She said she couldn't stay long down there, that he would catch on that she was down there telling the trouble.

Mrs. Haines had a theory about the source of the trouble between the Hossacks, based on a story she'd heard from John Hossack's mother. According to Grandma Hossack, her son had been in love with Margaret's sister, Jane, but "circumstances prevailed" upon him to marry Margaret. The union had never been a happy one. As Mrs. Haines put it, "Mr. Hossack was no angel in his family. [He] was aggravated an awful sight, and when a man don't like a woman there is lots of things comes up that makes them contrary to each other."

Other neighbors speculated that Hossack was especially strict with his children, and that his rage was often triggered when his wife took their side against his wishes; some thought that he was angry at the lack of discipline in the household.

Two of them suggested another motive: Margaret Hossack may have been jealous of her husband's relationship with someone else. The possibility was raised with Mary Nicholson, one of the only neighbors who claimed not to know about the Hossack family quarrels. John Hossack had visited her recently, she said, since he was helping her collect insurance after her husband's death. The questioners wanted to know about these meetings: How many times had he come? When had he arrived? Who else had been in the house during his visits? Mrs. Nicholson answered that she had seen John Hossack "about twice" since her husband had died. But six weeks later, at the grand jury hearing, her son John would testify that Hossack had visited their house "nearly every day" after Harvey Nicholson had passed away.

Later in the inquiry, the jurors asked Mrs. Nicholson a deliberately vague question: "Do you know anything that might be of interest in regard to the question that has not been brought up in the examination of you?" Mary Nicholson said she didn't, and then she was asked more directly:

"Do you know whether Mrs. Hossack was jealous of Mr. Hossack or not?"

"I never knew anything about it," she replied.

The same inquiry was put to the next witness, Mrs. George Grant, and she, too, denied any knowledge. Then the theory was dropped, and the topic was not raised again except to ask Margaret Hossack if her husband had ever, to her knowledge, had any "affection" for another woman. She replied in the negative; she said she hadn't known of any feelings like that on his part.

Whatever the reasons for the conflicts, many neighbors confirmed that Margaret Hossack had said she wanted to separate from her husband, claiming that she would have done so years before had it not been for the "disgrace" it would cause the family. Money was also a problem. John Hossack was a prosperous farmer, but he was not generous. As Rinda Haines put it, "Mr. Hossack always sold lots and had plenty of money, but that woman never got a cent of his money for anything." The property was in John Hossack's name. Margaret had told some neighbors that her husband had suggested dividing the farm: giving her and the children all the property except the west eighty acres, which he would keep for himself. She was in favor of the split, but the necessary legal steps were never taken. According to Conrad, "it seemed that about the time they were all agreed to divide the property, there would be a calm, and they did not do anything."

Talk of a separation had become more serious just one year before Hossack's death, when, according to testimony from neighbors and the Hossack children, a serious quarrel broke out between the couple on Thanksgiving Day. Hossack, angry with his daughters for making social plans without his knowledge, turned his rage on his wife when she took their side. When he went outside briefly, Mrs. Hossack left the house, and there was some suggestion that she escaped through an upstairs window. She fled to Will Conrad's house in the rain. Conrad described her visit:

> That evening I had gone to bed. I was asleep and did not dream anything until someone came and rapped on the door. Well, it sounded stealthy, was not an open rap. I waked up and says, who's there? No answer. I says, what do you want? No answer. Another little rap. I jumped out of bed and ran for the door, jerked the door open. Of course I was frightened; did not know what to expect. It was a wet rainy evening and I did not know what I was looking for.
>
> I was startled when she got near. I says, come in. She came in. Set a chair for her and says, set down. She said she did not have time. Once she walked to the window and

> looked out. She says, I want to ask a favor of you. . . . I want you to take me over to Ev's. I says, it is a pretty bad night to go over there. She says, I am going. I started on foot. It is worse than I thought it was. I did not have time to get my overshoes. I do not know whether I can make it or not. I says, you stay here until morning. She says, I cannot stay until morning; they would come for me. . . . She said she could not stand it any longer.
>
> We kept talking there. I told her I just would not go that night. She says, I must go. She could not go to bed; they would be after her. Finally, she started for the door and started out. I says, if you have got to go, it won't do for you to walk; you will never get there. If you have to go, I will take you. I had about concluded that maybe this was a good way out of it. I did not know what to do. So I went and hitched up and took her over to the Henrys.

Conrad took her to her daughter's house, and the next morning he gathered several men from the surrounding farms, including Frank Keller and Fred Johnston. Together, the men talked to Margaret Hossack and persuaded her to return home with Ev and Annie Henry. After Hossack had angrily confronted Ev Henry, insisting that his son-in-law leave his property, Keller and Johnston had themselves traveled to the Hossack farm to talk to the family and to urge reconciliation. In their testimony, the men admitted that their goal had been to convince the Hossacks not to divide the property and separate, and they believed that they had been successful. As Frank Keller told the inquest jury, "my understanding is that we got the children to agree to try and behave themselves, and Mrs. Hossack was to do the same and Mr. Hossack was to do the same and that they could try to live peaceably together."

Fred Johnston concluded the discussion by exacting a promise from the family members: They were to "let the matter drop and never mention it among themselves, or to me or to Mr. Keller, and I told them I never wanted to hear anything more about it, and they were not to talk to outsiders." Keller also emphasized the importance of secrecy, saying "that from that time forth, they should tell no man or woman, nor tell any person, about their troubles, were not to talk about it among themselves, were not to refer to it, and were, if possible, to forget it."

Johnston and Keller testified that they believed that all of the conflict had been resolved by the time they left the house. But Johnston admitted that Margaret had come to him as he was leaving:

> I had taken the children out in the kitchen and given them quite a lecturing, and Mr. Keller had his overcoat on ready to go, when Mrs. Hossack came in and begged me to stay all night; she was afraid after we got away it would break out again.

Johnston refused her request:

> I would not do it; told her I didn't think it would be the best thing to do under the circumstances; that they had all promised not to mention it again and I didn't think it was advisable for me to do it. She says, I want you to know one thing, that all he has told you is not true. I did not make her any answer.

During the year between this intervention and John Hossack's death, the neighbors who testified heard nothing of troubles in the family. When the Hossack children were questioned, they said that relations in the family had improved in those twelve months. As May said, "We have had some trouble since that, but nothing like we had then though."

Eight of the Hossack children, as well as two sons-in-law, were called as witnesses at the inquest. The five in the house on the night of the attack were asked to talk about that night and the preceding day. The questioners were most interested in their observations of their father's condition immediately after the attack, what he had said and the appearance of the wound. All the children remembered that he had spoken a few words, and Will had observed that his father's eye was swollen and his head was covered with a blood clot "about the size of a tea cup." The clot was smaller than that, according to Cassie and May, but they, too, had seen a lot of blood "piled" around the wounds, soaking into the bedclothes.

As with the neighbors, though, the inquiry primarily focused on the family during the years before the murder. For the most part, the children were reluctant to speak on the subject. The two youngest boys stated to the jury that they knew of no problems, while the others were only slightly more forthcoming. Will admitted that he remembered his father threatening Johnnie with a knife several years earlier. May confirmed that relations had been "quite bitter" between her parents at times, and Annie acknowledged that her parents sometimes used "very cross words," and that her father could be "quick tempered." But, she said, family members tried to refrain from discussing their difficulties with the neighbors and to bear them alone.

Annie and Ev Henry both claimed that they'd tried to keep the conflicts between her parents away from the public. As Henry said, "Before I married into this family, I thought there was not a family in the community got along as squarely, and that it went like clockwork." The questioner commended them, telling Annie, "We have found that you as a family done the right thing in trying to keep your quarrels to yourselves," although now, he stated, the family history was a main focus of the investigation and they were obliged to speak frankly.

Margaret Hossack was one of the last to testify. The questions about the attack on her husband were specific: How had she and her family spent the evening before? What had first alarmed her in the night? What had she done and said, seen and heard? Her answers were consistent with those of her children and with the reports she had given during the last two days to the neighbors, to the doctor, and to the authorities.

Eventually, the inquiries shifted. "Did you and Mr. Hossack ever have any trouble?"

She replied simply, "No sir, no more than we might some times get out of humor for a little bit, nothing much." The questioner seemed surprised: "You never really had any trouble?" She answered again: "No sir." The questions continued:

> "Did he ever abuse you?"
>
> "No sir."
>
> "Not at all?"
>
> "No sir."
>
> "Did he ever strike you with his fist?"
>
> "No sir."
>
> "Did you ever tell anybody that he did?"
>
> "No sir."
>
> "Did he ever abuse any of the children?"
>
> "No sir."
>
> "Did you ever tell anybody that he did?"
>
> "No sir."
>
> "Do you ever remember of his having any trouble with John?"
>
> "No sir, no more than some times John might not do things as he wanted, and he might scold him about it."
>
> "Did you know of his ever having a knife to kill John?"
>
> "No sir."
>
> "You never heard anything about that?"
>
> "No sir."
>
> "Did you know of his ever having a gun to kill John?"

"No sir. I never did."

"Did he ever make any threat toward John?"

"No sir."

"Did he ever make any threat toward you?"

"No sir." . . .

"Did you ever think that he might kill you?

"No sir, I did not."

"Or any other member of the family?"

"No sir."

"Did you ever tell any of the neighbors that you thought he might kill you . . . or kill any of the children?"

"No sir."

Margaret Hossack's denials continued. She denied ever having the conversations reported by the neighbors, ever seriously discussing the division of property, ever running away from home. She had never told anyone, she said, that she wished that her husband were dead; she had never even had such a thought as that.

The worst Margaret Hossack would say about her husband was that "sometimes he was kind of hard to get along with, but it would not take long to get over it." He could be "a hard man to care for when he was sick" and "when he got out of humor, he was a hard man to please." But he had been in better health during the last year, and it had been a good time for all of them; the boys had done everything to try to please him, and the family "never had a word of trouble." According to Margaret Hossack, her husband had been devoted to her and the children: "There was not a man who thought more of his family than he did or would do more for them."

Her questioners seemed incredulous as they listened to her testimony. One asked her, "Why in the name of God don't you tell us everything you know about it?" at the same time warning her, "The spirit of John Hossack . . . now listens to every question asked you." They persisted in asking about her difficulties with her husband, but she was consistent in her responses.

At the end of her testimony, she asked for permission to speak: "Well, gentlemen, I hope you don't think I killed him. I wouldn't do such a thing, I loved him too much." ☾

THE INTERROGATION OF witnesses concluded at 8 P.M. on Tuesday. Clammer, who was not permitted to join in the deliberations, left the room so that the three jurors could discuss the case with Coroner Dale. If the inquest jury named a suspect in its verdict, Dale had the power to immediately order that person's arrest.

The Hossack family remained in seclusion upstairs.

At 11 P.M., George Clammer was called to the sitting room to receive the verdict. It was a simple statement, signed by the three jurors: "We do find that said deceased came to his death by two blows on the head; one by a sharp instrument and one with a blunt instrument."

The jury had been unable to agree that Margaret Hossack should be named as a suspect. T. W. Passwater was in favor of identifying her as the person responsible for her husband's death, but neither C. D. Johnson nor Fred Johnston would assent to such a conclusion. The decision was unwelcome news for the county attorney.

Dale and Clammer separated themselves from the group to consult briefly. Then they jointly dismissed the members of the jury, thanking them for their services and telling them that their work was completed. Neither of the authorities, however, remembered to attend to one important matter—they did not take possession of the bloodied chemise.

4.

To any peace officer of this state:

Preliminary information upon oath having this day been filed with me, charging that the crime of Murder in the first degree has been committed and accusing Margaret Hossack thereof:

You are commanded forthwith to arrest the said Margaret Hossack and bring him [*sic*] before me at my office in Washington Township, Warren County, Iowa. Or in case of my inability to act, or in my absence, before the nearest or most accessible magistrate in this county.

Dated at Indianola, Iowa, this 5 day of Dec. A.D. 1900 —arrest warrant issued and signed by H. L. ROSS, Justice of the Peace

ON WEDNESDAY MORNING, December 5, the corpse of John Hossack was moved from the cooling board and placed in a pine coffin in the same small, downstairs bedroom where he had died on Sunday morning.

The Hossack family faced the preparations for the burial as well as the formidable task of confronting the people in their community. Many of the men summoned to the farm on Saturday night and Sunday morning—fellow farmers and Masons, members of John Hossack's church, his political and business associates—would attend the services and pay their final respects. There would also be the merely curious: spectators who, by word of mouth or from newspaper accounts, had come to know of the strange and terrible tragedy that had occurred at the Hossack farm.

At midmorning the coffin was carried out of the house and placed in the back of a farm wagon.

Margaret Hossack emerged wearing a black dress and a hat with a black veil. She was suffering from a head cold and fatigue, and her eyes were puffy and red. She walked to the buggy, stepped up, and sat on the front seat. One of her sons sat beside her, shook the reins over the backs of the horses, and the buggy started down the uneven road toward New Virginia.

At about the same time, Sheriff Hodson was meeting with Justice H. L. Ross, a magistrate in Indianola. Despite the jury's refusal to name a suspect, Ross had been persuaded by George Clammer earlier that morning to issue an arrest warrant calling for the apprehension of Margaret Hossack and accusing her of murder in the first degree.

Sheriff Hodson went home, hitched a team of horses to his buggy, and headed toward New Virginia. Seated beside him was his deputy, Grant Kimer. Marcia Bell Hodson, the sheriff's wife, joined the two lawmen for the twenty-two-mile drive from Indianola to New Virginia. ☾

IN 1900 THERE were no daily newspapers in Warren County. The six weekly papers in the county, three in Indianola, one each in Lacona, Milo, and New Virginia, were all published on Thursdays. With a circulation of 2,000 readers, the *Indianola Herald* reached the most citizens, but its coverage of the Hossack murder didn't begin until December 6, five days after the attack.

The first reports of John Hossack's murder appeared on Monday, December 3, in the four Des Moines daily papers, published with bold headlines such as FOUL MURDER NEAR INDIANOLA in the *Daily Capital* and PROMINENT FARMER ROBBED AND KILLED in the *Daily News.* Reporters, acting as fledging detectives, arrived in Indianola to see what they could uncover and to develop theories about the case. The sensational aspects of the Hossack murder—a leading citizen mysteriously killed with an ax in the dead of night—were guaranteed to attract readers. Given the rumors about family discord, the uncertainty about who might benefit from Hossack's demise, and the ongoing investigation, editors were optimistic about the story's longevity.

Competition was keen among the papers, and the *Daily News* was the clear frontrunner. With a circulation of 25,000, it was the largest daily in the state of Iowa, far surpassing its afternoon rival, the *Daily Capital,* which served 9,300 patrons. The *Daily Leader* was the premier morning paper. By 1900 its circulation had reached 17,000, which was more than double the figure for the *Iowa State Register* (later renamed the *Des Moines Register*). News dealers from Council Bluffs to Red Oak to Iowa City to Waterloo provided these Des Moines papers to their customers.

The reporter assigned to the story for the *Daily News* was a young woman named Susan Glaspell. She was twenty-four years old, bright, and ambitious. After graduating with honors from Drake University in the spring of 1899, Glaspell had been hired by the newspaper as a legislative reporter, covering politics and state government and writing whimsical social commentary in a column called "News Girl."

In an era when few women covered hard news or the affairs of men, the slender, attractive Glaspell was a distinctive presence. Born and raised in Davenport, Iowa, a small, riverfront community dominated by religious and traditional values, where the opportunities for success were limited by gender, family background, class distinctions, and money, she had started writing for a trio of local papers before going to college. At first she was designated to report on social and cultural life in Davenport—the comings and goings of the town's upper crust, openings of plays and musicals—but soon she was writing more distinctive essays: pungent and tongue-in-cheek critiques of life in the Midwest at the end of the nineteenth century. Expressing some of her own interests, her columns derided social conventions and customs that tended to stereotype women or limit their aspirations.

The killing of John Hossack was Glaspell's first murder case. Her initial report offered only a few brief facts and the theory that burglars had committed the offense, but the next day she emphasized the drama of the investigation and informed her readers that burglary was no longer thought to be the motive of the crime. People were "all at sea as to who killed Hossack or for what reason," Glaspell wrote, although one possibility had been suggested: "It is rumored that trouble had arisen in the Hossack household and that possibly some relative committed the murder."

On Wednesday afternoon, in her third article, Glaspell scooped her colleagues. Before Sheriff Hodson's buggy had reached New Virginia, afternoon readers of the *Daily News* were treated to breaking news:

SHERIFF AFTER MRS. HOSSACK

SENSATIONAL TURN TAKEN AT INDIANOLA.

Coroner's Jury Returns Its Verdict This Morning—
Mrs. Hossack Thought to Be Crazy.

INDIANOLA. DEC. 5. (Special.)—The Hossack murder case took a sensational turn today when the sheriff went to Medora for the avowed purpose of arresting Mrs. Hossack, wife of the murdered man. The departure of the sheriff was kept a profound secret for a time, but eventually some of the county officials were induced to reveal to your correspondent that the object of the trip was the arrest of Mrs. Hossack.

The evidence is by no means conclusive of Mrs. Hossack's guilt, but the testimony before the coroner's jury was such as to raise a suspicion of guilt and her arrest was decided upon as a matter of precaution.

Members of the Hossack family are understood to have

testified before the coroner's jury that the blood on the ax found under the corn crib was caused by chopping off the head of a turkey the day before the murder. It is now reported that a child admitted on cross-examination that he himself placed the ax in the corn crib the evening before the murder and that at that time there was no blood on it.

Friends of Mrs. Hossack are beginning to suggest that she is insane and that she has been in this condition for a year and a half, under the constant surveillance of members of the family.

The robbery theory has been wholly abandoned, as absolutely nothing was taken and no suspicious characters were seen in the neighborhood prior or subsequent to the murder.

The most suspicious circumstance in connection with the crime is the testimony of Mrs. Hossack that she lay in bed by the side of her husband while his skull was crushed in two places, and was not awakened in time to see any one leave the house.

The developments since the murder that the members of the Hossack family were not on pleasant relations with each other is a complete surprise, as Hossack was not supposed to have an enemy in the world. ☾

By the time Sheriff Hodson reached New Virginia, the Hossack funeral services in the Methodist church were under way. A large crowd had gathered in the street. Onlookers whispered to one another, nodding in the direction of the sheriff. Hodson's arrival meant that some legal action—probably an arrest—was imminent.

Hodson parked his buggy down the street from the church, trying to be as inconspicuous as possible, and waited for the service to conclude. To the extent he could, the sheriff ignored the crowd. It was a clear, mild December day, and he was in no particular hurry.

An hour later the church doors opened. The family of John Hossack emerged first and once again loaded the casket into the back of the wagon. Mourners streamed out of the church, milling about with the crowd.

Sheriff Hodson observed the scene from his seat in the buggy, but Deputy Kimer climbed down and crossed the street. Standing half a foot taller than almost everyone around him, Kimer angled through the crowd like a politician greeting well-wishers, moving amiably from one person to the next, shaking hands, exchanging a few words. The older Hossack boys eyed the deputy cautiously.

With the Hossack family leading the way, the mourners formed a long line of buggies, moving in the direction of the New Virginia cemetery a little more than 600 yards from the church. Kimer ambled back to Hodson's buggy and jumped up into the front seat. Hodson jiggled the reins and the buggy jerked forward, following the procession.

It didn't take the horses long to climb the low hill that led to the cemetery. The mourners halted their teams at the top of the rise and then tied them to the hitching poles by its gate. Hodson remained at the bottom of the hill, keeping a conspicuous distance from the funeral crowd.

Hodson watched as the pine box was pulled from the wagon. The Methodist pastor, solemn and serious, led the procession, his bare head bowed. Pallbearers followed the pastor, with Margaret Hossack walking directly behind them. She clung to the arm of her elderly brother, Donald Murchison, a former sheriff from Illinois. As the mourners filed through the gate, a few of them turned and glanced down the hill at the sheriff and his deputy.

In the northeast corner of the cemetery, the new gravesite had been prepared, a mound of soil to one side; the graves of John Hossack's parents and infant son were adjacent to the hollowed-out earth. The pastor signaled for the coffin to be lowered and the crowd moved closer, pushing in behind the family members.

As the observers settled into place, Sheriff Hodson moved his grayish-brown team of horses forward, driving them slowly up the hill. He turned them at the gate and stopped just in front of the hearse. Leaving Mrs. Hodson in the back of the buggy, Hodson and Kimer walked up the path toward the service, then separated. The sheriff positioned himself to the left of the crowd; the deputy stepped to the right.

Eventually the pastor concluded his remarks with the words "Dust to dust and ashes to ashes" and tossed a fistful of earth into the open grave. The clods drummed off the wooden casket.

People stepped away and lined the graveled path. The Hossack children formed a protective half-circle around their mother and, moving as a unit, slowly made their way toward the gate and the waiting carriages. Nervous friends and neighbors followed in silence.

As Margaret Hossack approached the gate, the sheriff planted himself directly in her path, facing her. She paused in front of him, took two steps forward, and stopped. Hodson advanced to meet her and spoke plainly and directly, telling her she was under arrest for the murder of her husband.

A murmur rippled through the crowd. Donald Murchison leaned over and spoke softly to his sister, explaining that it was necessary that she go with the sheriff. A few seconds passed as the terrible weight of that knowledge hung in the air between the sheriff and the accused woman. She lifted her veil and started to speak, and Hodson paused. He didn't intend to rush things. He could see that her face was twisted by emotion and that she was about to cry. The black veil dropped back in place, covering her features.

Then the sheriff reached out and put his hand on the widow's arm. Almost apologetically, he said, "This is not a matter of my choosing."

Donald Murchison stepped forward and, with Hodson, supported his sister in walking the few feet from the cemetery gate to the sheriff's carriage. She climbed into the backseat, where Marcia Hodson was waiting. There, the accused woman broke down. She put both hands to her face and sobbed, her body shaking convulsively as she wept.

The sheriff took her away. His buggy descended slowly and at the bottom of the hill turned east, on the road to Indianola. Left behind, the funeral crowd lingered for a few moments and then prepared to head for their homes.

Some of them felt a sense of relief that a suspect had been arrested for the slaying of their neighbor and that the process of justice was under way. Others believed that Margaret Hossack could not be guilty, and that another person, still at large, had committed the crime. For those who believed her responsible for the death of her husband—those who had listened to her stories and understood her fears—the moment of her arrest must have sent a shiver of shared guilt down their spines.

As the sheriff's buggy disappeared from sight, the mourners left the cemetery. The shuffling of horses' hooves beat an uneven rhythm as shadows began to fall in the dimming December twilight.

It was nearly 8:30 that Wednesday night when Sheriff Hodson's buggy carried Margaret Hossack into downtown Indianola. Aware of the public speculation the case had triggered, the sheriff was relieved that the scene was calm. The presence of an accused murderer in his custody—a woman, no less—was unusual enough to attract attention.

The county jail, located just one block south of the courthouse, was a small annex to his own residence, where Hodson lived with his wife and their young son, Paul. The jail wasn't used very often. Occasionally federal prisoners were housed there for safekeeping, but the average number of Warren County residents jailed in a year was fewer than a dozen, and most of those were for minor crimes.

Sheriff Hodson escorted his prisoner to her cell and let his wife check on her to see if she needed anything. Then Hodson took care of his horses and went to bed.

5.

In these days, when the laws of the land, and also the laws of the great Creator, are openly violated, and when those whose duty it is to bring offenders to justice, display such sympathetic feelings toward those who barbarously infringe upon the lives and property of their fellowmen, when such unnecessary expenses are incurred in prolonged, needless litigation to prove that which is too well known, is it to be wondered at when law-abiding citizens, feeling their insecurity of life and property, should form themselves into associations for self-protection? Neither is it to be wondered at that those associations thus formed should bring down upon themselves the abuse and slander of those who palliate with law and justice, and speak of them as the reckless vigilantes. . . . We have no code of laws governing the mode of punishing the offenders, but circumstances govern the case. Thus we stand before the world, asking that the laws be faithfully executed by those in authority, protesting also against unfair means to turn loose upon society those who have forfeited their lives by taking the lives of their fellowmen, pledging ourselves for the innocent, at the same time demanding that the guilty be punished.—*Indianola Herald,* March 9, 1876 (letter to the editors regarding the Warren County North River Detective Association)

ON THURSDAY MORNING, December 6, 1900, five men—Alexander and Johnnie, Margaret Hossack's two eldest sons; Ev Henry and Joe Kemp, her two sons-in-law; and Donald Murchison, her brother—arrived in Indianola to hire an attorney to defend the woman arrested for murder.

The community of Indianola numbered hardly more than

three thousand citizens. Townspeople lived within a few blocks of the town square, residing in comfortable frame houses with modest front porches, city dwellers with country roots. The town council in 1887 had decreed that livestock had to be restrained from running at large, but many residents continued to keep cows, pigs, chickens, and horses on their property.

The three-story county courthouse, built of brick and stone in 1868, was situated in the town square. Clustered around the square were the usual banks, churches, business establishments, and law offices. Just west of downtown, the campus of Simpson College sprawled over several acres. The town was laid out in an orderly grid; avenues extended east and west, intersecting streets that ran north and south. Sturdy maples and solid oaks stood like sentries in straight rows. The railroad linked Indianola to larger cities and markets. Evidence of progress had also appeared in the form of limited telephone service and electric lights. Utility poles, some tilting at precarious angles, lined the streets.

The representatives of the Hossack family tied their team to a hitching post near the southwest corner of the courthouse square, entered the Worth Savings Bank Building, and proceeded to the law offices of Henderson and Berry. The five-room suite occupied by the law firm was roomy and elegant by local standards. It was decorated with oiled sycamore woodwork and had indoor toilets, fireproof vaults, and hot-water heating.

Senator William H. Berry and his partner, Judge John H. Henderson, had been in business together off and on for nearly thirty years. They were a formidable duo, as successful in the backrooms of local politics as in the public sphere of the courthouse. Berry had served two terms as a state senator; Henderson, the first white male born in Warren County and the son of the county's legendary founding father, Paris P. Henderson, had spent ten years as a district and circuit court judge.

It was Senator Berry who greeted the men. Berry was a towering and robust figure, standing more than six feet tall and weighing over 250 pounds. At the age of fifty-one, he possessed a mass of dark, wavy hair on a large head. The handsome lawyer thrived in the public spotlight, and he was known as a powerful figure in the state Republican Party. He was experienced in legal practice, although he could not boast of extensive familiarity with murder trials. He had worked on only one such case: Four years earlier, he had been hired to assist the county attorney in prosecuting the McCuddin brothers for murder.

Berry talked to the Hossack men for two hours and finally agreed to take the case. The men paid him a $500 retainer. In addition, the family agreed that a bonus of $1,500 cash would be paid if he was successful in securing an acquittal.

By the time Berry signed on as the lawyer for Margaret Hossack, the murder and ensuing investigation had already aroused strong feelings among the populace. The crime was brutal and seemed premeditated; the victim, who had apparently had no chance to defend himself, was well known in the community. Berry could expect that many people would demand a swift resolution and severe punishment, and that the jury members who would decide his client's fate would be men who identified with John Hossack. Ample evidence existed to show that the couple had frequently quarreled in the past, and marital conflicts were often seen as strong proof of a motive for one spouse to kill the other.

On the other hand, no woman had ever before been arrested or charged with murder in the history of Warren County. On the cusp of a new century, fifty years after the beginning of the movement for equal rights for women, there were still deeply ingrained expectations about how women were supposed to behave. This might work in Berry's favor. Potential jurors, men with grown daughters and wives in their own households, might be reluctant to believe that a woman could act with such malice and violence toward a sleeping man. ☾

On the prosecution side, Coroner Dale and County Attorney Clammer were both young men. Neither was experienced in homicide investigations, and people in the community wondered whether the two were capable of doing their jobs in this case.

Warren County residents had good reason to doubt that justice could be found at the hands of the legal authorities. Many of them could remember the sensational "Tear Down" murders, which had occurred almost twenty-five years earlier, in 1876, when men in several different families had attacked one another with guns and knives one night after a church revival service. When the melee was over, three people lay mortally wounded, with another badly hurt. Over a four-year period, three separate trials were held, and three men were convicted of murder in the second degree. But the Iowa Supreme Court reversed all three convictions on technical grounds, and no one was ever punished for the crimes.

The McCuddin case had also raised questions about the competence of the authorities, though the failure was blamed on inconclusive evidence rather than lack of effort by lawyers for the state. After a young man, Ed Knotts, died under suspicious circumstances, two separate grand juries had brought indictments in the case, and three men, including the two McCuddin brothers, were indicted and tried. While incurring significant costs at taxpayer expense, the Warren County attorney had been unable to secure guilty verdicts. The mystery of the death of Ed Knotts remained unsolved.

Early in the county's history, as its justice system slowly evolved but was yet to be trusted, vigilante groups had formed to protect citizens. The groups operated openly; some published their charters and met publicly in schoolhouses. Other groups of men, less formally organized, came together and acted when they felt the situation demanded it.

While the trials following the Tear Down murders were in progress, in October 1877, a man named Reuben Proctor allegedly shot a young woman during the course of a robbery at her father's house. For several days, the woman, Augusta Cading, lingered near death. She named Proctor as the masked assailant who had attacked her. He was taken into custody and the crime was investigated, but the population was restless, eager for quick justice. A crowd of nearly three hundred men appeared at the county jail with a battering ram and tried to break down the doors to the jail to get to Proctor. Sheriff Joe Meek stood his ground and eventually the crowd dispersed.

A few days later, as Sheriff Meek escorted Proctor from the jail to a courtroom, a group calling itself the Concerned Vigilantes materialized and grabbed the prisoner from the authorities. They dragged him a short distance away, where they placed a noose around his neck and tied his hands behind his back. The rope was slung over the wooden beam of a livestock scale, and Proctor was yanked into the air and hung. The coroner cut down the body and convened an inquest next to the corpse, in an empty storeroom near the site of the lynching. The inquest verdict, rendered less than thirty minutes after Proctor had been seized by the mob, declared that Proctor's death had occurred "at the hands of parties unknown." Augusta Cading died the next morning.

Twenty-three years later, citizens in the county watched Dale and Clammer investigate the murder of John Hossack and wondered whether the legal process could be trusted this time. Some whispered that vigilantes were again prepared to punish the guilty party if the authorities were too slow. ☾

ON FRIDAY, DECEMBER 7, Deputy Kimer was dispatched to the Hossack farm to look for additional evidence. Several of the Hossack children recognized him and came out to meet him.

Kimer explained that, in particular, he was looking for the chemise Margaret Hossack had worn the night of the attack. Johnnie, Cassie, and Will offered to help with the search. Louie, pretty, dark-haired, and with a swollen belly, joined the group. Later that evening she would give birth to her first child in the downstairs bedroom where her father had died. The baby was named John after his murdered grandfather.

Kimer discovered the bloodstained mattress and bedclothes tossed in a heap in the yard. He searched the upstairs closets for Margaret Hossack's clothing. Downstairs, he looked in the couple's bedroom and noticed a container of embalming fluid resting on the sewing machine in the northeast corner.

At last he located the chemise. It was submerged under a few rags in a tobacco bucket filled with bloody water, on the ground under the Hossack's bedroom window. Johnnie Hossack used a stick to pull the saturated garment from the pail.

Given its condition, the chemise had almost no evidentiary value, and Kimer failed to turn up any other significant physical evidence. Still, Clammer and Dale would remain steadfast in their belief that Margaret Hossack had committed the crime. ☾

ACCORDING TO THE December 7 *Daily Leader*, the Hossack murder was "almost the sole topic of general conversation among the people of Indianola and the county" and public sentiment was divided: "While the trend . . . is apparently against the woman, there are many who insist that no woman of her character and standing could be so vicious and depraved as to commit a deed so revolting and unnatural." In an interview that accompanied the article, George Clammer made it clear that he felt no such doubt. He was certain that Margaret Hossack had killed her husband, and he outlined in detail his reasons, as if he were already arguing to a jury.

Clammer had reached his conclusion, the *Leader* reported, after a thorough investigation of the premises and interviews with the accused woman, her children, and her neighbors. Before conducting the inquiry, he had sought to "disabuse [his] mind of all bias or prejudice," and he proceeded with a "fixed determination . . . to allow the facts to develop the theory." He was rewarded by discovering many facts "pregnant with significance," sufficient to convince him that she was lying in her account of what had happened that night.

One example, according to Clammer, was the fact that Margaret Hossack was not touched by the ax. The bed that she shared with her husband was close against the wall on the side where John Hossack lay, and she claimed that she and her husband were lying in bed only six or eight inches apart. But, if that were so, the attacker would have reached across her with the ax. In Clammer's opinion "it would have been impossible . . . for a third party to have inflicted the wound on the right side of Hossack's head next to that of his wife, and not have struck her also," giving him clear evidence that her account was a fabricated one.

Other oddities in her story made it impossible to believe. She said that she was awakened by a loud noise in the night and then heard the door to the outside close, as if an intruder were leaving the house. By her own account, though, she made no attempt to awaken her husband at this point, although the man slept with a loaded Winchester rifle by his side, a weapon he could have easily reached. Instead, the woman called out to her children sleeping upstairs, in a voice that was so lacking in excitement that her oldest daughter told her to go back to bed. In Clammer's mind, the method of the attack also incriminated her: "The manner in which the wound was made was eloquent testimony. . . . It suggested having been made by a straight down stroke such as a woman would make, by seizing the helve and driving it downward in an almost straight line. The stroke, if delivered by a man, would have been overhanded."

And Clammer had discovered that the accused woman had a clear motive for murder. It had become apparent that the couple had lived in a state of long-continuing friction, with frequent and recurring quarrels. In Clammer's opinion, the woman had "brooded over these troubles until they bred in her a fierce hatred for Hossack which ended in his assassination."

Coroner Dale was quoted in the same article as saying that he, too, had concluded that Margaret Hossack was guilty. From a medical standpoint, the most significant evidence came from the Hossack children, whose testimony suggested that the woman had not called them immediately, as she claimed. When the children saw their father, within minutes of being awakened by their mother, he was semiconscious and talking in a rambling fashion. And yet, according to Dale, the victim would have been in a state of extreme shock, making speech impossible until at least eight to ten minutes after the attack. The children had also reported that they had seen a blood clot on their father's head; but the blood could not have coagulated immediately: a clot would have taken at least five to ten minutes to form. Based on this evidence, Dale believed that Margaret Hossack had wielded the ax against her husband herself, intending to kill him. When, after several minutes, she saw that he had returned to consciousness and "manifested alarming symptoms of revival," she began to fear "detection and exposure" for her act. Only then did she call her children, with a determination to "put on a bold front and claim the attempted murder was the act of some one bent on robbery."

In fact the evidence cited by Clammer and Dale was not as conclusive as it appeared in the reported interviews. At the inquest the doctors had disagreed about when speech would have been possible for John Hossack, and reports from the children about the appearance of their father's head were hardly consistent on the existence of a blood clot. Margaret Hossack's story of sleeping through the attack was difficult to believe, but dishonesty on that point wouldn't necessarily prove she was guilty of murder. Perhaps she had been out of bed at the time of the attack, and someone else had wielded the ax.

The inquest jury, of course, had heard the same evidence as Clammer and Dale, but it had decided not to charge Margaret Hossack with murder. According to the *Daily Leader,* Dale explained the jury's decision by pointing out that the two jurors who had refused to name her lived in the near vicinity of her sons-in-law. They wouldn't have wanted to "become embroiled in difficulties" with their neighbors. Dale didn't mention that *he* had chosen the three members of the inquest jury as men who could be objective.

After being quoted verbatim in print—and at great length—Clammer may have decided that it was unwise and impolitic to divulge so much of his thinking less than a week after the murder. Three days later, under the subheading "Much Hot Air Was Written," Susan Glaspell reported in the *Daily News* that, according to Clammer, the published interview in the *Daily Leader* was a fiction: "County Attorney Clammer stated today that the interviews . . . purporting to come from him were fake and that he has given out nothing concerning the case."

6.

The wife of John Hossack, arrested on the charge of having beaten out his brains with an ax, has employed Henderson and Berry as her attorneys and is preparing to fight the case to the end.

She was locked up in the county jail here last night at 8:30. She manifested no emotion, took her arrest calmly and absolutely declined to make any statement concerning her guilt or innocence.

Members of the Hossack family are standing by her solidly, but public sentiment is overwhelmingly against her.

Though past 50 years of age, she is tall and powerful and looks like she would be dangerous if aroused to a point of hatred.—SUSAN GLASPELL, in the *Des Moines Daily News*, December 6, 1900

THAT SATURDAY MORNING, Margaret Hossack was allowed to see her sons Alex and Johnnie, but only in the presence of Deputy Kimer. They discussed farm business, notably the appointment of Fred Johnston as the administrator of John Hossack's estate; according to Kimer, they didn't talk about the murder.

That afternoon, Senator Berry visited with his new client for the first time, talking privately with her for more than an hour. When Berry emerged from the jail, he was immediately questioned by waiting reporters. Of primary interest was the preliminary hearing, scheduled for the following Tuesday, when a judge would listen to evidence presented by both sides and decide whether the case should go forward. Senator Berry was coy, refusing to divulge anything about the nature of his conversation with Margaret Hossack or his defense strategy. As for speculation that the hearing would be waived, sending the case directly to a grand jury, Berry responded by deferring to the members of the community: "They know more than I do, then."

On Tuesday, December 11, a throng of several hundred gathered in the streets around the courthouse, hoping to catch a glimpse of the defendant on her way to court. A few minutes before 10 A.M., Sheriff Hodson, trying to protect his prisoner from the crowd, escorted her from the jail to the courthouse by way of a back alley, slipping into the office of Justice of the Peace H. M. Ross before the spectators realized what had happened.

With her children by her side, Margaret Hossack stood before the magistrate and listened as her attorneys indicated that she wished to waive the preliminary hearing. Her lawyers expected that the case would be heard by the grand jury at its next session, scheduled for January 8, 1901, with Judge James Harvey Applegate presiding. Justice Ross refused to release the defendant on bond but took the matter under advisement, promising to make a decision within the next few days. The proceeding was over in a matter of minutes, and Hodson, unable to avoid the eager onlookers this time, returned his prisoner to the safety of the county jail.

Susan Glaspell was among those outside the courthouse, and she saw Margaret Hossack in person for the first time. That afternoon, Glaspell secured an interview with Justice Ross. She asked him directly whether or not he intended to allow the prisoner to post bond. "Judging from the evidence submitted at the coroner's inquest," he told Glaspell, "I regard Mrs. Hossack's offense bailable." ☾

BY THE TIME she reported on the Hossack murder, Susan Glaspell was well acquainted with the history and ideals of the movement for women's rights, which evolved out of a meeting in Seneca Falls, New York, in July 1848. Three of the most prominent members of the movement, Lucy Stone, Elizabeth Cady Stanton, and Susan B. Anthony, lectured and campaigned in Iowa as early as 1871 in support of a woman's suffrage amendment to the state constitution. In particular, the presence of Anthony was felt in Iowa over the course of the next three decades, as she passionately argued for women's rights: to divorce, to own property, to be protected from abusive husbands, to vote, and to sit on juries. She spoke in all major cities in the state, including Davenport, where she lectured five years before Glaspell's birth, and her appearances were widely reported in Iowa newspapers. For thirty-eight years Anthony had been president of the National Woman Suffrage Association, an office she relinquished in 1900 at the age of eighty. Carrie Chapman Catt, raised and educated in Iowa, was selected to succeed Anthony. Catt had been active in the struggle for a state woman's suffrage amendment, but the Iowa legislature continued to reject the change. In 1900 the General Assembly again turned it down, despite petitions from across the state bearing more than 100,000 signatures.

Glaspell would become more radical in her thinking and writing in later years, but by 1900 she had not yet written anything directly in support of the cause. A subtle turning point in Glaspell's thinking about women, however, occurred in the first week of her reporting on the Hossack case.

A few days after Margaret Hossack's arrest, Glaspell visited the scene of the crime, probably on the same day that Deputy Kimer searched for evidence at the farmhouse. It was a moment that stayed in her memory for the rest of her life. Reflecting on that event twenty-seven years later, Glaspell wrote, "When I was a newspaper reporter out in Iowa, I was sent downstate to do a murder trial, and I never forgot going into the kitchen of a woman locked up in town."

Glaspell was approximately the same age as Margaret Hossack's daughters, but in terms of the arc of her experience and education, she represented a different generation. She was employed in a job she had chosen, and she was self-supporting. She was independent and single, unburdened by a husband or children or the daily chores required of farmwomen. Despite the small world of Davenport in which she'd been raised, Glaspell had attended college, where she was exposed to literature and trends of intellectual thought that thrust her toward the twentieth century as a modern woman. She saw herself as someone with choices to make about her future and her career, and she continued to nurture a deep desire to be a writer.

As Glaspell stood in the Hossack kitchen that day, it became clear to her that Margaret Hossack had lived a completely different kind of life. The harsh realities of the other woman's experience affected her perception and her future reporting.

In her early articles, written during the first days after the crime and prior to setting eyes on Mrs. Hossack or the scene of the murder, Glaspell focused on the investigation. She included portrayals of Margaret Hossack as unemotional, seemingly unrepentant, powerful and possibly dangerous. According to Glaspell, "friends of Mrs. Hossack are beginning to suggest that she was insane."

As the *News* vied with the *Daily Capital* for the most complete coverage, Glaspell's early articles were designed to hook readers and sustain their interest. Glaspell reported the facts—though not always accurately—and also speculated about theories and suspects. In her first piece she hypothesized that the murderer was an intruder intent on robbery. Two days later, when Margaret Hossack was suspected of involvement in the crime, Glaspell suggested that perhaps the motive was an alleged $5,000 life insurance policy carried by the victim. In other articles, she seized on the reasoning favored by the legal authorities:

John Hossack was hated by his wife and family and killed by one of them.

Glaspell related the story as a kind of evolving mystery in which various people took the stage as either major or supporting characters in the drama. Margaret Hossack's arrest made her the obvious target of the investigation, but Glaspell also reported the history of quarrels between John Hossack and his neighbor William Haines, as well as Hossack's longstanding conflicts with his older sons. Any one of these people, Glaspell suggested, could have been the murderer. Glaspell even put herself into the script. In several of these early articles, playing the role of a detective reporting directly on the clues she uncovered as the investigation proceeded, Glaspell referred to herself in the third person as "your correspondent," a device that she'd previously employed in her "News Girl" features.

But the tone of Glaspell's reporting changed after she visited the farmhouse and when, a few days later, she saw Margaret Hossack in person at the courthouse. Glaspell's descriptions became more sympathetic, evoking empathy more than animosity. On December 11 she described the prisoner as "worn and emaciated" and reported that "Sheriff Hodson says that within the past few days she has begun to show signs of weakness and at different intervals he has noticed red and swollen eyelids indicating that she has been weeping."

On December 12, Glaspell wrote her longest article yet on the case, with the headline MRS. HOSSACK MAY YET BE PROVEN INNOCENT: TIDE OF SENTIMENT TURNS SLIGHTLY IN HER FAVOR. The story started with an image of Margaret Hossack hearing the news that she would, in all probability, be released on bail later that week; the woman, according to Glaspell, "looked up into the officer's face, smiled and remarked that she would be glad to get home again with her children, but did not manifest any great joy at the news." On its second page, the article included an artist's depiction of Margaret Hossack sitting in the courtroom. She looked subdued and matronly in a high-necked dress and with her hair covered by a tight-fitting cap; her arms were crossed, her head was bowed. Under the drawing, the caption noted that "she kept her eyes almost continuously on the floor." Glaspell described her:

> She is intelligent and to visitors who had occasion to go to the home even only a few months prior to the murder she was attentive to her husband, seeming to anticipate his wants, and saw that he wished for nothing. She is said to be a woman who is quick tempered, high strung, like all Scotch women, but of a deeply religious turn of mind.

Glaspell went on to rehash the details of the case, suggesting again that Berry and Henderson might attempt to mount an insanity defense and mentioning that Johnnie Hossack was the source of many of the family quarrels. The boy, Glaspell reported, had a particular interest in seeing "that the matter be cleared up as quickly as possible, so there can be no finger of suspicion pointed . . . in his direction." Noting that authorities believed a family member was guilty, Glaspell again made the point that John Hossack's children might also be considered suspects.

The article ended with a brief comment on the relationship between Margaret Hossack and her husband: "No one ever regarded the quarrels between the couple as serious." ☾

RUMORS AND THEORIES about the crime circulated throughout the community, initially by word of mouth and soon reaching full public exposure in sermons and newspaper articles. The first news story in the *Indianola Advocate-Tribune*, which appeared on Thursday, December 6, five days after the murder, stated the facts of the crime and also raised suspicions that Mrs. Hossack had not told the truth at the inquest. Three days later, a local minister preached a sermon proclaiming his own belief in Margaret Hossack's innocence and asking his parishioners to regard her as so unless she was convicted of murder.

In its next issue, on December 13, the *Advocate-Tribune* published a long, unsigned editorial entitled "The Moulders of Public Opinion." Responding to the charge that the press was making a case against the accused woman, the author of the editorial asserted that it was "just as censurable" for the pulpit to "manufacture feeling" on her behalf. The circumstances surrounding the case were too suspicious and incriminating to indulge in a presumption of her innocence without further explanation on her part. The article concluded:

> We should not allow our sympathies to prompt us to attempt to thwart the ends of justice. . . . John Hossack's blood cries out for vengeance. . . . It behooves the people of this country to spare no effort to search out and convict the criminal. Mrs. Hossack is entitled to receive and will receive the benefit of every reasonable doubt. Yet all the known circumstances seem so incriminating that the public can not reasonably be expected to be content with less than a satisfactory explanation at her hands.
>
> In our sympathy for the prisoner we must not forget that John Hossack was murdered, brutally, foully murdered, and by her own declaration he was thus murdered while in bed with her. For the sake of humanity we pray God she may be able to establish her innocence—satisfactorily explain every incriminating circumstance and that the real criminal may prove to be outside the murdered man's own household. But whether without or within his household the public has a right to demand and does demand that the murderer be searched out and punished.

7.

> There is every indication that the Hossack case will be hard fought in the courts. The fact [is] that all of the evidence against Mrs. Hossack, as far as has been given out, is purely circumstantial; that the family has lived in the vicinity for more than thirty years, and has numberless friends. The family is well-to-do and will have plenty of money at its command to fight the case.—*Des Moines Daily Capital*, December 6, 1900

WILLIAM BERRY HAD always been an ambitious man. In June of 1872, shortly after his graduation from Simpson College, he declared, "I go now to the bar and the political fields. . . . There I shall seek my fortune and fame." By 1900 he had achieved a measure of greatness in both fields.

Born in Illinois in 1849, Berry moved to Iowa with his parents and three siblings in the fall of 1867, establishing residence the same month that John Hossack arrived to purchase his farm in Squaw Township. For two years, Berry farmed with his father north of Indianola, developing an appreciation for agriculture and a love of horses. But he grew restless with rural life. Eager for a formal education, he moved back to town, enrolled at Simpson College, and graduated with honors. He read law under the tutelage of John H. Henderson and was admitted to the Iowa bar in September 1873. The two men soon formed the partnership that was to become the county's most prestigious law firm. Berry and Henderson also became involved in state and local politics and were recognized as the most prominent politicians in the county for nearly half a century.

In 1874 Berry married Alice Barker, a proud and self-confident woman who had graduated as valedictorian of their class at Simpson College two years earlier. Petite, with dark hair and gray eyes, she came from a prominent Indianola family. Her father, John Barker, was a local merchant, the founder of Barker and Johnson Dry Goods Store. Her uncle, Anselm Barker, moved west and was known for building the first dwelling in the town that became Denver, Colorado.

The Berrys settled in a modest one-story frame house at 105 East Third Street. Their only child, Don, was born in 1880. He was a smart, devoted boy, and when he turned four, Alice gave him a brightly colored primer from which he learned the alphabet and how to read a few words. She enjoyed teaching him, and she continued to educate him at home until he was old enough to enter Simpson College. Alice also involved herself in local activities, serving as treasurer of the Indianola chapter of the Women's Foreign Missionary Society and as secretary of the Simpson College Alumni organization. In 1886 she founded Indianola's first women's group, the Monday Club, an organization that met regularly to discuss the issues of the day.

In 1890 William Berry built a house at 713 West Ashland Avenue, about a half mile west of the town square. It was a splendid two-story dwelling with a large attic, two covered porches, and four gables. A central chimney allowed for fireplaces in the four main downstairs rooms, and there was a parlor for entertaining special guests, which featured a handsome hand-carved cherry mantel above the fireplace. Alice's father provided moquette carpet for the downstairs. A double door decorated in gold leaf opened from the front porch into the parlor, an entrance that was used only on special occasions. A rail fence surrounded the property, and a small barn behind the house provided shelter for the family horse, Billy; Don's pony, Pet; and a milk cow named Old Moqui. Soon after the house was built, hard maples and elms were planted around the property, and a Russian mulberry hedge was installed on the west edge. The house cost $6,000, a significant sum in those days, and was one of the finest homes in the county.

William and Alice Berry hosted many dinner parties and family gatherings, enjoying long evenings of conversation and political debate. William Berry was renowned for his homemade oyster soup. Ministers and lecturers who passed through town were invited to visit, as were district court judges and politicians. Alumni of Simpson College frequented the Berry residence, which became a kind of unofficial meeting place for them and other people associated with the college.

Senator Berry was affluent and influential, and he loved being in the public eye. One historian labeled him the "the most colorful, and perhaps the most versatile of Warren County residents." He made his presence felt in various ways throughout the community. On Thanksgiving and Christmas, Berry made it a tradition to provide food to others in the neighborhood who were less fortunate. Usually he carried the food himself to a needy family before sitting down at his own table. He founded the Worth Savings Bank, served as a member of the board of trustees of Simpson College, and held the position of superintendent of the Methodist Sunday school, where he taught Sunday school classes for thirty years.

He was elected to the Iowa State Senate in 1896 and reelected two years later. As a senator, Berry was both a pragmatic politician and an advocate of moral principles. While championing various causes of his constituents, he also authored a bill to outlaw the death penalty, a proposal embraced by few of those who had voted for him. Though his proposed legislation was soundly defeated, Berry remained a passionate opponent of capital punishment. In 1900 political wrangling at the county level forced him to give up his seat. But he had not yet given up his political ambitions. It was not out of the question, or out of Berry's mind, that one day he might be elected governor.

The Hossack case thrust Berry back into the public spotlight. Reporters from Des Moines newspapers were knocking on his door, seeking quotes, asking about legal strategies. They told their readers to anticipate a sensational and dramatic trial. Berry knew that everything he said in the courtroom would be well publicized; thousands of Iowa residents would read about his opening and closing arguments.

As for George Clammer, the Hossack trial would be his first big on-the-job test, an opportunity for the county attorney to make an impression on the community. Clammer had ambitions of his own. Recently reelected, he would be judged by how well he performed against Senator Berry. The previous county attorney, L. L. Mosher, had been soundly rebuked in the newspapers for failing three times to get a conviction in the McCuddin case, and if Clammer stumbled, his own political career could be in jeopardy. On the other hand, if he were able to convince twelve jurors of Margaret Hossack's guilt, he might take the first big step toward the kind of recognition and respect that Senator Berry now enjoyed.

Clammer was not among the many Simpson College students who came from wealthy Indianola families. He earned his recognition by hard work and competition, playing football and excelling in the classroom. Despite his size (at just 143 pounds, Clammer was the smallest member of the football squad), he emerged as the star of the team, tough and pugnacious. He was the team punter as well as being a running back and hard-hitting tackler. Off the field he won honors as an orator and served as the first sports editor of the college newspaper, *The Simpsonian,* eventually assuming the editorship of the paper.

After graduation, Clammer worked in a local law office, studied law, and obtained his license in early 1898. He set up a practice of his own, advertising in the Indianola newspapers and renting a room above the hardware store on the south side of the town square. In one of his first cases, Clammer represented George Huss, a plaintiff who was suing the Chicago Great Western Railway Corporation after some of his livestock had been killed by a train. Clammer argued against Henderson and Berry, lawyers for the defendant. The case was hard-fought, ending only when the jury, after eighteen hours of deliberation, announced that it was unable to decide.

In October 1898 Clammer married fellow Simpson student Tella Talbott, and the president of Simpson College officiated at their wedding. A month later he was elected to the position of county attorney.

Now Clammer, who was labeled "one of the rising young attorneys of this city" and "a young lawyer of marked ability with a bright future ahead of him," was ready to oppose William Berry in a murder trial that had the potential to determine the political futures of both men.

Although the two were of different generations, they shared some common attributes and experiences. Both were Republicans, members of the era's dominant political party in Iowa; both were Methodists; both had attended Simpson College. Their paths crossed not only on the courthouse steps but also in meetings and at rallies where the political issues of the day were discussed. Each of them had married a college classmate from a prominent Indianola family, and Clammer had served on a Simpson College alumni committee with Alice Berry.

The battle in the courtroom would highlight their differences. Berry was old enough to be Clammer's father. Physically, Berry towered over the younger man. Clammer was handsome and well-dressed, with a precise, studious manner. Like a scholar or a professor, he was most comfortable addressing an audience from behind a lectern. Berry had an energetic manner in the courtroom, the look of a country lawyer, a folksy manner, and a resonant baritone voice. In the midst of legal argument, he stripped himself of formal attire. He frequently yanked off his suit coat and unbuttoned his vest, flinging the garments aside as he strode from one side of the room to the other. His thick fingers tugged at his shirt collar until it loosened. Jurors already knew about Berry as a man and as a political legend. He had set the standard for Warren County lawyering. ☾

CLAMMER KNEW WHAT he would be up against in court, and he wanted to bolster his case against Margaret Hossack with as much physical evidence as possible. As he developed his arguments, he realized that he needed a sample of hair from John Hossack's corpse in order to prove that the three hairs taken off the purported murder weapon at the Hossack farm were in fact hairs from the head of the victim. Clammer instructed the sheriff to exhume the body and collect the hair samples.

Sometime in mid-December, Sheriff Hodson and George Moore, the undertaker, traveled to the New Virginia Cemetery to dig up John Hossack's coffin. With shovels and pick axes, the men chopped through the icy dirt, piled clumps of earth in a mound to the side of the site, and uncovered the wooden box containing the remains of John Hossack. Carefully, they brushed the dirt off the top of the coffin. The cold wood gave a shiver and squeaked as they pried off the lid and revealed the corpse.

Moore bent over and used scissors to clip a few strands of white hairs just above the gash on the right side of Hossack's head. The hairs were, as Hodson later testified, "as near to the wound" as they could get. The evidence was deposited in a small vial, which Hodson put in his pocket.

The men hammered the lid back on the coffin, shoveled dirt back into the hole, and stomped it down with their boots.

A little less than a week later, Hodson and Clammer visited

Professor John Tilton in his office at Simpson College and handed him two vials; one contained the three hairs from the ax and the other the hairs obtained from the corpse. Tilton, a geologist and a well-respected member of the Simpson College Science Department, was asked to examine the hairs and determine, if he could, whether or not they matched.

8.

"I was at the Hossack place one evening when he just got back from Des Moines. He asked her to get supper for him. She said you ought to have been here when the rest of us ate. She did not get his supper for him. One of the girls got his supper. My aunt was with me and also Neil Morrison was there."—testimony of L. STICKEL, 19-year-old farmer and neighbor of the Hossacks, before the Warren County Grand Jury, January 1901

"Reporters love murders."—CALVIN TRILLIN, in *Killings*

A FEW DAYS before Christmas, the Hossack family finally succeeded in raising the bond to obtain Margaret Hossack's release so that she could return home to spend the holidays with her family.

The Warren County Grand Jury met behind closed doors from January 9 through January 17. Clammer solicited testimony from more than fifty witnesses, including the Hossack children. Margaret Hossack was not required to give testimony, and her attorneys were not allowed in the grand jury sessions.

On January 17 the grand jury returned an indictment against Margaret Hossack, charging her with murder in the first degree. Sheriff Hodson once again arrested her and took her back to the county jail, where she was to remain until her trial at the Warren County Courthouse. ❨

FOR NEARLY ELEVEN WEEKS, from the time she was indicted until the start of her trial, Margaret Hossack was confined in the jail. The days of winter passed inexorably, one after another. From the grated window in her cell, she could glimpse the sky and watch the people of Indianola passing on the street.

The person Margaret Hossack saw most often during these months was Marcia Hodson, the sheriff's wife, who tended to the prisoner's daily needs, doing her laundry and taking meals to her. Cheerful and friendly, Marcia Hodson was about the same age as Annie, the oldest Hossack daughter. The Hodsons had one child of their own, an eleven-year-old boy named Paul, who was just two years younger than Ivan. Sometimes Margaret heard the sound of the boy's voice or saw him playing outside.

Like her husband, Marcia Hodson had been raised in Ackworth, a farming community dominated by Quakers, and she was a birthright member of the Ackworth Friends Church. Her husband's election to sheriff took her to Indianola. Marcia Hodson's rural upbringing helped her envision the kind of life Margaret Hossack had lived: the daily routines of housework and farm chores and the clamor of young children constantly underfoot. She also knew that farmers could be abusive in their treatment of livestock or their families.

Several times a day, the sheriff's wife turned the key in the lock of the cell door, listening to the metallic click and looking in on the prisoner, whose health seemed to worsen with each week that passed. A bad case of influenza drained her of energy. When she spoke, she talked about her children and her life on the farm, never mentioning the legal case pending against her; she occasionally mentioned her late husband, referring to him simply as "Pa"; but for long hours, Margaret Hossack passed the time reading and sewing, waiting in silence for her trial.

In the community, there was intense curiosity about the woman who was housed in the county jail. Some felt compassion, especially when the newspapers reported that Mrs. Hossack had been mistreated by her husband, but there was also horror at the brutality of the attack. It was not unheard of for women to kill their husbands, but the means was usually poison. Slipping a lethal dose of rat poison or arsenic into a man's food was easier for a wife than shooting or stabbing him.

In fact, only a few months before John Hossack's death, in September 1900, a man in Keokuk County, seventy-five miles east of Indianola, had died of strychnine poisoning. His wife, nineteen-year-old Sarah Kuhn, was tried for first-degree murder.

Most of the facts in that case were not in dispute. Sarah Kuhn and her husband, Charles, had traveled by buggy a few miles from their rural home to the town of What Cheer, Iowa, where they bought beer and bologna to eat on the return trip. After dark, near the town of Delta, Charles Kuhn became violently ill, complaining of severe pains and crying out for help. Wesley Snider, a local farmer, heard the cries as the Kuhns passed his house and ran out to the road to investigate. Sarah Kuhn called, "Come quick, my husband is dying," while her husband screamed, "I am dying, I am dying. She has poisoned me." A doctor was summoned but Kuhn died a short while later.

An autopsy revealed evidence of strychnine in his stomach. Strychnine was also found in one of the two beer bottles, and a traveling salesman found a small bottle, partially filled with the poison, alongside the road between What Cheer and Delta.

It was a tantalizing story, with more juicy tidbits appearing in each day's paper. The press coverage—available to all the potential jurors who might soon judge Margaret Hossack—focused not only on the evidence, but also on the appearance, character, and demeanor of the accused.

The Des Moines newspapers had featured daily accounts of the trial. The *Daily Capital* depicted Sarah Kuhn as an innocent girl: "The defendant is self-possessed, calm and smiling as usual. She is a very pretty blonde, with wide, child-like blue eyes." In another story, she was described as "young and beautiful."

The reports changed in tone as the evidence against her accumulated. MRS. KUHN UNMOVED, declared one headline, and she was described as listening to the report of her husband's autopsy "with serene indifference" and "without betraying the slightest sign of horror, guilt, or emotion of any kind." According to the reporter, "her fair, sweet face retained its expression of childish interest through all the sickening details."

The defense offered the court an intriguing story: Charles Kuhn was insane and had committed suicide, taking the strychnine of his own volition. The prosecution claimed that the tale was absurd, especially since Kuhn repeatedly claimed that his wife had poisoned him.

According to evidence presented by the prosecution, the defendant had wanted to rekindle her romance with a former lover, a railroad worker named Andy Smith. Several witnesses claimed they'd seen the two in clandestine meetings and overheard Sarah Kuhn say that she couldn't live with her husband any longer. The accused woman, testifying in her own defense, denied that she'd committed the murder. But she admitted that she and her husband had quarreled just days before, when she'd complained about his impotence and inability to have sexual intercourse.

The evidence, especially the accusatory words of her dying husband, was overwhelmingly against Sarah Kuhn. In addition, the defendant's personal conduct violated the moral strictures of the community. This was a woman, pretty and wily, who had a young lover, talked about sex with her husband, drank beer, and appeared emotionless in the courtroom. The prosecution's argument was clear: No matter how childlike she appeared, no matter how young and beautiful, this was a woman who was capable of murder.

The jury settled on a verdict within a few hours. The *Daily Capital* article reporting the decision left readers with a final image of the woman, who, in the view of many, was well-deserving of punishment: MRS. KUHN IS FOUND GUILTY, read the bold headline, and, underneath, DEFENDANT SMILES AS THE FOREMAN READS THE VERDICT PRONOUNCING HER GUILTY OF THE MURDER OF HER HUSBAND. ☾

SARAH KUHN WAS convicted of using poison to kill, but accusing a woman of an ax murder was not completely without precedent either. Eight years earlier, another woman had been charged with one of the most famous crimes in American history: the bloody double murder of Andrew and Abby Borden in Fall River, Massachusetts, on August 4, 1892. The case received widespread publicity across the nation, including front-page coverage in the *Des Moines Daily News* on the very day that the bodies were discovered.

Andrew Borden was socially prominent and rich, although stern and dour in manner and known to be exceptionally frugal. After the death of his first wife, the mother of his children, he remarried. At the time he was killed, he was living with his second wife and his two daughters, by then both middle-aged spinsters. Lizzie, at age thirty-two, had made no secret of her dislike for her stepmother and her frustration at her father's reluctance to spend money on luxuries or to move the family to a more prestigious house in town.

On the morning of the attacks, Lizzie Borden and a housekeeper named Bridget Sullivan were alone in the house with the elder Bordens. Shortly before noon, Lizzie called to the housekeeper, who was resting upstairs, "Come down quick! Father's dead. Somebody's come in and killed him." A neighbor was summoned, then the police. They found Andrew Borden, who had been attacked while he napped on a downstairs couch and struck directly in the face and head nearly a dozen times with a hatchet. His features were almost unrecognizable. The dead body of his wife, Abby, was then discovered upstairs, where she'd been bludgeoned, apparently with the same weapon. Doctors determined that Mrs. Borden had been slain at least an hour before the attack on her husband. Although Lizzie claimed to know nothing about what had happened, saying that she'd been outside in the barn when her father was killed, she was suspected at once. There was ample reason to think she might be guilty, including her possible motives, her inability to prove her whereabouts during the killings, and the lack of evidence that an outsider had entered the house. The evidence was circumstantial, but it pointed directly to Lizzie Borden, and she was arrested, indicted, and tried for first-degree murder.

The public, however, refused to believe she was guilty. Just days after the murder, a prominent clergyman preached an entire sermon on the case, warning the press not to besmirch the good name of Lizzie Borden, the "poor stricken girl . . . at once innocent and blameless," and this image of the defendant took hold. The press, as well as feminist organizations, various religious groups, and much of the citizenry of Fall River, treated the defendant as a victim: a refined, well-educated, upper-class woman unfairly accused by police and prosecutors. Despite the strong circumstantial evidence against her, many thought that it was impossible that Lizzie, the "poor defenseless girl," as her lawyers called her, could have committed such a violent and bloody crime.

The depictions of Lizzie Borden during her trial reinforced the view of her feminine nature—and of her innocence. According to the "Cult of True Womanhood," a popular phrase during those years, a true woman possessed four cardinal virtues: piety, purity, submissiveness, and domesticity. With her tears and her downcast eyes, her fainting spells and her devotion to her home and church, Lizzie exhibited these traits in her mannerisms, dress, and actions. And it was her womanliness, according to her lawyers, that made it unthinkable that she could have committed the crimes. The twelve men on the jury listened as her lawyer argued that "it would be morally and physically impossible" for his client to have swung the ax that killed her father and stepmother. Convicting her of such a crime, he said, would go against the laws of human nature. "To find her guilty, you must believe her to be a fiend," the defense lawyer shouted to the jury at the end of his argument. "Does she look it?"

The jury was convinced. Without a glance at the boxes of exhibits, the jurors voted immediately and unanimously for acquittal. They waited ninety minutes—presumably to give the impression of more sustained deliberations—before emerging with their decision. After the foreman said the words *not guilty*, the courtroom exploded in cheers, and the defendant, wearing a great plumed hat, staggered backward into her chair and began to cry.

The community celebrated the jury's finding. Friends called that evening to offer Lizzie their congratulations, and a band serenaded her with its rendition of "Auld Lang Syne." The judge announced that he was "perfectly satisfied with the verdict." To a reporter from United Press, Lizzie proclaimed herself "the happiest woman in the world." Lizzie Borden had gone from being an accused murderess to being a celebrity—and, with the money she inherited from her father, a very wealthy woman.

Eventually, the euphoria diminished. The Fall River police, convinced that the real killer had been acquitted, declined to investigate any further. Then the newspapers, some of which had been instrumental in convincing the public that Lizzie was innocent, began to raise questions about the verdict. Just days after the trial ended, the *Providence Journal* called upon Miss Borden and her friends to come forward with information that would point to the real murderer. She did not respond, and her supporters, so vocal during the courtroom battle, now had nothing to say. Skepticism in the media increased with the publication of editorials and interviews that were highly critical of the courtroom procedures, the judge's rulings, and the jury's decision. The community began to reappraise the evidence.

If Lizzie wasn't guilty, then who was? No other suspects came readily to mind. ☾

Lizzie Borden could be portrayed as a "true woman," but could Margaret Hossack?

She was a fifty-seven-year-old farmwife, sturdy and hardened by outdoor work. From the beginning, descriptions of her in the newspapers frequently employed masculine terms. To the reporter from the *Daily Capital,* she was "tall and erect," "well built and muscular," with "high cheek bones, and a look common to the Hossack family that bodes no good to the enemy."

According to the *Daily Leader,* "there is a set look about the mouth which betokens determination. In this respect she resembles her dead husband. In fact, all the Hossack family have a look of bull dog tenacity."

The next day, the *Daily Leader* ran a longer portrait of the accused woman:

> Mrs. Hossack . . . has manifested no unusual emotion, and if she feels the prickings of an uneasy conscience or deep sorrow for the death of her husband, it is not manifested by an outward expression of word or act. She denies having committed the murder, and receiving, as she does, the united aid and sympathy of the children, she will be able to put up a stubborn contest in the courts. She was married to John Hossack in Illinois, thirty-one years ago. Like Hossack, she was of Scotch stock. In stature she is about five feet, seven or eight inches, and while lean and angular, she will weigh 160 pounds. Her face is rather broad and, to a degree, rendered sinister by a pair of small, steely blue eyes, which give her an expression of subtle

> cunning, coupled with reserve and unflinching resolution of purpose. Wonderfully self-possessed, she needs not the caution of attorneys to keep her from talking at a time when silence is golden. Her square, firm set jaw and thin lips compressed over a fine set of teeth proclaim her a woman of determination and unflinching courage.

In many ways, the media portrayed Margaret Hossack as a model farmwoman—reserved, self-possessed, and determined. Yet these were not the characteristics enshrined in the "Cult of True Womanhood," the image that was purveyed to the public as ideal through newspapers, periodicals, advertisements, schoolbooks, and church sermons. Given the difficulty and strenuousness of their lives on the farm, it was almost impossible for rural women to adopt stereotypically feminine appearance and dress. Still, the less visible traits of a "true woman"—piety, purity, submissiveness, and domesticity—held remarkable power as goals toward which all women, even those in rural communities, should strive. When a woman was held up for judgment, her success or failure in measuring up to the paradigm was something that would be noted.

Although Margaret Hossack's lack of womanly beauty or charm may not have been damning, suggestions in the press that she was not properly devoted to her husband were more significant charges against her. Reporters frequently noted that she shed few tears and rarely showed other signs of grief. She was seen as "stern" and "unfeeling," and, as the *Daily Capital* noted, "one can scarcely detect that she is worried or mentally disturbed." The criticism—that she was not reacting appropriately to her husband's death—was implicit.

There were also strong hints in reports from the neighbors, which were often repeated by the press, that she had fallen short in other ways as well, such as lacking the feminine virtues of obedience and submissiveness. If she suffered from domestic difficulties, whose fault was that? It was the wife's responsibility to create an agreeable sanctuary for her husband and children and to show, as the Agricultural Report of 1862 put it, a "self-denying devotion . . . for the comfort, prosperity, and respectability" of her family. According to *Godeys Lady's Book,* a widely read periodical, "A good wife, a true woman . . . puts her own grievances out of sight to drive away with pleasant smiles the clouds that gather around her husband's gloomy brow." If Margaret Hossack had been unhappy at home and mistreated by her husband, perhaps it could be believed that she was to blame.

9.

The morning of the 30th of April was not very bright; but neither was it very gloomy. Rain might come within an hour, but the sun might come out—I would not consent to delay our departure for fear of the weather. Had I not made up my mind to encounter many storms? If we were going, let us go, and meet what we were to meet, bravely. . . . That afternoon wore quietly away, the weather being rather brighter and warmer than in the morning—and now night was coming on. No house was within sight.

Why did I look for one? I knew we were to camp; but surely there would be a few trees or a sheltering hillside against which to place our wagon. No, only the level prairie stretched on each side of the way. Nothing indicated a place for us—a cozy nook, in which for the night we might be guarded, at least by banks and boughs. I had for months anticipated this hour, yet, not till it came, did I realize the bleak dreariness of seeing night come on without house or home to shelter us and our baby-girl. And this was to be the same for many weeks, perhaps months. It was a chilling prospect, and there was a terrible shrinking from it in my heart; but I kept it all to myself. . . .—SARAH ROYCE, pioneer woman, writing in her diary in 1849, on beginning the journey westward with her husband and small child

Ah, *marriage is a lottery*. How full of Deceit do they come with their false tongues and "*there is no one as dear as thee*" until after one is married then "*you are mine now we have something else to do besides silly kissing*."—EMILY GILLESPIE, Iowa farmwife, writing in her diary on April 25, 1887

IN FACT, OF COURSE, none of the journalistic portraits of Margaret Hossack accurately defined her or the circumstances of her life. The superficial images disseminated in the media concentrated on her physical appearance and made guesses about her personality and attitude based on her outward demeanor. The images conformed to what the writers—and the public—expected a female murderess to look like. Not surprisingly, the truth was far more complex.

Margaret was born in Scotland on November 19, 1843, the youngest child of Alexander and Ann Murchison. At the age of five, she sailed to America, crossing the North Atlantic on a voyage that lasted fifty-seven days, with her parents and three elder siblings: Alexander, who turned eighteen during the passage; Jane, sixteen; and Donald, fourteen.

The family settled in Stark County, Illinois, near the town of Elmira, and soon earned a measure of respectability. They worked hard, lived frugally, and were accepted into the community, where they were instrumental in the founding of the United Presbyterian Church, in Toulon.

In the spring of 1866, the elderly Alexander Murchison employed a fellow Scottish immigrant named John Hossack as a new hired hand. Both of Murchison's sons had moved off the farm, and only his daughters remained. Hossack joined five or six men, who also lived on the property, and helped with the farm work.

Hossack was twenty-five years old and unmarried. He labored for the Murchisons until the summer and returned a year later. After several months, in October of 1867, Hossack traveled west, crossing the Mississippi River, to explore the new state of Iowa. He found acres and acres of inexpensive land with rich black soil, rolling land that looked more like his native Scotland than like the flat terrain of Stark County. On October 28, he purchased a farm: 120 acres of land and a small house located in Warren County, in the south central part of the state. Hossack paid $480 in cash for the property and returned to the Murchison farm.

There is no clear record of what transpired between John Hossack and the two Murchison daughters in the months before he left again for Illinois. If the rumors that followed him to Iowa are true, he was originally interested in his employer's eldest daughter, Jane, despite her being nine years older than Hossack and clearly past the prime marriageable age. In any case, eventually Hossack turned his attentions to Margaret. By late November or early December, she was pregnant, and on January 29, 1868, she and John were married. The wedding, however, was not held in her family's church, a fact that may well have indicated the displeasure of her father. It took place in the home of Margaret's brother Donald, with Reverend N. C. Weede performing the ceremony. No notice of the union appeared in local papers.

That spring Margaret Hossack left her family's farm in Illinois and moved to Iowa with her husband. Her pregnancy forced the Hossacks to lie about the actual date of their marriage. To friends and neighbors in Iowa, they would claim November 19, 1867, nine months prior to the birth of their first child, as their wedding day, and that was the date noted in public records about John Hossack and his family. The date was an easy one to remember: It was Margaret's twenty-fourth birthday.

Margaret Murchison Hossack left behind her past—her Scottish birth, her Illinois childhood. She also left behind her parents and siblings, her in-laws, nephews, nieces, and cousins. With the exception of her brother, Donald, she would never again see any of the Murchisons. When her father died four years later, his will divided his considerable property among his three children still in Illinois, leaving only a small cash bequest of $500 to his daughter Margaret. ☾

LEAVING A FAMILY FARM to travel west with a new husband wasn't an uncommon experience for young women in the latter half of the nineteenth century. In the diaries and journals of these women, one often hears a plaintive voice describing the constant hardship of their lives and a longing for the people and places from their past. For many young brides who departed the comfort of their childhood homes, the anguish of leaving friends and relatives could be profound, a separation that left a void some women compared to death. "Our hearts [are] torn at the loss of dear ones," one woman wrote. Some eased their homesickness by writing letters to their families and dreaming of future reunions, either in life or death. For Margaret Hossack, the estrangement from her family in Illinois was such that she knew she could not retrace her steps.

The Hossack farm was located in Squaw Township, more than sixteen miles from Indianola, the county seat. Medora, a crossroads with a general store and a blacksmith, two miles to the east of the Hossack farm, was the closest approximation of a town. Six miles to the west was New Virginia, a larger and older town. A few farms were nearby, but roads between farms were little more than narrow trails, so travel by foot or even horseback was difficult. Still, conditions had improved significantly since the first inhabitants had lived in covered wagons, sod huts, and log cabins. In 1869, the annual report for the Warren County Agricultural Society remarked on some of the changes:

> Improvements are to be noted on every hand. The original sheds and shanties of the pioneers are fast giving way to commodious houses and substantial barns. Picket fences that enclose front yards, dotted with flowers and shrubbery, indicate greater taste and refinement.

During that first spring and summer, a new life emerged for Margaret Hossack. The small house occupied by the Hossacks was crowded by the arrival of her husband's elderly parents, Alexander and Catherine Hossack. Unlike the relative comfort of her father's home in Stark County, where there were hired men and a close-knit extended family to share the work, life in the most rural reaches of Iowa was full of difficult challenges, with few opportunities for social interaction outside the household. Her husband was busy getting his first crop of corn in the ground. Margaret was pregnant and tending to the domestic responsibilities of a farmer's wife. According to one memoir, the routine work for a rural woman at home included "water carrying, cooking, churning, sausage making, berry picking, vegetable drying, sugar and soap boiling, hominy hulling, medicine brewing, washing, nursing, weaving, sewing, straw platting, wool picking, spinning, quilting, knitting, gardening and various other tasks."

On August 16, 1868—six months and nineteen days after her marriage—Margaret Hossack gave birth, at home, to a healthy son. The boy was named Alexander, after both his grandfathers and his maternal uncle, a Civil War hero. ☾

THE FIRST SETTLERS had been allowed to stake their claims in Warren County in 1845, and the population grew steadily in the next few years. In the 1850 census, which counted livestock along with people, pigs outnumbered humans 1,331 to 961, but by 1868 more than 15,000 citizens resided in the county.

The work of the pioneers was evident. Early settlers had cleared the fields of timber, and almost all of the land in the county was under cultivation. Squaw Township was now a patchwork of farms, sections of acreage that abutted one another like pieces of fabric in a quilt. The original owners still lived on many of the farms. Although mechanization was years away, hand tools had largely been replaced by reapers, mowers, and plows, all drawn by horses or oxen.

That first summer Hossack quickly made friends with some of the neighboring farmers, most notably Frank Keller, who'd moved to the county in 1854. Hossack devoted himself to his new farm. In time he came to play a visible role in the community, joining fraternal organizations, including the Masons and the Woodman's Association, and actively participating in his church and local politics. He was perceived as a leader, selected as a church elder and a trustee of the township. A biographical entry in the 1879 History of Warren County acknowledges Hossack as one of the area's most prominent citizens.

Hossack had achieved the goal that the historian Stephen Ambrose described as that of thousands of early American settlers who had moved westward: "American immigrants and emigrants wanted their share of the land—free land—a farm in the family—the dream of European peasants for hundreds of years—the New World's great gift to the [O]ld."

For men like Hossack there were social and economic rewards for such prominence. They felt the pride of ownership, and they developed camaraderie with other farmers. Although much of a man's work on his farm was done alone or with his sons and other relatives, some of the more physically demanding tasks required cooperation. Neighbor men sometimes traveled in groups, working from one farm to the next. As they became acquainted with one another, they established places away from home—the trading post, the blacksmith shop—where they would congregate to discuss the weather or talk about farming problems.

The United States Department of Agriculture, created by an act of Congress on May 15, 1862, issued its initial annual report on January 1, 1863. The first Commissioner of Agriculture, Isaac Newton, made the following observation about the appeal of farming:

> The farmer, if not absolutely rich, is, at least, independent. He has a home which his labor and his taste have

> adorned; he has broad acres, not held by lease, as in many countries, but as a freehold. In the Old World land is generally divided into large estates, and owned by few proprietors. In England, for instance, the number of acres is 32,342,400; the number of proprietors about 44,000; in Scotland, 19,738,930 acres and 4,000 proprietors. Such is not the case in our country. No law of entail or primogeniture fosters the accumulation of large estates. It is one of the blessings of the American farmer that he owns in fee simple the land which he cultivates. He has not to stoop and cringe and stand in awe in the presence of those whom he calls master. He has no master. . . .

Like other nineteenth-century immigrants, John Hossack was poised on the brink of his future. The rich promise of America loomed before him. ☾

LABOR ON THE FARM was broken down by gender. Men and the older boys were responsible for the heaviest jobs, including clearing and plowing the land and construction and maintenance of the buildings and fences. The men usually tended the livestock, although care of the chickens and milking the cows were delegated to the women.

Men typically worked the fields. Spring was consumed with planting, whereas the long days of late summer were occupied with difficult physical work: cultivating, threshing, and harvesting. Winter provided a break from the most strenuous tasks. There were still animals to be fed, barns and stables to be cleaned, and machinery to be repaired, but the colder months meant more leisure for the men, giving them time for trips to town, political and Masonic meetings, and social visits to neighbors.

While men focused on the commercial operations of the

farm, women were primarily responsible for feeding the family and maintaining the home, tasks that varied less with the season. Food preparation, the most time-consuming activity, was a constant and daily duty that involved not only cooking but also planting and harvesting a large garden, often an acre or so in size, to provide most of the family's meals. Collecting eggs, butchering chickens, milking cows, and churning butter usually fell within the woman's domain, as did the long, hot tasks of preserving and canning fruit and vegetables for the winter months.

But preparation of meals, with the carrying of water and dishwashing that inevitably followed each one, took up only part of a woman's day. She was also responsible for clothing the family—sometimes spinning or weaving the cloth, and at all times sewing and repairing the garments and keeping them clean. Laundry was one of the most exhausting weekly jobs, involving long hours of hauling and then heating many gallons of water, scrubbing the clothes on a board, wringing them, often by hand, and then hanging the heavy, wet fabrics out to dry. Most items, including bed linens, were ironed, using flatirons heated in the fireplace, and the women had to make soap, a process that required boiling grease and wood ashes together to make lye. To light the house, they made candles. Cleaning the house was also a woman's task. People were constantly coming in and out, bringing dirt and dung from the fields and yards, and insects and bugs were pervasive. Most farmwomen attempted to keep their houses looking as nice as they could, dusting furniture and sweeping and cleaning floors, but these latter tasks, monotonous and repetitive, were often the most thankless of all.

As hard as women worked, their lives were made even more difficult because their labor was rarely recognized as making an economic contribution to the family. Sometimes their products, such as butter or eggs or garments, were sold or bartered, but more often their tasks were dictated by usefulness to the household.

Men were also involved in subsistence farming, but when they produced a surplus—something that was common in John Hossack's time—they were the ones involved in trading or selling and making contacts with the broader community. In most cases, women's work was taken for granted or overlooked, and it was the accomplishments of men that were viewed as responsible for financial stability and success.

The domestic responsibilities could be physically overwhelming for any farmwife, especially when combined with pregnancy and childbirth. And Margaret and John Hossack had more children than most, even by the standards of that time. During the first twenty years of her marriage, Margaret gave birth ten times. Less than a year after Alex's birth in 1868, Margaret was pregnant again; Anna Jane was born in February of 1870. Shortly after Christmas of 1871, a baby boy, named Donald, was delivered, though he was to die in infancy. Catherine, called Cassie, was born in February 1874. Johnnie was conceived about a year after Cassie's birth. Margaret Lucretia, nicknamed Louie, was born thirteen months after Johnnie. Three years passed between the births of Louie and May; two years between May and Will, and another two years between Will and Jimmie. When Ivan, the last Hossack child, was born in September of 1887, Margaret was almost forty-four years old.

With extended family living far away and their work done almost entirely at home, rural women, unlike their husbands, had few opportunities to socialize or to share their experiences with others. Friendships were difficult to establish, especially in the more isolated environments. Women sometimes visited one another, but the journeys often were possible only on foot. The nearly constant demands of caring for small children and infants made travel difficult and time hard to spare, even though the distances might be small. With the men typically responsible for business matters, farmwives seldom had occasion to go to town.

Unable to vote or hold leadership positions in the community, they had no public role to play. In their own homes, they were dependent on their husbands. It was the men who usually owned the property, controlled the finances, and made the decisions. As one song expressed the female plight, women were

> Always controlled, they're always confined.
> Controlled by their family until they are wives,
> Then slaves to their husbands the rest of their lives.

In a study of the condition of farmwomen, included in the first report of the Department of Agriculture, Dr. W. W. Hall expressed grave concerns about their health:

> In plain language, in the civilization of the latter half of the nineteenth century, a farmer's wife, as a too-general rule, is a laboring drudge; not of necessity by design, but for want of that consideration, the very absence of which, in reference to the wife of a man's youth, is a crime. It is perhaps safe to say, that on three farms out of four, the wife works harder, endures more, than any other on the place; more than the husband, more than the "farm-hand," more than the "hired help" of the kitchen. Many a farmer speaks to his wife habitually in terms more imperious, impatient, and petulant than he would use to the scullion of the kitchen or to his hired hand.

Dr. Hall suggested that physical overwork and the emotional toll of isolation could have brutal consequences, including insanity, and his warning was prophetic. By the 1880s, farmers' wives made up the largest percentage of people in lunatic asylums. Stories about women being taken away from their homes to be institutionalized were widespread. One woman, describing her life on a Midwestern homestead in the late 1800s, remembered the women "screaming all night long in the jail after the first spring thaw. Their husbands brought them into town in wagons from the sod huts where they had spent the terrible Dakota winter; they were on their way to the insane asylum in Jamestown."

No evidence exists that Margaret Hossack kept any written record of her experiences. If she maintained a journal or wrote letters, the pages have not survived. Yet there is another diary that has been preserved, which shows a life—and a marriage—with remarkable similarities to those of Margaret Hossack. ☾

EMILY GILLESPIE WAS an Iowa farmwife and a contemporary of Margaret Hossack. Born in Michigan in 1838, Emily was five years older than Margaret and better educated, having taught school for some years before her marriage. In 1862, at the age of twenty-four, she left her family with her new husband, a young Iowa farmer of Scottish-Irish descent named James Gillespie. They moved in with his elderly parents in Manchester, Iowa, a farming community forty miles west of Dubuque, until the couple acquired a farm of their own. Within a year, Emily gave birth to a boy, Henry, and less than two years later to a girl, Sarah.

Emily started her diary on her twentieth birthday and continued her entries on an almost daily basis until a few weeks before her death in March of 1888. Her words describe both the mundane details of everyday farm work and the dynamics of family life.

Emily was committed to being a good wife and mother. Like most women of her day, she saw homemaking and the moral education of her children as her most important responsibilities. She longed for a peaceful and happy home, praying that "no discord ever enter our family circle." She blamed herself for any small conflict with her husband and reminded herself to work harder and never to express "an unkind thought or word." She and her husband occasionally quarreled over chores and money, but they toiled together at the cycle of farm and domestic tasks.

Her diary during these early years is a report of endless and repetitive tasks, day after day and year after year. James took care of the animals and the crops, while Emily sewed and raised poultry and sold the eggs to supplement the family income. In precisely maintained ledgers, she kept a record of her earnings.

Gradually the young woman's frustrations emerged. She missed her family. She complained that her work and contributions were not appreciated or fairly valued, and she was concerned about finances. She resented her husband's superior ownership rights and his attempts to assert authority in the home. On occasion, when the couple had "angry words," James sulked and remained emotionally distant for days. She felt that he didn't respect her opinion; as she wrote in one entry, "get real mad at James because he never seems to want me to go anywhere or to say anything at all about his things (which he calls *his* affairs). It makes it very disagreeable. . . ."

As she struggled with her own emotions, Emily Gillespie was also affected by the personal crises and catastrophes of her neighbors. When one man's wife left him and took their young child back to Scotland, Emily commented to her diary: "O dear, tis a sad affair for a husband and wife to part." Another neighbor hanged himself. One of Emily's uncles was maimed in a reaper accident, and several years later she received the grim news that a cousin in Michigan had killed herself after murdering her four young children, slitting their throats with a knife. When she heard about an acquaintance who was being taken to the insane asylum, Emily wrote: "I only wonder that more women do not have to be taken to the asylum, especially farmers' wives: no society, except hired men to eat their meals, hard work from the beginning to the end of their years, their only happiness lies with their children."

In the late 1870s the Gillespie family became increasingly prosperous, eventually building a large new house, which was carefully furnished by Emily. But outward success was accompanied by private turmoil, and her diary recorded growing discord in her marriage, marked by her husband's increasingly erratic behavior. James Gillespie's moods were characterized by silence or by threats of violence against his family. On occasion Emily observed him abusing the farm animals, and sometimes he threatened to kill himself. Emily struggled to keep her family troubles out of the public view and to protect her son and daughter from his anger. She was sustained by the loyal attachment of her children, who bonded closely with their mother as their father's behavior became more threatening.

As her children grew older and more independent, Emily continued to yearn for domestic peace, but she was oppressed by her years of constant work and increasingly afraid of her husband. Her feelings come through in selections from her diary during the last decade of her life:

> AUGUST 16, 1881. Do general work, indeed I can not do work as easily as I could twenty years ago. it seems sometimes as though I would have to give up were it not that Henry and Sarah help me. . . . tis as ever, not much Happiness for me, when James has any extra work to do. I sometimes think of words which different women have told me in my girl-hood—that—"woman is always lovely—until her strength & beauty fails, then—she is—only in the way"—it seems almost invariably true, yet we will try to say & think—all is well.

> OCTOBER 8, 1881. [W]e retire to sleep, our hearts filled with sorrow, yet with a prayer and trust that all will end well. James has one of his fits of—well I do hardly know what—whenever he has to pay out any money for any thing he seems to think, I ought to get every thing for myself & the Children without calling on him for it. Henry & Sarah went out & got him to come in, they were afraid he would hang himself—well he did—as he has done many times be-

fore—get a rope & threaten. Alas! the trial to get along with such a disposition. we can only know & trust that God will help us to brave it through. he does not want the Children to go to school. Thinks there is no need of it—but wants them to stay at home & work. . . .

MAY 21, 1882. James has another freak of being *ugly* to his horses. 'Tis *too mean* to tell. I—well I did get very angry at him—am sorry tis so, yet I can not endure the seeing of kind animals abused.

AUGUST 5, 1882. . . . we are all tired. . . . Im sorry I get so nervous when I am warm cooking over the hot stove, it seems just as if I burned up twenty years of my life by the heat off the stove. but for all I must try to always be pleasant. Tis so much better for the Children and me too.

MARCH 25, 1883. . . . James is at the barn, he went without his supper because of a very unpleasant time we had—tis too bad—but I can not always endure everything he would turn us all out of doors if he could. (when a man lays his hands hold of his wife & Children I think tis time something was done.) . . . we must not despair.

MARCH 27, 1883. I finish my night-gown &c. go to Town with James. he feels better natured—I am thankful he does. I sometimes think tis a real disease that some people have to have a time every so often. they seem to get so full of some undefinable thing they must explode. . . .

JUNE 1, 1883. Friday. Half past seven. well I begin this June morning in sadness. James did not come in to supper last night nor to his breakfast this morning. he will not answer when spoken to. he has done his chores and gone with the team up west, but I do not know where. It is indeed trying to my nerves to live as I have had to for years. I am sorry it is so but I think something will have to be done. . . . I did not sleep but a little while last night. laid awake till after two—and then woke at every sound. Yes I have not dared to go to sleep many a night, and it wears me out—I feel it is not right to live so. . . .

AUGUST 10, 1883. Half past eight. I am real grieved. I started to take the girls . . . to school. we had gone about half a mile, they said they rather go on foot than ride. James jerks and hits Beauty with the pitch-fork and hollows at her so much that she is almost uncontrollable. she jumps & scringes at every noise & every move as if afraid she was going to be kicked or pounded. I may talk & reason—tis of no avail—and my tears for the team seem all in vain. I can only hope & trust it may be better sometimes, though I fear that cruel spiteful disposition of James' will never allow him to have a nice team.

OCTOBER 4, 1883. . . . James chore and chop wood. he is tired & has one of his bad spells again. I am sorry and hope he will feel better in the morning. it makes my blood run cold & I shake like a leaf as did Sarah, too. James said—"give me what you have of mine & you may have the rest." I said, "I do not consider I have any thing of yours"—"don't eh, then you & I are done forever on earth." I sometimes hardly know what to do.

JANUARY 17, 1884. . . . I was speaking . . . to James this evening—when he said in one of his tones, which means he does not like to hear a word said, "It seems to me your voice has a peculiar whang to night." I asked him why? he did not reply. Dear old journal, none but you greets me a welcome, when Henry and Sarah are gone. it is not very pleasant, to always keep still & only listen.

APRIL 19, 1884. I went with James last evening to Mr. Richmonds to settle calf-keeping account. . . . we were coming home through a brushy dismal place and talking about the calves &c. all as I thought was good nature & all right. When to my very unpleasant surprise he said "Emily I believe you mean to kill me sometime, I want you to tell me if you do, I want to meet my God prepared."—I was perfectly terror struck, & though I did not really fear him, I was afraid he might attempt something wrong. I only said, "you have no reason for such unjust talk," "I have my reasons," he said. I asked him "what are they," but he would not say. I was very thankful when we arrived *safe* home. it seemed like riding with a maniac in a dark dark night alone. . . .

AUGUST 8, 1884. . . . I was alone all day; horses got in garden. Sarah came back to help get them out. am tired of so much work. I sometimes wonder what *was* designed for woman to do, seems as if there is no end.

OCTOBER 22, 1884. . . . James looks at me with such a stare sometimes it almost makes me feel a fearful dread to see him. why, O, why is it & what can he be thinking of.

AUGUST 10 1885. I have never seen a happy day since less than two weeks after we were married. he told me how he had been tempted to kill himself as far as to get a rope & go the barn to hang, he has threatened it many time since. O what an anxious heartbreaking sorrow to me it has been and for it I have spent many sleepless nights.

AUGUST 17, 1885. . . . I will try, as I have done, to keep our little family together just as long as possible. yet—sometimes—yes often, I think it is dangerous to be with him alone. O if he could only be & do all right. . . . I told [a

> neighbor] how we were so near being separated, how very disagreeable & unpleasant it was for us. he said he was perfectly astonished and if I did not say it, he would not believe it, that every one thought Mr. Gillespie to be one of the best men to his family that ever lived & that I had kept our trouble to myself & kept the children from ever saying a word & we always seemed so happy & pleasant, that it would be apt to throw the blame on me. I fear not, for I am right. At least I feel that I am. I only regret that I did not go away and leave him when I first knew and found out what a terrible despondent disposition he had.

Emily considered the possibility of leaving her husband, although she feared the public scandal of a separation. His behavior continued to frighten her, and finally, after an especially bad episode, she took action against him. James, acting like a "raving maniac," went after their grown son, first trying to choke him and then threatening him with a pitchfork. Emily went to town that day and talked to a lawyer, who eventually was able to persuade James to leave the farm, allowing his wife and adult children to remain there without him.

Soon after their separation, Emily wrote in her diary:

> SEPTEMBER 25, 1886. The heart sometimes is broken by trouble. . . . I tried so hard to live through it without it being known by the outside world, suffered untold sorrow by hearing his abusive language, yet I did not dare to displease him. I have written many things in my journal, but the worst is a secret to be burried when I shall cease to be. God alone knows I have prayed every day that I might have Wisdom, that I might know the right way, & *do* right in all my words and doings.

Emily lived apart from her husband for the last two years of her life, first at the farm and then, as her physical health worsened, in a rented house in town. Emily was convinced that her poor health was the result of years of overwork. She was confined to her bed and cared for by her daughter. Suffering from growing paralysis—at the end, she could no longer move the muscles of her face—Emily Gillespie died in 1888. She was not yet fifty years old.

Emily Gillespie's marriage was not one of the worst of the time. Her husband was a respected member of the community, and he seemed to be a responsible provider for his family. He was not in debt. He did not drink. Although he threatened his wife and children when he was angry, he never physically hurt them. Her concern for her son's safety finally drove Emily Gillespie to separate from her husband, but she never took legal action to terminate the marriage.

Margaret Hossack's marriage seems to have followed a path similar to Emily Gillespie's, with outward success accompanied by internal discord and turmoil. Just as James and Emily Gillespie did, the Hossacks worked hard together to build a successful farm, and after more than two decades of marriage, John Hossack marked their prosperity by building a new house for his family. He and his neighbors worked through the summer to construct a sturdy two-story structure with a steep roof and a covered front porch; there were five bedrooms in the house, a large kitchen, and a sitting room. A split-rail fence surrounded the house and yard. It was a homestead befitting one of the county's leading citizens.

Hossack had purchased additional land and now owned 200 acres, one of the larger farms in the township. He focused on two of the most profitable products in Iowa: corn and red hogs. He also had dairy cows, shorthorn Angus beef cattle, and poultry.

In the community, Hossack had earned the respect of his peers, who regarded him as a knowledgeable farmer and a shrewd businessman. To his fellow farmers, he was friendly and usually in good spirits. He was a God-fearing man, praised for his integrity. He was also careful with his money—some called him tight-fisted—and he paid his debts on time. Though he smoked a pipe on occasion, he didn't drink, nor did he approve of playing cards or dancing.

But the private John Hossack could be difficult. At home, he was sharp tongued, moody, and humorless. He complained that his family was united against his will and wishes and that they didn't respect him. He often felt sick and unloved. He was strict with the children and scolded the older boys for their poor work habits. Ev Henry commented that "he was very particular how everything should be done" and if his sons did things differently, the boys "would have to take a jawing."

Hossack's disputes with the children spilled over into his relationship with his wife. One of the older boys, Will, called the arguments between his parents "the rackets." The quarrels were loud; they shook the farmhouse walls. Tensions mounted in the household when Margaret Hossack interceded on behalf of her children. In the worst of his rages, Hossack called his wife "bitch" and "whore" and threatened her and the children with physical harm.

The summer when Hossack moved his family into the new house, his oldest son, Alex, went to work for a neighbor. Some people whispered that Hossack had thrown him off the farm.

Emily Gillespie told her secrets to her diary; Margaret Hossack confided in her neighbors. She denied it at the coroner's inquest, but according to numerous reports from others, Margaret Hossack had talked about her husband's mistreatment of his family for more than a dozen years. The neighbors lent sympathetic ears. Many of the men—Will Conrad, Neil Morrison, Frank Keller, and others—visited the farm on occasion to calm Hossack when he was agitated. None of the neighbors recalled seeing

Hossack in the midst of these rages (usually they arrived to find him sullen and brooding), but they did recall unusual behavior.

Will Conrad remembered that, on occasion, Hossack would get "kind of wild and cross" with his family, but conversation with outsiders seemed to relax him. Conrad thought that he could tell when Hossack was suffering a particularly bad spell; at his worst, Hossack "would have a wild look to his eyes" and they would look "restless and brighter."

Frank Keller and Fred Johnston spoke of Hossack's emotional fragility. Keller noted that his friend had "nervous spells"; Johnston observed that Hossack was prone to "something a little more than temper, something about his nerves that he would seem to be all unstrung and excited."

In the parlance of the era, Hossack suffered from "spells" and "tantrums." Although his family and friends often thought that he seemed unwell, they would not have expected that treatment was possible. Most mental illness went undiagnosed in those days, and medical expertise or facilities to treat mental conditions were scarce, especially in rural areas. Those who were obviously dysfunctional and delusional, presenting a clear danger to themselves or to others, could be brought before the County Board of Commissioners of Insanity and, if found to be insane, committed to an asylum. They would be kept under lock and key until they were deemed healthy enough to return to mainstream society.

In John Hossack's case, though many in the community listened to the complaints from his wife, they acted only occasionally, and then by distracting Hossack until his rage passed. A visit from a friend, a few soothing words—these seemed to help well enough. The neighbors told Margaret Hossack not to worry, reassuring her that her husband would never hurt his family.

Knowing they had few options, the neighbors hoped that the

situation at the Hossack farm would get better. A few of them discussed arresting Hossack as a way to protect his family, but he had done nothing against the law. In private conversation among the neighbors, the insane asylum was also mentioned as a possibility. But steps were never taken toward that end. To bring a man of John Hossack's stature before the Commissioners of Insanity would have been almost unthinkable.

10.

The audience that storms the box office of the theatre to gain entrance to a sensational show is small and sleepy compared with the throng that crashes the courthouse door when something concerning real life and death is to be laid bare to the public.—CLARENCE DARROW, in "Attorney for the Defense"

The Hossack trial comes on for hearing next [week]. Both the counsel for the state and defense have been working industriously since Mrs. Hossack was bound over to the grand jury for the murder of her husband, and one of the most sensational trials that has ever occupied the attention of a Warren county criminal court is promised when the case opens. . . .

No one has ever been able to gain access to the exhibits which will be introduced as evidence at the trial. The bloody ax . . . is kept locked in the vaults of the state attorney. . . . Locked up in the attorney's vaults is also the chemical analysis of the blood found on the blade of the ax. There is a question as to whether or not this blood is human. The ax was sent to [a chemist] for his analysis and he, together with County Attorney Clammer and the midnight assassin are the only persons who know whether the blood is that of John Hossack. . . . —SUSAN GLASPELL, in the *Des Moines Daily News,* March 23, 1901

ON MONDAY MORNING, April 1, 1901, four months to the day after John Hossack was violently attacked in his bed, the trial of Margaret Hossack commenced in district court with Judge James Gamble, of Knoxville, assigned to the case.

The day was dreary and overcast, with rain predicted, but a large crowd formed in the town square more than an hour before the courthouse doors were officially opened at 8:30 A.M. Indianola residents walked from their homes, while horses and buggies brought farmers dressed in boots and heavy coats from throughout the county. Farm work had already been delayed by frequent storms in March; snow, sleet, and rain made labor in the fields almost impossible. Now it looked as if early April would be plagued by wet and inclement weather as well.

When the doors opened, the crowd pushed into the courthouse and climbed the stairs to the second-floor courtroom, quickly filling the rows of seats, anxious to catch a glimpse of Margaret Hossack. The defendant was not present, but her family was grouped near the defense table: all nine of her children, plus her two sons-in-law and half a dozen grandchildren.

Judge Gamble was seated in a high-backed chair at the front of the courtroom, with various law books stacked on his desk. He was dressed in a judicial robe and wore a vest and a small bowtie. Sixty-four years old and white-haired, with deep-set eyes and a thick mustache, Gamble was a veteran of the Civil War, a devoted Mason, and an able jurist with a stern demeanor. Though he had been on the bench for only four years, he was well versed in criminal law, having previously served as Madison County Attorney.

A criminal trial was a kind of spectator sport in the community. Anticipating a packed courtroom, Judge Gamble had appointed two additional bailiffs, charging them with maintaining order and security. He'd also instructed them about seating: He wanted the defendant's family to be segregated from the gallery and seated inside the bar of the courtroom. Unrelated observers could occupy the rows behind and would also be allowed to stand in the aisles and in the back of the room. One block of seats at the side was reserved for members of the press.

Nearly a dozen newspapers, including all the local papers and some from as far away as Chicago, sent reporters to cover the trial. Except for Susan Glaspell, all the reporters in the courtroom were men. Another notable presence in the press section was a young man with a narrow face and large ears. His name was Don Berry. Covering the trial as a correspondent for the *Iowa State Register*, Berry was a student at Simpson College and the son of Margaret Hossack's defense attorney.

Judge Gamble understood that selecting a jury would be a difficult task. Under state law, only male property owners over the age of twenty-one could serve on juries, and the lawyers would be looking for individuals who were not well acquainted with the principals in the case and did not hold firm opinions about the outcome. Expecting that many men in the community would be unable to fulfill either category, Judge Gamble increased the size of the usual jury pool. Typically, twenty-two men were called to be questioned when a jury of twelve was to be chosen; for the Hossack case, the judge ordered that fifty additional men be called.

Jury selection took a day and a half. One by one, the prospective jurors were called to the witness box and questioned by the lawyers. Just as Judge Gamble had feared, many admitted that they'd already decided that the defendant was guilty—or, in a few cases, innocent—and so were excused from further service. By late morning on Tuesday, April 2, a jury had been impaneled, and the names of the jurors were published in the *Daily News* that evening: D. Agard, J. P. Anderson, J. B. Biting, J. W. Bruce, J. W. Hadley, George W. Lewis, F. E. Miller, John Niles, W. C. Pittman, J. W. Poland, William Powers, and S. R. Richards.

The jurors were relatively prosperous and educated; all of them could read and write. Most were farmers, although one was a brick mason and another was a teamster. The eventual foreman, J. P. Anderson, was a well-respected local merchant. Ten of the jurors were forty-five or older. Eight had been married for at least twenty years; five had seven or more children.

In short, the men selected to determine the fate of Margaret Hossack constituted a jury of her husband's peers.

> INDIANOLA. April 2. (Special.)—The opening of tomorrow morning's session will be marked by the introduction on the part of the prosecution and defense of such facts as they intend to prove when they will at once proceed with direct examination of witnesses.
>
> It is understood seventy-eight witnesses have been subpoenaed, fifty-three in behalf of the prosecution and twenty-five on the side of the defense.
>
> A conspicuous feature so far is the large attendance of women in court. Over half of the spectators present today belong to the gentler sex. The bright array of Easter hats lent a novelty to the scene, giving it much the appearance of some social function.—SUSAN GLASPELL, in the *Des Moines Daily News*, April 2, 1901

Shortly before noon on Tuesday, a side door to the courtroom opened and Margaret Hossack, escorted by one of the bailiffs, entered the chamber. Dressed in a high-necked black dress and matching gloves, her gray hair pulled away from her face in a tight bun and covered with a black hat tied under her chin, she walked to the defense table and took her seat, close to her children. By her side sat Marcia Hodson, the sheriff's wife, who had been with her more than anyone else since the arrest.

With a bang of his gavel, Judge Gamble called the court to order and asked the defendant to rise. Margaret Hossack stood with her lawyers and faced the bench. Behind her the gallery stirred anxiously. A row of white-haired farmers, contemporaries of John Hossack, sat in a line near the front of the courtroom, bent forward and attentive, like watchful birds on a rail.

Gamble had a stern look on his face as the clerk rose and read the indictment, charging that Margaret Hossack had killed her husband with two deadly blows, "unlawfully, feloniously, willfully, deliberately, premeditatedly, and of her malice aforethought." The defendant, the jury was told, had pleaded not guilty to all charges. As the accused woman listened, her eyes filled with tears and her heavy body shook with emotion.

When the clerk finished, the judge nodded to the two lawyers for the state, George Clammer and Harry McNeil, a prominent Indianola lawyer who had been hired to assist the prosecution. Clammer, meticulously dressed in a suit and tie, rose to give his opening statement.

As for any prosecutor in a criminal trial, the county attorney's goal in his opening was to give the members of the jury a simple and chronological narrative as a connective thread or framework for the evidence to come. Just as important, he wanted to offer an explanation of what had happened that would be consistent with the jury's notions of how people behave. Hatred was central to Clammer's tale, the passionate hatred that a wife had borne her husband for thirty years, a smoldering emotion that had finally overwhelmed her one night, driving her to the brutal act of which she stood accused.

To craft this story, he would use the words and recollections of his witnesses. One of his key witnesses, however, would be absent from the trial: William Haines, the neighbor who'd been questioned at the inquest about Mrs. Hossack's attempt to engage him in a plot against her husband. It was reported that the man had "gone insane brooding over the tragedy" and been committed to an insane asylum at Chariton, Iowa, just nine days before the start of the trial. The news was broken in a story written by Susan Glaspell on March 23, shortly after she had interviewed William Berry in Des Moines. Glaspell did not mention—and perhaps she did not know at the time—that the mental breakdown had occurred just a few days after Berry had visited Haines to question him about the case. When Berry left, Haines had become distraught, saddling his horse and riding wildly from farm to farm. It had taken the efforts of several neighbors to subdue him so that he could be transported to the asylum.

Clammer had only recently learned the news about Haines. He'd had to reshape his strategy to depend on Haines's wife, Rinda, to supply the important testimony about Margaret Hossack's plot to kill her husband.

Clammer began by establishing the scene. He produced a large diagram of the Hossack homestead, the first of many physical props he would rely on throughout the trial, and placed it on an easel in the front of the courtroom. Immediately, Berry was on his feet at the defense table, arguing that it was not drawn consistently to scale. But Clammer assured Judge Gamble that a uniform scale had been used, and the judge ruled that the exhibit could remain.

Clammer's style was confident and self-possessed as he went on to talk about the evidence of the defendant's motive. He noted the many witnesses who would testify to the domestic difficulties in the family and to Margaret Hossack's wanting her husband dead. He said he would prove that her animosity had lasted right up to the night of the murder. Clammer declared that "the testimony of James will show, after the rest of the family had retired, the father and mother were quarreling for some time. . . ."

It was a dramatic assertion, containing a statement that had not been reported by the press. The newspapers had written that all nine of the Hossack children supported their mother and denied recent family arguments; now Clammer claimed that the story of one of them was different.

Clammer continued with his account of what happened the night of the murder, providing the jury with a vivid narrative that he hoped would be difficult to forget.

According to Clammer, the defendant plotted the murder of her husband while she lay in bed next to him after their final quarrel, and then she retrieved the family's ax from inside the granary. She struck the sleeping man twice, first with the blade and then with the blunt end, "crushing the bones of his skull deep into his brain." Walking across the sitting room, she carried the bloody ax, "holding her hand, or perhaps a rag, beneath the ax so that drops of blood would not stain her rug." She rinsed it and put it away, but threw it underneath the granary instead of replacing it inside the shed. She was dismayed to find that Hossack was not yet dead when she returned to the bedroom. When he began to groan aloud, she decided on the lies to tell her children and then summoned them to their father's bedside.

The evidence, Clammer admitted, was circumstantial, but it would prove beyond a reasonable doubt that the defendant was guilty of murder. The jury would see physical evidence to incriminate her: photographs of John Hossack's body; the bed where the attack occurred, still covered with the bloody pillow and other bedclothes; and hair and blood samples from the family ax. Expert testimony would show that the ax was the murder weapon, a fact that would discredit Margaret Hossack's story of an intruder. Wouldn't an intruder have brought his own weapon to do the deed? And there was the family dog, strangely quiet on the night John Hossack was killed. Wouldn't Shep have alerted the family to the presence of an outsider?

The jury would hear from other experts: scientists and doctors whose testimony would show that the defendant was lying in another critical aspect of her story—specifically, that she had been in bed when her husband was attacked and that she had called her children immediately after the attack. Medical testimony and physical exhibits, as well as simple common sense, would show that her claim was impossible to believe. Most significantly, neighbors and members of the Hossack family would testify to an irrefutable aspect of the case: Margaret Hossack hated her husband and she wanted him dead. ☾

COURT ADJOURNED FOR thirty minutes before William Berry addressed the jury on behalf of the defense. Over the past few months, Berry had come to understand the facts of his client's life. She had lived for thirty-two years with a husband who was harsh and abusive to his family, prone to irrational rages, and, quite possibly, mentally ill. But Berry would not tell that story in court. These details of her life might generate support in the minds of some, but they were the same ones that the prosecutor would use to prove that she had a motive for murder.

So Berry took a different tack, focusing on Margaret Hossack's character, describing her in familiar terms: as a hard-working wife and mother who was devoted to her husband and children. Berry knew many of the older farmers in the room by name; some of them had been friends of his own father. They were among the original settlers who'd come to Warren County when it was first organized, men who also knew John Hossack and had done business with him. Speaking in a strong and powerful voice, Berry told a straightforward story about the Hossacks, which was bound to resonate with jurors because it was a story that many of them could have told about their own lives.

Margaret Murchison had been born in Scotland and traveled to America with her parents when she was just a toddler. On her father's farm in Illinois, she'd met John Hossack, a man who had come to this country from Canada with nothing but "his hands, his head and good health." The two married and moved to Warren County, where John had purchased land and built a house. They had struggled together, Berry said, as helpmates, to make a life for themselves, with John laboring on the farm and Margaret keeping the home and raising her family. As Berry spoke, the defendant sat at the defense table, her head bowed, the sheriff's wife at her side.

Berry conceded to the jury that the couple had argued. Many neighbors would testify about that. And it was true, Berry said, that Margaret had left home on one occasion after a quarrel with her husband during the Thanksgiving weekend in 1899. She was upset, and she'd gone to her daughter's house.

But Clammer was wrong in saying that the ill feeling between the couple had continued. As the jury would hear, Margaret Hossack had returned home the very next day. She'd wanted to remain with her husband, and the two of them had reconciled, agreeing to live together in peace. It was the result that Margaret Hossack, as the good wife that she was, had greatly desired, and both she and her husband had abided by their agreement. Their reconciliation had been a complete success, and they had lived without conflict for the entire year before John Hossack was killed. Just days before the murder, the Hossack family had come together with friends and neighbors for Thanksiving, with John and Margaret celebrating the restored condition of their marriage and their love for each other and for their children.

By midafternoon, the skies outside the courtroom had darkened and a driving rain pounded against the long windows of the courtroom. The steady drumbeat of the downpour echoed throughout the room as Berry spoke. When he came to the night of the murder, offering the jury an alternative to the story Clammer had told, he raised his voice so that he could be heard over the sounds of the storm.

"You will hear from the defendant," Berry told the jury, "that she was awakened by a noise shortly after midnight on the night of the attack, and then, her children at her side, discovered her husband, wounded in his bed. Throughout the long hours of the night, she stayed next to her husband and nursed him until he died the next morning."

Berry stood before the jury box and spoke in ringing tones. The killing of John Hossack was an awful act, and it was also a mysterious one. In order to convict the defendant of murder, the prosecution had to prove her guilt beyond a reasonable doubt, and that would not be possible. The defense would show that Margaret Hossack was an innocent woman.

> Fully 1200 people flocked out of the court house when court adjourned yesterday at the close of the second day of the Hossack murder trial. During the afternoon session, which began sharply at 1:30 o'clock, the seating capacity of the courtroom proved inadequate to the demand and scores of people crowded into the aisles and stood packed in about the railing separating the attorneys, witnesses and defendant from the promiscuous multitude. . . .
>
> When Attorney Berry yesterday afternoon addressed the jury for the defense and took up the events of the day preceding the night of the murder and detailed them in their proper sequence, the stillness in the courtroom became oppressive. Carefully, he went over the actions of each member of the family. He told how on the night of the killing five of the children were asleep in the house; how at the side of the death bed eight of the nine children gathered while the mother, stunned by what had happened, attended to the wants of the sufferer, frequently administering water to the parched lips and bathing the wounded head.
>
> During the description of this scene, Mrs. Hossack, who occupied a seat by the sheriff's wife, surrounded by three of her daughters and all but one of her sons, broke completely down and wept bitterly. Grief was not confined to her alone, it spread until the weeping group embraced the family and the sympathetic wife of Sheriff Hodson, who frequently applied her handkerchief to her eyes.—SUSAN GLASPELL, in the *Des Moines Daily News*, April 3, 1901

11.

"On Wednesday, the 19th of December 1900, I met Young John Hossack on the street in Indianola. I took from his conversation that he wanted me to go on the bond. I told him that the way my business was situated that I could not. He asked me what the people at New Virginia thought of the matter. I said I didn't know, that they were at sea about the matter. And then he said "the public don't know as much as we do and we won't tell what we know and we couldn't and you don't blame us do you?"—testimony of J. B. FELTON, 55-year-old farmer and Hossack neighbor, before the Warren County Grand Jury, January 1901

CLAMMER CALLED WILL HOSSACK as his first witness. A large and awkward youth, unused to speaking in public, Will testified for an hour, sitting in the witness box and directly facing his mother.

He said that he'd used the ax the day before Thanksgiving to kill the turkey and, on the night of the murder, had told Ivan to put the ax away inside the granary. Then Will described being called by his mother in the middle of the night and seeing his father for the first time after the attack. According to Will, he'd seen a clot of blood on the right side of John Hossack's head that was "nearly as big as a tea cup." The area around his father's eye was blue, and the eye itself was swollen shut.

Clammer then questioned Will about the history of the family's domestic quarrels, but the boy was reluctant to answer.

> "I will ask you if you know of any trouble having been between your father and mother?"
>
> "I don't remember of any trouble much for a year."
>
> "For a year. You do go back beyond that time?"
>
> "Yes sir."
>
> "How far back can you remember of there being trouble?"

At this point, Berry interrupted and objected to Clammer's questions. The troubles were too far in the past, Berry argued, and therefore irrelevant to the crime as charged. Given the ample evidence that the couple had reconciled at Thanksgiving of 1899, the court should not allow the jury to hear testimony related to previous arguments.

As he would throughout the trial, Judge Gamble overruled Berry's objection, allowing the jury to hear about past conflicts in the Hossack household. Whether they were relevant to the murder was a question for the jury to decide. The judge instructed Will to answer Clammer's question, and the boy continued:

> "I don't remember what the first rackets were. I don't remember how far back I can remember difficulties between my father and mother."
>
> "I would ask you to use your best judgment upon this and state how far back you can remember, one year or fifteen. . . ."
>
> "I don't remember of any rackets, or remember what they was or anything. There has been trouble I guess about as long as I can remember. I have heard talk between them of a separation. About a year ago. Have heard none since that time."

Will talked more about his parents under Berry's cross-examination. The conflicts, he said, were occasional and over quickly. They would argue about something around the house or the farm, but "then very soon it would be over as if nothing had ever happened. You would not know or notice that there had been any disagreement between them." A year earlier, according to Will, his parents had reconciled; the family "agreed to let bygones be bygones and pay no attention to what had gone before." After that, "everything went very quietly and nicely." ☾

IN HER NEWSPAPER report later that day, Susan Glaspell described Rinda Haines as "a small woman, who looks to be suffering from some nervous ailment." Mrs. Haines had good reason to feel under stress. Her husband had previously been identified as a "star witness" for the state, but he was now hospitalized indefinitely in the state insane asylum, and the prosecution expected her to testify in his place. As Rinda Haines saw it—and as she had told others—her husband's involvement in the case was against his will, and his inability to testify was the fault of the defense lawyer who had visited him, triggering his breakdown. Although she was interrupted several times on the witness stand by Berry, who claimed that her stories were too remote in time and not sufficiently connected to the offense as charged, Rinda Haines answered the questions at length:

> We neighbored back and forth with Mr. and Mrs. Hossack, and I was friendly with Mrs. Hossack, and the families were friendly [and] frequently visited back and forth. We would go to their house and stay until bed and they would come to ours. We would go to places in the neighborhood to visit and to the schoolhouse. It continued along through all the years. . . .
>
> It was some two or three years ago that I had the conversation with Mrs. Hossack when she came down to the road to talk to me and my husband. We were coming by there and she come down to stop and talk with us about the middle of the forenoon. We had been to New Virginia. At that time

> she told us that Mr. Hossack was giving them trouble. Neither Mr. Haines or myself first suggested better get two or three neighbor men to come in also. Nothing said about that by either of us. She mentioned it first. I think we went up there that night. Nobody else went. Just Mr. Haines and myself. Mr. Hossack was quiet. He didn't talk to us unless it would be when we were about ready to go away. I suppose he spoke to us when we went. He was not discourteous. Seemed to be still. Didn't say much. . . .
>
> She once told me about them quarreling, and . . . he hit her and she stepped out of the glass door, and she pulled the door to and broke the glass out; she said that he hit her at the side of the head, and she run out the door and shut the door behind her and broke the glass out. She told that he throwed stove lids and hit her on the foot and knocked her toenail off.

The next witness was Dr. Dean, the physician who had tended to John Hossack in the last hours of his life. As Dean settled into his seat in the witness box, George Clammer approached and handed him a model of the human skull. Pointing to the location of the wounds on the skull as he spoke, Dean described Hossack's condition:

> I arrived there about half past four. Found him unconscious, with a wound in the head, and with a thready, rapid pulse, shallow and irregular breathing, and the body was covered with a cold, clammy sweat. There was an incised wound of a considerable extent, and the skull was crushed. . . . He was not conscious any of the time after I got there. He articulated a few words, but he held no conversation.

Clammer asked for a medical opinion from Dr. Dean: Was it possible that Hossack could have spoken at any time after the attack? Dean couldn't tell him that, claiming that there was no "hard and fast rule." In answer to another question from Clammer, Dean stated that there was no way he could know how much time had elapsed between the attack and his examination.

When it was Berry's turn, he asked Dean about the appearance of Hossack's wounds. Will had seen what he thought was a large blood clot on his father's head. Had Dean seen such a clot? No, Dean responded, he was quite sure that no solid clots had formed by the time he examined Hossack at 4:30 A.M., and certainly not a clot the size of a teacup. He had seen an enlarged place on Hossack's head, just as Will had, but that was "the entangling of the brain matter as it oozed out of the wound . . . with the blood and with the hair lodging on the ear."

Berry asked about Hossack's brain injuries. Wasn't it possible that the wounded man could speak soon after the injury? Dean agreed; speech several minutes after the attack was surely possible, with the ability to speak declining over time due to bleeding and the resulting pressure on other parts of the brain. In other words, it was more likely that Hossack could have spoken soon after the injury rather than later, when more time had elapsed.

At a break in the testimony, Berry spoke to reporters, saying he regarded the testimony of Dr. Dean, a witness for the prosecution, to be of enormous value for the defense. ☾

ON WEDNESDAY CLAMMER called thirteen-year-old Ivan Hossack to the stand to tell his story about putting the ax away on Saturday night. Ivan said that he thought he'd placed it inside the granary.

Under Berry's questioning on cross-examination, Ivan remembered the evening before the murder as a peaceful one. "After supper Will took the cushion and whip . . . and we were playing and cutting up, and father was jolly, laughing and joking and playing with us that night before we went to bed," Ivan said. "I saw no indication of any disturbance or quarreling between father and mother that evening. He and ma were playing with the children. Heard no trouble after I went to bed."

Undaunted, Clammer continued to pound away at the theme of family troubles, calling a procession of Hossack family members to the stand. Cassie, May, and Annie, as well as Annie's husband, Ev, marched to the witness box and answered questions about the history of the quarrels. Like Will, they acknowledged conflicts in prior years but claimed that arguments had ceased after the reconciliation at Thanksgiving in 1899.

With each cross-examination, Berry stressed the contrast between the two Thanksgivings. At times, when addressing the Hossack children, Berry grew expansive in his questions, often lacing his inquiries with details, and then requesting that the witness simply affirm that his descriptions of the reconciliation and subsequent holiday dinner were accurate. Clammer objected strenuously to Berry's use of description in his questions; the defense attorney, Clammer stated, was acting as a witness.

> Upon the cross-examination of each of the girls Senator Berry kept rubbing in the fact that a reconciliation had taken place between Mr. and Mrs. Hossack around Thanksgiving day [1899] and that this reconciliation was complete. In fact Senator Berry is playing upon the Thanksgiving reconciliation to such an extent that the attorneys for the state say they can smell the turkey. Every time there is a Hossack on the stand Senator Berry turns to the Thanksgiving stories and in the questioning regarding it he displays marked descriptive powers. In fact when Senator Berry gets on the turkey story there is little left for the witnesses to do. Some times they give an occasional "yes" but even this is sparingly employed. The county attorney this afternoon rather objected to Senator Berry acting as witness in the case when he had not been sworn. This did not embarrass the big sen-

> ator, however, and he proceeded to regale the judge and jury with Thanksgiving dinner stories until all that has ever been said on Thanksgiving dinners had been exhausted. Thanksgiving day is the time of all times in the Hossack trial. The county attorney talks unfailingly of the stormy time of Thanksgiving, 1899, and Senator Berry then follows with tempting morsels of the anniversary of 1900.—*The Daily Capital,* April 4, 1901

The next witness, Dr. Harry Dale, the coroner, had publicly declared that he believed that Margaret Hossack was guilty of the murder of her husband. When he was called to the stand as the final witness on Wednesday afternoon, Dale seemed eager to support the prosecution's case, responding to Clammer's inquiries with assurance and conviction.

After initial questions about Hossack's wounds, Clammer asked Dale for a medical opinion regarding Will's claim that his father's eye was swollen and bluish in color. How much time, in Dale's opinion, would have elapsed before this condition would occur?

"At least a quarter of an hour," Dale responded with certainty.

Clammer knew how the coroner would respond to the next question. The county attorney's voice strained with excitement as he asked it:

"Where a man is found suffering from two such wounds as you describe; where there is a clot of blood as large as a teacup and as thick as your hand; where the blood has ceased flowing; where the eye is discolored and swollen, and where the man when found asks and answers questions, what would you estimate as the length of time that had elapsed since the blow was struck?"

The courtroom was still as Dale responded in theatrical fashion. He paused, seeming to consider his response. Then he turned and looked directly at Margaret Hossack as he spoke.

"I should think," he said slowly, "at least half an hour must have elapsed."

A smile of satisfaction crossed Clammer's thin lips as he sat down.

The implication of Dale's opinion—that the defendant was lying in her claim to have called her children immediately—caused a stir in the courtroom. Reporters busily scribbled in their notebooks.

At the defense table, Senator Berry leaned over to his co-counsel, and the two men bent their heads together in a whispered consultation. John Henderson then rose to conduct the cross-examination.

Henderson was tall and thin, with a long, stylish, black mustache meticulously groomed and curled up at either end. He stood for a moment in front of Dale, his hands in his pockets, looking at the coroner almost defiantly.

Henderson's objective was to demonstrate that Dale's conclusions, particularly as to the length of time after the attack before the victim could have spoken, were highly subjective, no better than educated guesses. Had Dale ever treated a patient who exhibited the same condition and head injuries as John Hossack? No, Dale admitted, he had not treated anyone with both incised and contused wounds. Then Dale's knowledge of the shock suffered by Hossack must be based on reading, Henderson surmised, more than his own experience? Yes, Dale said, that was the case. But could he then tell the jury anything conclusive? No, Dale had to admit, only a physician who was there with the patient could say with certainty when he returned to consciousness. Wasn't it true, then, that Dale was only guessing when he answered the hypothetical put to him? Dale could not deny that this was so.

Henderson then brought up the American Crowbar case: a

man who had suffered perforation of his brain, when his head was pierced completely through by a large thirteen-pound iron bar, three and one-half feet long and one and one-fourth inches in diameter. Unbelievably, the victim did not lose consciousness, but immediately walked upstairs, telling the story of what had happened to him, and then lived for twelve years without ever losing his mental power.

How, Henderson asked, could this case be explained? That was an exceptional case, Dale stated, as were others where victims suffered severe injuries to the brain without loss of their senses. Wasn't it possible, Henderson asked, that the same could be true of John Hossack: that it could be an exceptional case, in which the victim never lost consciousness? It was possible, Dale admitted.

The exchange between Henderson and Dale on the subject of Hossack's wounds ended with two final questions and answers:

> "Isn't it a fact that as a result of all this you are compelled to say to this jury that you don't know anything about when he could have recovered consciousness, whether he ever did, how long it would be, or anything about it, as a fact?"
>
> "I would not make any definite statement as to the fact."
>
> "It might have been early or late, or between times, or any other, isn't that true?"
>
> "Yes."

Predictions of the ultimate outcome of the case swung back and forth, and the relevance of key testimony was debated outside the courtroom as well as within. Front-page stories in the *Daily News* and *Daily Capital* were carried under provocative headlines: HOSSACK BEGGED WIFE TO AID HIM in the *Daily News* and HOSSACK CASE HANGS UPON A SINGLE POINT: COULD JOHN HOSSACK SPEAK AFTER BEING HIT? in the next day's *Daily Capital.*

With both morning and evening editions being published in the Des Moines area, thousands of readers who were unable to attend the trial in person were kept updated on the day's events with new reports appearing just hours apart. By midweek the trial had taken on the ebb and flow of a prizefight.

12.

It must be admitted, however, that the prosecution has not thus far furnished any direct evidence and it is extremely doubtful if the chain of circumstantial evidence thus far offered will be sufficient to eliminate all doubt of the defendant's guilt from the minds of the jurors. Unless more positive evidence of threats or desire on the part of the defendant to get rid of her husband are offered, it begins to look like the defense will be able to sustain its claim of easy acquittal.

On the other hand, however, it is known the state has not by any means exhausted its efforts and it is claimed by the prosecuting attorney that the best evidence is yet to come. The prosecution was never more confident of securing a conviction.—SUSAN GLASPELL, in the *Des Moines Daily News*, April 4, 1901

ON THURSDAY MORNING, Clammer turned to a topic that had generated intense speculation in the community ever since the murder: the blood and the hairs on the ax.

The public knew that reports from the men who'd found the alleged murder weapon differed. Had both the blade and the handle been covered with fresh blood and hairs, or were there only a few spots of old blood on the handle and a few hairs stuck to the blade? Of course, people understood that blood and hairs didn't necessarily establish the ax as the murder weapon, especially given Will's testimony that he used it to kill a turkey only days before. But experts had analyzed the blood and hairs to determine if they were human or animal, and their conclusions were eagerly anticipated.

Dr. John L. Tilton, professor of natural sciences at Simpson College, was a native New Englander with a distinctive accent. His manner of speech was unfamiliar to most Midwesterners. Tilton was, however, widely respected as a teacher with a great deal of scientific training. A former student described him as "precise to the finest point, sometimes bookishly theoretical."

In answer to Clammer's questions, Professor Tilton explained in long and tedious detail the difficulties of his analysis, stating finally that he had found no satisfactory evidence of human blood. Some of the blood had come from a fowl; Tilton was certain about that. That conclusion was, of course, consistent with Will's testimony about killing the turkey for Thanksgiving, but established nothing whatsoever about the use of the tool for any other purpose.

Professor Tilton had also studied the hairs. In great detail, he described his analysis of the three hairs from the ax. The first two hairs had characteristics common to dog hair and human hair, while the third was "unlike that of any dog whose hairs I have been able to examine," justifying his conclusion that "that hair was probably from a human being." Given that all three hairs were said to come from one source, Tilton said, he thought that they all probably came from a human being.

Were the hairs taken from Hossack's head from the same human being? In response to Clammer's question, Tilton conceded that they "could" have come from the same head.

In Berry's mind, the hairs on the ax were a significant issue. He knew that Clammer would rely heavily on the hairs to establish that the Hossacks' ax was the murder weapon, especially given the lack of definitive evidence regarding the blood. It was important for the defense to challenge Tilton's conclusions on several grounds, and Berry was prepared to do just that.

Berry's cross-examination focused on the certainty of the professor's opinions. Under Berry's questioning, Tilton conceded that his conclusion that the human hairs came from the same individual was little more than a guess. It was practically impossible, he said, for a scientist to take a few hairs of unknown origin, compare them with hairs from a particular man, and then to conclude without a doubt that the hairs were from the same man. The most that a scientist could say is whether the hairs under comparison resembled one another. He thought that the hairs in this case did, although hairs from two different individuals could also do so.

Tilton's lack of certainty was good for the defense, but Berry had another, more important goal in mind; Berry wanted a ruling that the testimony about the hairs should be entirely disregarded by the jury. The challenge was a procedural one, based upon the requirement that physical evidence could be admitted only after its chain of custody had been established. In this instance, the prosecution had to prove that the hairs introduced in the courtroom were the identical ones that the sheriff had removed from the ax, and Berry didn't think that the state could do that. And Berry knew that Clammer would be especially sensitive to this challenge, since it directly implicated the conduct of the county attorney during the murder investigation.

With the cross-examination of the next witness, Berry raised that issue: Sheriff Hodson was called to the stand, and Clammer took him through his story of obtaining and transferring the evidence. On the morning after the murder, Hodson said, he'd taken three hairs off the ax and placed them in his pocketbook. Some days later, he went to Clammer's office, and the hairs were put in a vial. After that, he participated in exhuming the body of John Hossack and put the hairs collected then in a second vial. Both vials were eventually delivered to Professor Tilton for analysis.

When it was his turn, Berry wanted to know more details. Exactly how long had the hairs from the ax been in the sheriff's pocketbook? Hodson thought that it was a week or ten days, but he couldn't be certain. Who had placed the hairs in the first vial? Hodson didn't remember that either, but he thought it was Clammer or Dr. Dale. Clammer had kept the first vial in his possession until about five or six days later. Then Hodson and Clammer had gone together to Professor Tilton's office, Hodson had given Tilton the vial with the hairs from Hossack's body, and Clammer had given him the other vial. But did Hodson know that the hairs in the vial Clammer handed to Tilton were the same ones he had taken off the ax? No, Hodson said, that would be impossible for him to say. He knew nothing for sure about what had happened to the hairs he had taken out of his pocketbook after he'd given them to Clammer.

Berry fixed on Hodson's response. Immediately after Margaret Hossack had been arrested, the county attorney had gone on record to say that he was convinced of her guilt—at the very time that he had in his private possession the hairs from Hodson's pocketbook. Unless Clammer were to testify under oath, which Berry knew was extremely unlikely, how could the jury be sure that the hairs examined by Professor Tilton were, in fact, the ones Hodson had taken from the ax? Establishing a chain of custody was an essential precondition of introducing any tangible object into evidence. If the hairs were inadmissible, it seemed obvious that Professor Tilton's testimony, based on those hairs, should be disregarded as well. With no evidence to consider as to the hairs, and only inconclusive evidence as to the blood, how could the jury conclude that the Hossacks' ax was the murder weapon? In Berry's mind, he had scored an important victory for the defense. He made a motion to withdraw the hairs from the jury's consideration, and Judge Gamble agreed with the defense and sustained the motion. The hairs from the ax could not be shown to the jury.

Berry then made his second motion: If the hairs themselves

were not proper evidence, he argued, the expert analysis of them must also be inadmissible. But Judge Gamble did not agree with this contention, and ruled that Professor Tilton's testimony, which had come before the defense challenge to the relevance of the hairs, could stand. The jury would be allowed to consider his conclusions. Berry silently noted that if the jury convicted his client, Gamble's ruling would be grounds for an appeal. ☾

JIMMIE HOSSACK, AT SIXTEEN, was tall and lanky. When his name was called, Jimmie walked awkwardly from his seat near his mother to the witness box, then stood with his hand on the Bible, swearing to tell the truth.

Before Clammer started the questioning, Jimmie looked directly at his mother. She sat quietly in front of him, her eyes fastened on her son. Jimmie put his large hands on the armrests on either side of his chair, bracing himself for what was to come. He breathed heavily, shuffling his big feet under the chair.

Clammer started the questioning innocuously, asking Jimmie about the night of the murder: where he slept and when he went to sleep. Jimmie said that he knew his parents were still in the sitting room when he went to bed between seven and eight o'clock that evening. Clammer paused then, and asked the significant question: "Did you hear them quarreling for about an hour after you had gone to bed?"

Jimmie stared hard at the county attorney. The boy's eyes narrowed and the muscles in his face twitched. In a firm voice, he answered, "No."

Clammer appeared to be taken aback by the boy's answer. He turned to the prosecution's table and retrieved a sheaf of papers. He shook them slightly in Jimmie's direction as he asked him the next question.

"Didn't you swear before the grand jury that you had heard them quarreling before they went to bed?"

Jimmie looked at his mother and then down at the floor. "Yes," he said.

Clammer leafed through the papers, then pulled one out and extended it toward Jimmie.

"For the purposes of refreshing your memory," Clammer said, "I will ask you to read these lines from your testimony before the grand jury." Jimmie's hands were visibly trembling as he took the paper and looked down at the print. He handed it back to the county attorney.

Clammer read the page aloud: "'I heard Ma and Pa quarreling after I had gone to bed. I did not hear what they said. He was blaming her for something. On Thursday evening they had also been quarreling for about an hour.' "

Clammer paused and then asked the boy, "Did you not also testify that he was blaming her for something and that she said he was almost driving her crazy?" Clammer's face was stern as he looked at the boy, waiting for his response.

"Yes, I did," Jimmie said, in a low voice.

"And you said, too, before the grand jury, did you not, that you did not pay much attention to them, as it was such a common thing for them to have quarrels?"

"Yes, I said that then. You got me to say it." The boy was choking back sobs at this point, and his face, as described by one of the reporters, had a look of agony upon it, "like [that of] a hunted animal."

"Do you not so testify now?" Clammer asked.

"No," Jimmie said, "I do not."

At this point, Berry stood and objected to Clammer's examination of Jimmie. The prosecutor was cross-examining his own witness, Berry argued, asking leading questions, which would normally not be allowed. And Clammer should not be permitted to read testimony from the grand jury hearing once Jimmie denied that it was the truth. Judge Gamble overruled Berry's objections, saying that Clammer could continue.

But Clammer could not sway the boy from the course he had chosen. Several more times, Clammer read aloud from Jimmie's prior testimony about hearing his parents quarrel on Thursday night and again on Saturday, the night of the murder. Each time, Jimmie said that his previous statements were false. Clammer had scared him, he said, making him say things that weren't right. The truth was that he hadn't heard his parents arguing either night. He didn't remember hearing anything between them after he went to bed. Yes, he said again and again, he had testified differently before, but he would not say those things now. He'd heard nothing that night until May woke him up to tell him of the attack on their father. By the time Clammer sat down, Jimmie was crying openly.

Berry rose for his cross-examination. His large frame shielded Jimmie from the sight of many of the observers in the courtroom, but others could see that the boy, still crying and gulping for breath, seemed to calm down. When he spoke, Berry's voice was gentle and kindly.

> "Do you remember how many times they called you in and out of the grand jury room?"
>
> "No, sir, but it was a great many. They would send me out and then after a while they would send for me again."
>
> "Now, while you were being examined at some one of those times before the grand jury, Jimmie, Mr. Clammer told you, did he not, that if you didn't change your testimony and testify differently from what you did before the coroner's jury, and tell all you knew about this, you would be prosecuted?"
>
> "Yes, sir."
>
> "And that you would be put under arrest?"
>
> "Yes, sir."
>
> "Now, Jimmie, I will ask you if you were alarmed and scared by this statement of the County Attorney?"
>
> "Yes, sir."

The courtroom was still as Jimmie was excused and stumbled back to his seat. Judge Gamble adjourned the court for a brief recess.

When the court reconvened, Judge Gamble announced: "Let the record show that all of the testimony of the witness, James Hossack, as to what he testified to before the grand jury, is by the Court, on its own motion, stricken from the record and withdrawn from the consideration of the jury, and the jury is, by the Court directed, in its further deliberations in this case to pay no attention to, or refer to what the witness, James Hossack, testified to before the grand jury."

Whether or not the jury believed that Jimmie was now telling the truth, the newspaper reporters were cynical. In the *Daily News,* Susan Glaspell described Jimmie's testimony:

> [It was] so palpably an effort to shield his mother as much as possible as to have just that much greater effect on the jury. . . . The introduction of the evidence as given before the grand jury by this witness is thought to be a great point in favor of the prosecution as it is generally thought the boy on more mature deliberation is making an endeavor to shield his mother.

The reporter for the *Daily Capital* shared Glaspell's view, describing Jimmie's denial as

> a tragedy which could well form one of the soul stirring chapters of a Victor Hugo romance . . . and one of those instances where humanity defies ethics and where the dictates of the heart throw the promptings of conscience to the winds.

No other family member in the house on the night of the murder—including Ivan, who had been sleeping next to Jimmie, and Cassie and May, sleeping upstairs in the room directly over the sitting room—testified to hearing John and Margaret Hossack argue on Saturday night or, in fact, at any time during the Thanksgiving weekend. Perhaps, if Jimmie was telling the truth to the grand jury, the voices of his parents had not been loud, or the discussion had not been prolonged and had ended well before the couple settled into bed.

Jimmie's recantation of his prior testimony might have been a blow to the prosecution, but it did not stop the county attorney from hammering away at the theme of the Hossack family troubles. On Thursday afternoon, Clammer presented Neil Morrison, Will Conrad, Nora Cart, and Eleanor Keller—various Hossack neighbors who told the jurors about their conversations with Margaret Hossack over the years. Berry was on his feet many times, objecting to the line of inquiry. The information Clammer was seeking, Berry continued to argue, was immaterial, unconnected with the offense charged, and too remote to be relevant. Each time, Judge Gamble overruled Berry's objections and the jury was allowed to hear the evidence.

Eleanor Keller repeated what others had said: She'd heard the defendant say on several occasions that she thought her husband was "very dangerous to his family" and "kind of crazy." She had "no peace and . . . she wished he was dead." Mrs. Keller's testimony was particularly significant because she had also talked to Margaret Hossack in January 1900, after the reconciliation arranged by her husband and Fred Johnston. Mrs. Keller described the conversation:

> I don't know just how it commenced, what was said first, but I don't think I asked her anything about it till she commenced talking. I could say that I wouldn't ask her for anything at all; she talked about her troubles that night and cried, she always cried to me about it, seemed like her heart was touched very much, and we got to talking, and I says,

> ain't you getting along better now, and she says, no it ain't any better than it always was, Mrs. Keller, not a bit, it is just as bad as it ever was. You know this was after the settlement.

Had the defendant said anything about wishing that her husband were dead? asked Clammer.

"Yes," Mrs. Keller answered, "I think that was the last time she said that, she wished him dead, that is the last time I talked with her."

On cross-examination, Berry asked whether Mrs. Keller thought that the woman was having a "pretty bad time."

"Yes," Mrs. Keller responded, "I did, I used to feel it when first she told me more than afterwards . . . I don't know what came over me. I didn't somehow—"

Was Mrs. Keller about to mention having a sense of guilt and regret about not helping Margaret Hossack, a woman whom she knew to be in a dangerous and unstable situation? Before she could finish her sentence, George Clammer was on his feet, objecting. The witness was unresponsive. She wasn't answering the question that had been asked.

Judge Gamble agreed with Clammer and addressed the witness directly: "All you are asked for, Mrs. Keller, is the conversation between you and Mrs. Hossack, not what you thought." Mrs. Keller's testimony ended moments later. ☾

THE NEXT DAY Clammer was rewarded with articles in the Des Moines newspapers noting the growing strength of his case against the defendant. Under the headline WOMEN TESTIFY AGAINST HER, the *Daily Capital* described the Thursday afternoon session:

> The testimony of the neighbors and especially of the women of the neighborhood, which was given yesterday afternoon, was extremely damaging to Mrs. Hossack. The ev-

> idence that was introduced during the afternoon showed that family quarrels were much more numerous than had been previously indicated. These troubles had been communicated by Mrs. Hossack to the women of the neighborhood, who now took the stand against her. To several of them she had said she had no peace at home and that she wished Mr. Hossack was dead. It also became evident that quarrels had not ceased with the reconciliation of Thanksgiving, 1899, as during the last year Mrs. Hossack had still told her friends of how hard it was for her to get along at home. . . .
>
> The testimony so far has not indicated that Mrs. Hossack was popular in the neighborhood. She is not a woman, in fact, who would make warm friends. In some of the testimony yesterday afternoon there seemed to be a note of animosity. The women either did not realize the weight of their testimony or else were not averse to making a strong case against the defendant. Some of them had to be called down on the stand for expressions of opinion as "we thought a good deal of Mr. Hossack."

In the *Daily News,* Glaspell's first reports had been succinct and objective in describing, witness by witness, the testimony elicited by Clammer and Berry. Her articles were marked by occasional dramatic flourishes, but she offered only brief analysis of the evidence until, after the inconclusive medical evidence on Wednesday, she wrote that "it begins to look like the defense will be able to sustain its claim of easy acquittal." On the following day, however, Glaspell, like the reporter for the *Daily Capital,* recognized that the prosecution was making headway in its case against Margaret Hossack. At the same time, her increasing empathy for the defendant was becoming evident:

LOOKS BAD FOR MRS. HOSSACK

> INDIANOLA. April 5. (Special.)—Slowly but surely the prosecution in the Hossack murder case is weaving a web of circumstantial evidence about the defendant that will be hard to counteract. The examination of each additional witness leaves a perceptible effect on the jury and their faces become more and more set and stern. Mrs. Hossack is bearing up well under her trying ordeal, but day by day her countenance becomes more haggard and drawn. She may come out of the trial a victor, but the terrible strain cannot but have the effect of permanently undermining her health and bringing her to an early grave. To many it seems her hair is turning perceptibly lighter, and the gray is gradually giving away to silver.

During most of Good Friday, Margaret Hossack sat impassively at the defense table with her granddaughter, Ethel May Henry, cuddled in her arms. The toddler was three years old, a quiet child with curly hair and large, innocent eyes. To some in the courtroom, one of the main points of Berry's argument seemed obvious: This elderly woman, showing such affection to the grandchild in her lap and surrounded by her loving and supportive children, could not conceivably be capable of violent murder.

That afternoon the county attorney called Frank Keller, the neighbor and longtime friend of the Hossack family, as the fortieth and final witness for the prosecution. Described by one reporter as "a man who looks as though he had stepped down from the shelves straight out of a volume of Dickens," Keller sauntered to the front of the courtroom, swinging his arms at his sides. Tall and thin-faced, with a mane of uncombed white hair, he took the oath and sat down, arranging his long legs until he felt comfortable.

He began his rambling testimony by describing in detail his arrival at the Hossack home early Sunday morning, just before John Hossack's death. As he spoke, he turned in his seat and faced the jurors directly, waving his arms for emphasis. Keller repeated the story Margaret Hossack had told him about what had happened; it was consistent with the reports of others. But Keller had new information to divulge—that after the murder, the defendant had known where the ax was to be found. He'd asked her where the ax was, he said, and she had answered, without hesitation, that it was under the granary. And she was right, of course; Keller and some other men had found it in that very place.

When Clammer encouraged Keller to tell what he knew about the Hossack family troubles, the witness obliged with a lengthy account. Senator Berry, as usual, objected to the line of questioning, and Judge Gamble again allowed the witness to testify about conversations he had with the defendant about her husband. Many times, Keller said, the defendant had talked to him about her husband's erratic behavior, and she'd told him that her husband had threatened to kill the family. On one occasion he had suggested to her that he should accompany her home and speak to John Hossack, but she'd refused. Keller recalled:

> I then said, Mrs. Hossack, what can I do, you won't allow me to speak to your husband about this thing, nor you won't allow me to go with you, what can I do? Why she says, I will tell you what I want you to do, I want you to gather up two or three men, come in some night and beat him pretty near to death for abusing his family, tell him when you leave him, that if ever you hear of such an occurrence again, that the next time you will finish him up. I told her I couldn't do such business as that. She said she couldn't live with him, she wished to God he was dead. . . . She

> turned around to go home . . . cried and says, O, why is it the good Lord don't remove him out of our way?

Keller's story was eerily similar to the one told by Rinda Haines on the first day of the trial. Was Keller's memory clear on this point? Or was he mixing up his recall of past conversations with the testimony he knew Rinda Haines had already given? At the coroner's inquest, Keller had said nothing about being asked to beat or assault his neighbor.

It was hard for Keller to answer Clammer's questions without digressing, adding extraneous opinions or theories about the case. Keller's responses provided some degree of entertainment for the audience but frustrated the judge. At one point, Keller started to discuss how some Masons in the community had come to him and urged him "not to make certain statements on the stand," but Judge Gamble quickly silenced him and admonished the witness to respond only to specific inquiries. Keller's conversation with the unnamed Masons was not to be revealed in court.

Eventually, Clammer steered Keller to Thanksgiving of 1899. Keller's memory was consistent with that of Fred Johnston, who had testified the previous day, except for one thing: Keller remembered that Hossack had referred to a secret between himself and his wife. As Keller recollected, Hossack said, "I want you to understand that there is a hidden secret in this family that nobody but me and Maggie and my God knows anything about. When I die I will die with this secret in my breast."

Keller went on to say that he'd never learned what the secret was. It was something, he believed, that was known only to the murdered man and his wife.

With her young grandchild now asleep in her arms, Margaret Hossack visibly shuddered at Keller's words.

Henderson conducted the cross-examination. Keller's willingness to talk was evident. He told the defense attorney that "if there is anything you want to know, just jump in."

Mostly Henderson wanted Keller to discuss his relationship with the deceased: how they had met and become friends, how they'd participated together in various social and political activities. In the course of the testimony, Keller acknowledged that John Hossack was sometimes emotionally unstable, "subject to tantrums or spells," and that Mrs. Hossack had frequently requested that Keller or her husband's other friends come to the house "for the purpose of cheering him up." On only one occasion, Keller admitted, had Mrs. Hossack suggested to him that the neighbors should consider beating John Hossack so that he would "quit abusing his family."

At the conclusion of the examination, Henderson asked Keller what he and Johnston had told the Hossack family at the time of the reconciliation. Keller responded:

> We suggested that from that time forth, they should tell no man or woman, nor tell any person, about their troubles, were not to talk about it among themselves, were not to refer to it, and were, if possible, to forget it. He and they all agreed to it.

At the end of that Friday afternoon, the prosecution rested its case.

13.

"I do not think that John Hossack had an enemy in this county. He is the last man on earth that I should have thought would have met his death that way."—*Des Moines Daily Capital*, April 8, 1901, quoting T. T. ANDERSON, Indianola resident, speaking to a group of John Hossack's longtime associates in the offices of the *Indianola Herald*, April 6, 1901

It has been long since any trial in the state of Iowa has attracted the statewide attention that has been given the trial of the Hossack murder case. The fate of the woman accused of the killing of her husband will be read with eagerness by many thousands to whom she is a stranger. It has been so strange and horrible that it has fascinated many who are not ordinarily interested in the proceedings in a criminal court. An old woman on trial for the murder of her husband is far from an every-day sight. . . . The Hossack murder trial will be a story long told in the state of Iowa.—*Des Moines Daily Capital*, April 11, 1901

SATURDAY MORNING WAS CHILLY, with temperatures just above freezing, as William Berry left his house to walk up Ashland Avenue to the Warren County courthouse. The ground was still damp from Friday's downpour, but Berry could hear songbirds in the Russian mulberry bushes and see new buds on the trees. Gray wood smoke curled from chimneys. It was the day before Easter, and a hint of spring hung in the air. Court would be in session for the morning only.

For the defense to succeed, Berry had to convince the jury that it was at least possible that an intruder had killed John

Hossack. That morning, he had one particular issue in mind that he knew could be problematic for the jurors. If someone had entered the house and committed the murder, why hadn't Shep barked and wakened the family? Berry planned to argue that the dog had been drugged, and he wanted to call the witnesses to support that claim right away.

Several obstacles, in addition to the silence of the dog, stood in the way of an acquittal. Clammer's story succeeded because no other suspects had been named, no motive but the wife's hatred for her husband suggested. The defense wasn't obligated to prove that another person was guilty, but it would certainly help its case if the jury could at least imagine a specific alternative to the prosecution's story. William Haines was an obvious choice—the man, who was certifiably crazy, wasn't there to defend himself, and Berry intended to bring his name back to the jury's attention in his closing argument.

The prosecution's arguments were effective because they appealed to common sense: How could the defendant have been in bed when the blows were struck and not have awakened? How could she have been in bed without also being hit by the ax? These aspects of her story were difficult to believe, and the defense would have to depend heavily on Margaret Hossack's performance on the stand. She would have to persuade the jury that she was telling the truth.

The prosecutor's evidence of motive was the most damaging to the defendant. The twelve men on the jury were not apt to forget the many reports by neighbors that Margaret Hossack had said on frequent occasions that she feared her husband and wished him dead. The defense could only argue that her feelings had changed since then, stressing the reconciliation and relying primarily on the testimony from the children. Their honesty was, of course, subject to doubt, since their mother's life was at stake. But, now that Jimmie had changed his story, they were at least consistent in what they said, and perhaps the show of the strong and emotional support by all of her children would have some effect in swaying the jurors in Mrs. Hossack's favor.

As Berry crossed the street, he came abreast of the crowd of spectators who appeared daily outside the courthouse doors in hope of gaining access to the day's proceedings. Horses and buggies encircled the square, tied to the chains that stretched between the hitching posts. A few well-wishers and colleagues greeted Berry as the crowd parted and let him enter the building.

Berry opened his defense of Margaret Hossack by calling an expert witness to the stand: Dr. T. S. Parr, a physician who'd been practicing medicine in Indianola for thirty-two years. Dr. Parr gave his opinion in great technical detail, but his conclusion was relatively simple: If Hossack had spoken at all, it was likely that he would have done so very soon after the injury.

Next, Berry turned to the evidence about Shep, presenting witnesses who described the dog's behavior Sunday morning, claiming that he was not acting naturally. William Anderson, a schoolteacher who had once boarded with the Hossack family and who'd taken Shep hunting, noticed that the dog was behaving strangely, as did Will and John Hossack. All of them remembered that the dog was acting stiff and unusual, certainly not his regular self.

Donald Murchison, Margaret Hossack's elderly brother, also testified about the strange behavior of the dog: "I thought his eyes looked kind of strange . . . and he looked kind of languid and out of sorts." He'd asked one of the boys about the dog, but the boy said he didn't know what was the matter.

Berry didn't expect Murchison to be one of his strongest witnesses about the dog. After all, as Clammer brought out in cross-examination, Murchison hadn't visited the Hossacks for more than twenty years, and he had never seen Shep before. But Murchison could also speak about the early life of John and Margaret

Hossack, bolstering the story in Berry's opening statement. He told of young John Hossack's having worked on the Murchison family farm and then marrying his sister and traveling with her to the newly purchased land in Iowa.

It was in this context that Berry asked a simple question, one to which he thought he knew the response: "When was the Defendant, Margaret Hossack, married?"

Murchison hesitated in his answer, saying: "I am not quite positive; I think it was in the fall of 1868."

Berry didn't acknowledge anything irregular in Murchison's response, although he knew that the Hossacks had always claimed they were wed in the fall of 1867. Murchison went on to say that the couple had moved to Iowa in the spring of 1868, after their marriage. Berry either didn't notice the inconsistency or perhaps thought that it wasn't worth pointing out. In any case, the sworn statement by the defendant's brother—that the Hossacks had wed in the fall of 1868—went uncorrected, becoming part of the official transcript.

Clammer, however, noted the marriage date as stated by the defendant's brother. Only moments later, when Alex Hossack was on the stand, Clammer asked his birthdate, and Alex responded that he had turned thirty-two in August 1900. Clammer did the math to himself—that meant that the oldest Hossack child had been born in August 1868. To Clammer, the secret known only to Margaret Hossack and her husband had just been revealed. Here was something that the prosecution could use to its advantage.

Although unaware of Clammer's thinking, Berry addressed the issue of the secret between the Hossacks on Saturday morning with his final three witnesses. According to Frank Keller, Hossack had told him that he and his wife had a secret, and, as Keller related Hossack's comment, it seemed that there was something more between the couple than just domestic quarrels, something bigger and more unique—perhaps a secret that warranted murder. But Berry hoped to refute that interpretation and replace it with another: Hossack meant only that his troubles were private matters; he didn't want others to know about his conflicts with his wife and family. Berry had witnesses who would testify to that effect.

Berry produced three people in quick succession who said that they had overheard the conversation between Hossack and Frank Keller, and they had not heard it as Keller remembered. Louie Kemp had heard her father say that his troubles were a secret he would carry with him to the grave, but nothing about a secret known only to himself and his wife. Cassie Hossack confirmed her sister's recollection, and so did Fred Johnston, the neighbor who had joined Frank Keller in his conversations with the family. According to Johnston, Hossack had said

> His troubles were a secret within his own breast, that he would carry them with him to the grave. . . . There was nothing said by Mr. Hossack about there being any secret known between him and Maggie and their god and that it would die with him. No mention of Maggie in connection with any particular secret at all.

At noon, Judge Gamble adjourned the trial for the remainder of the Easter weekend, reminding spectators that court would be back in session on Monday morning. ☾

THAT AFTERNOON THE large headline in the *Daily Capital* proclaimed DEFENSE HOPES REST UPON HOSSACK DOG. Noting that a review of the evidence presented by the prosecution strongly supported the state's case, the reporter cautioned the public not to jump to premature conclusions. The defendant was being represented by two of the finest lawyers in Iowa. Senator Berry had done his best that morning to challenge the logic of the prosecution theory and to suggest that Margaret Hossack's story about an unknown intruder was plausible. The possibility that the dog had been drugged lent another angle to the case. More surprises, the article suggested, might lie ahead.

Over the weekend, people in Indianola and in the outlying farming communities discussed the case against Margaret Hossack. In the streets, in stores, and in homes, as families worked together and gathered for meals, men and women, husbands and wives, argued about whether or not she was guilty of murder. Would the jury convict or acquit, and if convicted, would she be sentenced to death, as the prosecution was asking? If she did receive the death penalty, she would be the first woman ever to be executed in Iowa and would die by hanging.

People were fascinated and repelled by the facts of the Hossack case. The murder, although one of the bloodier ones of the time, was not the most horrible; other crimes reported in Midwestern newspapers at the turn of the century included a woman who killed her lover's wife by slitting the wife's throat with a razor; a young wife who, after her husband took steps to annul their marriage, shot him four times and then kicked his dead body; and a wife who blinded her husband by throwing carbolic acid in his face, forced her ten-year-old daughter to drink of the poison, and then committed suicide by drinking it herself. There was also Sarah Kuhn, who had poisoned her husband—but that case seemed somehow more understandable. Not only had she killed in a more feminine way, by slipping something into his food, but that defendant had had a lover and so had already stepped over the bounds of propriety.

Margaret Hossack, in contrast, seemed by all reports to have been a typical farmwife. Perhaps she'd suffered abuse at the hands of her husband, and maybe she had carried her woes to the neighbors and talked too much about her domestic situation, but committing a violent crime seemed out of character. She'd been steadfast in her claim of innocence, and her family stood squarely behind her. Still, there were no other suspects, at least none that the legal authorities identified.

The *Daily Capital* reflected on the community's obsession, commenting on its "exceedingly great strangeness":

> It is not that it is so horrible, but that it is so weird, so hard to understand. People listen to it because it baffles them. On their faces are constantly the questions: "Could she really have killed him like that? What drove her to such a thing? What was that secret in the Hossack house that John Hossack said he would keep in his breast until he died? If she did not hit him with the ax, who did and why?"

On Saturday night, a group of older men gathered in the offices of the *Indianola Herald* to discuss the case. Most of them had been in the courtroom every day for the past week, and they wanted to speculate about the evidence and the likely outcome. Some had been acquainted with John Hossack since his first years as a landowner. They could only guess what would happen in the trial, and so, eventually, the talk turned to their memories of the murdered man.

They acknowledged that he was a flawed man who could be sullen and hardheaded, but mostly they remembered him as an honorable leader in the community. He was a good farmer. He kept his word and paid his debts.

The elderly farmers remembered Hossack's candidacy for county treasurer only months before his death, an election that he'd nearly won. No one, the men agreed, had ever breathed a word against Hossack during the campaign or made any insinuations about his character. They talked of his loyalty and his devotion—to his friends, his church, the Republican Party, the Masons. As far as they knew, he hadn't had an enemy in the county. His death, as one man put it, was "one of the most awful things that ever occurred in the state of Iowa." ☾

ON EASTER SUNDAY, Indianola went to church.

The day was sunny and warm, with the brightest of blue skies. The churches in town were lavishly decorated with flowers, and the streets around the courthouse were crowded with women dressed in their best finery and elaborate Easter hats, enjoying the weather and greeting friends and acquaintances as they passed.

With the trial in recess, it was a day for the Hossack children to go to church instead of the courthouse. After breakfast together at their boardinghouse, they dressed for morning services. Later they would go to the jail to visit their mother.

As the Hossacks walked to the Presbyterian Church, they were recognized by passersby who'd been among the crowds at the courthouse. People turned to look and pointed them out to others. They entered the church and filed, one by one, into a pew near the back. The word that the Hossack family was in attendance circulated around the room, and people twisted in their seats to stare.

To many congregants, one of the minister's prayers—that all be given the strength to handle whatever was to come—seemed to have a special significance, and tears were in many eyes when, with bowed head, he prayed for special strength for those worshipers who were dealing with a sorrow that was even greater than death.

> At the Presbyterian church, some of the singers who were to take part in the special service that evening gathered in the afternoon for a rehearsal. A woman with a rich contralto voice was singing "The Holy City" when a door at the rear of the church opened slowly, and a girl stepped

timidly inside. She sat down in a far corner of the rear seat and bent her head low on her hand as though endeavoring not to be seen. The church was almost empty, it was near evening and the sinking sun was sending strange, beautiful lights into the half-darkened building. The full rich chords of the organ swelled richly out and then melted away to meet the shadows. The music seemed to give the girl courage, for she raised her head and looked around. The empty pews all around her, the dim light falling through the colored windows and the rich strains from the organ that seemed coming for her alone, lifted her out of herself and her apparent sorrow and she sat there with folded hands, only listening.

After a time the last glorious "Hosanna" died away and then the singer began another song, a song that was softer, more appealing than the first. It seemed to be a song that was written for heavy hearts and it was sung slowly, sympathetically. It closed with the words:

For earth knows no sorrow
That heaven cannot heal.

The voice of the singer stopped, but the notes from the organ still came. Just as they were sinking lingeringly away the solitary girl rose from her seat and stepped noiselessly out. She was not crying, but the look on her face was a strange one for so young a face to wear. She walked slowly a block west and then stopped at a building where there were bars across the windows.

The girl who had crept all alone into the church on that beautiful Easter afternoon was May Hossack. She had stopped on her way to the county jail where she was going to see her mother. She went from the church, heavy with the perfume of Easter lilies, to the padded cell, where that perfume could not enter and where songs of praise had not found their way.—*Des Moines Daily Capital*, April 8, 1901 ☾

SUSAN GLASPELL SPENT the weekend in Indianola, walking the streets and enjoying the fine weather. Her mind, like those of others in the community, was on Margaret Hossack.

On the Tuesday after Easter, she published the following in the *Daily News:*

HER DREARY EASTER DAY

MARGARET HOSSACK SAW NOT THE SUNSHINE NOR BIRDS

Residents of Indianola Promenaded Past Her Cell and Stared at the Lonely Woman.

INDIANOLA. April 9. (Special.)—Seldom, if ever, have the people of Indianola seen such an Easter Sabbath as Sunday. It was not so much the beauty of the day, for, although it began and finished with ideal Easter conditions, there has been many another as balmy, as full of the freshening vigor of spring. There were other elements at work than those of external nature; other influences beside those arising from the deep significance of the day. Blended with it was the spirit of tragedy, and it penetrated and permeated all classes and found vent in the intensity with which the questions: "Is she guilty?" "Will they convict her?" were asked.

It was the atmosphere of tragedy surrounding Mrs. Hossack who, shut in from the world in a narrow, padded cell in the gloomy interior of the county jail, listening throughout the day to the inspiring clanging of church bells or catching the half lost strains of chanting choirs, which even heavy walls and iron-grated windows could not entirely exclude.

Spring had come and with it, as if by magic within a day, many an emerald spot, fresh and vigorous with the new life of summer, shown brilliantly against the sober brown, where winter yet reigns. But they were not for the eye of Mrs. Hossack.

In churches great banks of delicately colored flowers buried pulpits and adjacent aisles and exhaled upon the air a perfume that will linger in the vaulted roofs and shadowy pews until another Easter shall come. But they were not there for Mrs. Hossack to enjoy.

On the streets, especially those most remote from the jail, a throng of gaily dressed people enjoyed the warmth of an ideal Easter. Then they were merry; they laughed and chatted and walked; they talked and jested, but less as they approached the jail, until, when parading beneath its grated windows, a hush would fall upon them.

Was there something fascinating in those walls that they could so suddenly silence the gay interchanges of the day, or was it for the woman within, for Mrs. Hossack, invisible to the multitude, that they felt a sympathy, which no evidence could entirely destroy?

But about and beyond the jail, far enough away that it might not be heard within, there was that buzzing of human voices which always accompanies public excitement, and in it could be heard that question which lingers on the lips of everybody here: "Is she guilty?" and the answer is lost in the discord, but the discord has an ugly sound.

Mrs. Hossack spent the day quietly. Other members of the family attended one of the churches during the morning and some of them visited the jail in the afternoon. They are remaining in town during the trial, perhaps they will never go back to the farm again. Wherever they went yesterday they were pointed out; they had become curiosities;

they awaken speculation, and following each came those questions: "Is she guilty?" and "Will they convict her?"

Were it possible to obtain a consensus of opinion representing the entire community it might present Mrs. Hossack as an innocent woman, but that which can be gathered does not do so. That she has the sympathy of many people is certain; why, unless it be because she is a woman? When asked to express an opinion as to her guilt they refuse.

It is possible the general condemnation of the woman is due to the few who talk it so incessantly. Perhaps it is these thirteenth jurors who are responsible for the public verdict.

14.

One thing it is entirely safe to say. Margaret Hossack is a very unusual woman. She has a face that defies analysis. Sometimes it is hard and sometimes appealing. It is scarcely possible to tell whether the look upon it is put there by remorse, by fear, or by a broken heart. Hour after hour she sits in the courtroom and scarcely moves. She makes fewer nervous motions than any one within the bar. For whole days her only display of emotion will be in the twitching of her hands.

And yet it cannot be said that she does not feel or that she does not understand the significance of the testimony that is given. She is a Scotch woman and one whose powers of self control are developed to a rare degree. She seems to be one who could suffer to an intense degree and give no sign. On the other hand, it does not seem hard to believe, looking at her at other times, that she would be capable of brutality. She has not in any sense what could be called a fine face. Her smile, which has been seen less than a half dozen times this week, while not soft, is peculiarly pathetic. The lines about her mouth are hard, and when they do relax they create strongly the impression that she is a woman who has been abused. She is either a very strong character or a very thorough criminal. With it all there is no way of telling to what extent she feels the ignominy of her present position.—*Daily Capital,* April 6, 1901

THROUGHOUT THE MONTHS preceding the trial, Berry had declined to say whether or not the defendant would take the stand, but the possibility had been rumored. It was a dramatic moment when, at 10 A.M. on Monday morning, April

8, Senator Berry called Margaret Hossack as the final witness for the defense.

In the crowded courtroom, people whispered to one another and craned their necks to see as Margaret Hossack rose from the defense table and made her way to the front of the courtroom. Chairs scraped on the wooden floor as spectators rearranged themselves to get a better view.

The defendant had aged before their eyes during the course of trial. The weathered features of her face sagged; her steel gray hair seemed to have whitened. For exactly a week now, she had sat erect and composed at the defense table, her hands usually clenched in her lap. On most days, she wore a shawl draped protectively across her shoulders, and sometimes she raised a black-bordered handkerchief and held it to the corner of her mouth. Her sharp, blue eyes stared straight ahead, and she did nothing to acknowledge the crowd in the courtroom. She walked deliberately to the witness box, her steps slow and steady, like those of a person in no hurry to get from one place to another.

The defense lawyers knew that Margaret Hossack's appearance on the stand would be memorable for the jurors. They'd seen her sitting in the courtroom, and they'd watched her crying as her children testified, but they had not yet heard her speak. They still had to be convinced that she was just the kind of woman the defense claimed her to be: a hardworking farmwife and mother, committed to her husband and her children, incapable of committing the violent act of which she was accused.

This was the opportunity for the jury to relive the night of the murder from Margaret Hossack's perspective. Berry wanted her to tell her story in a simple and chronological fashion. He would not ask her about her relationship with her husband, either about their conflicts over the years or about their reconciliation.

At the inquest, she'd denied that she and her husband had ever had serious quarrels, and now, in the face of sworn statements to the contrary from so many neighbors, such testimony could only hurt her credibility.

Speaking in a low but firm voice, Margaret Hossack answered questions without faltering or contradicting herself. Several times during her two hours on the stand, she cried and had to stop speaking until she could regain her composure.

When asked about the night before the murder, she described preparing supper for her husband and Ivan on their return from the coal bank, milking the cows with May, patching and darning while her husband played with Ivan and then read the newspapers. Later she rolled the butter in the pantry. Several times she heard the dog barking, fussing as if something had disturbed him, and at one point she went out to the porch, thinking some cattle from one of the neighbors might have come onto their property. But she didn't notice anything strange.

She'd talked with her husband that night, she said, about the work to be done on the farm. He wanted to butcher one of the hogs and build a new platform on the wells, and they'd discussed the boys' going back to school. As she remembered their last conversation, her voice began to shake and tears ran down her cheeks. He'd told her, she said, that he felt better that night than he had in the morning, and that he was looking forward to church the next day.

Berry waited for several minutes until the witness indicated that she was again able to speak. Then she recounted what had happened after she went to sleep, telling the story as she had at the inquest. She was awakened by a noise that sounded like two boards hitting together, and, thinking that it was the children or something that had broken, she jumped out of bed. Outside the bedroom door, she heard sounds from her husband, and she thought that he, too, must have been disturbed in his sleep by the noise. But then she saw a light and heard the door to the outside shut. She ran to the door and found that it was not fully closed. It was then, she said, that she called her children, saying that she thought there had been someone in the house. She also called to her husband several times, but he didn't answer, and, hearing that he was breathing hard and choking, she realized he might be hurt. When her children came downstairs, she lit a lamp and followed Will into the bedroom, where they found John Hossack mortally wounded.

Margaret said that her husband first asked why Ivan was crying and then claimed that he was not hurt but only sick. He called for her—"Ma," he said—and later for Will and for Johnnie. As she recalled her husband speaking the names of her sons, she again began to cry. She paused, then bowed her head and sobbed, gasping as she sought to catch her breath. The courtroom was very still as people listened to the sound of her weeping and watched as she sought to regain control of herself.

Finally, Berry asked her a series of pointed questions. Margaret Hossack did not hesitate in her answers to him:

> "Mrs. Hossack, I will ask you to state to the jury whether or not you that night struck Mr. Hossack any lick with anything?"
>
> "No sir, I did not."
>
> "Or any one to your knowledge strike him that night that you knew of?"
>
> "Not that I know of more than this noise."
>
> "All you know is the noise you heard?"
>
> "Yes sir."
>
> "Did you see anyone in the house that night until after you had aroused the children, after you went to bed, except Mr. Hossack when he went to bed?"
>
> "No sir."

"Was anyone in the house during the night that you know of?"

"No sir."

"I will ask you to state to the jury, Mrs. Hossack, whether or not you had that ax [holding up the ax marked Exhibit A] or any other in your hand that night?

"No sir, I did not."

"State to the jury whether or not you had any sharp instrument in your hand that night, after you went to bed and after the children had gone to bed."

"No sir, I did not."

"Or any blunt instrument?"

"No sir."

"And whether or not you struck Mr. Hossack a lick with anything?"

"No sir, I did not."

"Or know who it was that did strike him?"

"No sir, I do not."

Berry concluded his direct examination with her answer, saying that he had no further questions for the witness at that time. ☾

HARRY MCNEIL ROSE to conduct the cross-examination, and, for more than an hour, he took Margaret Hossack again through her story of the hours surrounding the attack. He asked her to repeat much of what she'd said in response to Berry's questions, challenging her memory at times and requesting more details. Margaret responded calmly, speaking in a low monotone and without appearing disconcerted or confused. Only once did she contradict herself, but it was on a point that seemed insignificant: when she had gone into the pantry to prepare the butter.

On a more critical issue, McNeil asked several questions about her testimony that she had heard the dog barking. Did she really hear him barking for an hour and a half? That was her recollection, she said.

Just as on the direct examination, the questions were limited to the hours surrounding the attack. The prosecutors hoped to challenge her story, but they weren't relying on her testimony to supply them with evidence of a motive. The neighbors had already given the prosecution what it needed on that score.

When Margaret Hossack was finally permitted to step down from the witness stand, it was close to noon. She nearly stumbled from exhaustion as she walked the few steps back to her chair.

It was reported that Margaret Hossack was a superb witness for herself and that, as Susan Glaspell phrased it, "there seemed to be the impression on the audience that she had told the truth." Don Berry complimented the defendant, writing in the *Iowa State Register* that "at all times her voice was soft and her manner womanly, not at all evidencing the shrewish character that some of the witnesses would lead one to believe." He echoed Glaspell's sentiments: "No flaws were found in her story and it had every appearance of being absolutely true."

15.

"She did it, Gentlemen, and I ask you to return it to her in kind, that having considered all this case as honest, honorable men, knowing as you do your enormous responsibility that you will return to her a debt at the hands of the law. She has forfeited her right to live; she should be where John Hossack lies, rotting beneath the ground."—GEORGE CLAMMER, in his closing argument, April 8, 1901

ON APRIL 8 a crowd congregated outside the courthouse during the lunch recess, and this time, fewer than half of those waiting could be admitted to the afternoon session before all the seats were taken. People stood three and four deep, pressing together and filling the standing room.

The dry facts of the case had been presented, and the testimony of the investigators, neighbors, and family members had been heard. Now the lawyers had the stage to themselves.

Clammer was the first to address the jury. He spoke for four hours that afternoon, arguing the case for the prosecution with conviction and force. He returned to his theme of hatred—an emotion that he claimed had festered for years in the defendant's heart—and the images he painted of what happened on the night John Hossack was killed were vivid and terrible.

Clammer reminded the jury first of the proof of motive; over a period of years, he told them, the neighbors had heard the defendant say that she feared her husband. She complained about him to others and sought to humiliate him by her stories. According to Clammer, she'd brooded for years over the idea that she would be better off without him and had even tried to get a neighbor to kill him. When he refused, she decided to do the deed herself.

In dramatic fashion, Clammer recreated the events of the night of the attack, when the defendant had been transformed from a typical farmwife into a wicked and evil spirit. As he talked, he reminded the jurors of various pieces of evidence that were consistent with the story as he told it.

"That night after they had gone to bed she lay thinking it all over; how it would never be any better; how for years she had hated John Hossack. The man she despised was lying beside her in a deep sleep, she could hear his breathing; she wanted to stop it; she wished she could kill him. She thought herself into a passionate fire that night on December 1, when she said she was nervous and could not sleep and in a fit of desperation she got up. She walked about the sitting room; everybody in the house was asleep. She lighted the lamp and by that time there was a demon in possession of her soul. With livid face she stood in the door of the sitting room and looked at John Hossack—how she hated him.

"She had never been a loving wife, she had never been a woman of strong affections, and that night murder crept into her strange soul. She did the deed as a woman in such a moment of desperation and barbaric determination might be expected to do it, crazily, clumsily, with the family ax. She knew where the ax was, she had heard Ivan say in the evening that he was going to put it in the granary. She opened the door and walked out into the night. The good old family dog rose to meet her and she gave him a vicious cuff. She walked down to the granary with her heart full of hate. She did not stop to let herself think; she had but one purpose, she was going to get rid of John Hossack. She could do it, for every one was asleep and no one would ever know who struck him.

"She came back to the house, and left the ax in the kitchen. Her husband might have awakened and he might have seen her with it. But, no, he was still asleep, sleeping soundly, and no sound disturbed the quiet of the night in the lonely farmhouse. She took the ax and walking through the sitting room, stopped a minute at the bedroom door. She was now crazed with her evil purpose, and scarcely knew what she was doing. With that instrument in her hand and with that man sleeping there alone she could not go back. She would kill him with one well-directed blow and no one would guess who did it. Then she would be rid of him. She had borne it for thirty-two years; she was tired of doing it any longer. So she advanced to the bedside of the man who was sleeping with his back to her. With his back to her, it was a coward's blow, for John Hossack, an honest man, turned his back on the world, and had gone quietly to sleep, little expecting that a murderer, and that his own wife, would steal up behind him and kill him with an ax.

"She struck the first blow with the sharp end of the instrument, who but a woman would have done that? She struck it far into the head, but that was not enough. She drew the ax back over the bed and rested it for a minute on the piece of carpet at the side of the bed, where it left its bloody mark. Then she threw it again over her shoulder, and it dripped down over the right shoulder and back of her skirt, just where the examination showed the blood spots to have been. Some of it spattered on those pillow shams which were on the machine cover just behind her, and some of it was spattered on the walls. She struck the second blow and then she was satisfied. She turned to take the ax from the house. She held her hand on it as she was carrying it, through the sitting room, a housewife's instinct, perhaps, but when she reached the porch she let it drip. Then she stuck it in the barrel of water at the side of the house. The fresh blood was wiped off, the fowl's blood which had already been on the blade, was freshened. Most of the hairs washed off, but a few of them stuck. It was all done in an instant, and done well. But in every crime there is some mistake, and one mistake was made by Margaret Hossack. When it was all over she could not remember whether she got the ax out of the granary or under it. She hesitated a minute and then she stuck it under. She hurried back to the house and removed all marks of guilt. Then she heard her husband groaning; he was not dead. She gave the alarm.

"No human eye witnessed the killing of John Hossack. No man saw the light which flooded the sitting room and bedroom where he lay. No man saw the stealthy figure creep to the side of the bed, no one saw that ax raised. No one saw the edge cleave his skull. No one saw the defendant step back a moment and set that ax upon a piece of carpet. No one saw that second blow, which crushed in the head of John Hossack; no one saw the murderess walk stealthily from that house through the bedroom door across the sitting room door out across that porch; none saw the direction taken by the murderer.

"And yet how are they going to explain it away? He was killed, and by what argument can you say he was killed in any other way? Will you kindly tell me how a stranger would know where to find the family ax? Would he use that ax at all; would he not bring his own instrument? The blood spots . . . show that the ax was carried to the granary after the deed was done. The granary is one hundred and twenty feet from the house. A murderer slipping away in dead of night would never have gone there. He would have taken the shortest road to get away. . . .

"The accuracy of those blows shows that they were never struck in the dark. I will merely leave it to your common sense. Would any man take a light into that house and raise an ax to strike John Hossack when he had to raise it over the wife's sleeping body and with her face toward him. We know he would not, and we know if he had, Margaret Hossack would have been awakened."

At one point, Clammer returned to Shep and offered the jury an explanation for his unusual behavior:

"When the defendant went out of the house first he perhaps gave some sign of recognition, made some effort to jump up, and she cuffed him, giving him a scolding. He lay there and he realized what was happening to his master; he heard what was going on inside. Perhaps the dog crept in after her. He was a dog which came in the house; he may have followed her right through the door and he may have seen the deed. The dog felt the shame which the family has not shown on the stand; felt the shame which has often been shown a dog possesses; it was that which made the dog unwilling to follow the boy; he perhaps had seen and followed her down to the granary, saw the ax put away, went back and lay down there with a heaviness of heart which this family does not show, a heaviness of heart because his master had been killed."

Partway through his argument, Clammer came to a dramatic revelation. He wanted, he said, to return to the question of the defendant's motive.

"Now, gentlemen, I have looked over this evidence, I have wondered what is the underlying cause of this trouble, hatred and malice by this defendant: What could cause a man and woman who had agreed to love and cherish each other, who lived in a community all those years, who raised up a family of children, what cause could make them hate each other so terribly, as is shown in this case? I have conjectured; I have wondered if it might not be some secret cause; something unknown away back in their early lives. I have wondered over and over upon this. You gentlemen may have done the same thing. Was it a loveless marriage? Did something arise between these parties in their early acquaintance which caused them after to loathe each other?"

At this point, the courtroom was very quiet. Margaret Hossack sat very still in her chair, her eyes fixed on Clammer as he continued to speak:

"I want to call your attention to this and we will do a little bit of arithmetic before we get through with this. If you subtract from the number 1900 the number thirty-two, what is your result? 1868. If you will remember, the brother of this defendant Donald Murchison, testified on the stand that Mr. Hossack and Mrs. Hossack were married in the fall of 1868. The next witness on the stand was Alex Hossack.

"'How old are you?' asked the defense. 'Thirty-two years old.' When it came time for the cross-examination, 'When was your birthday last?' 'It was in August, 1900.' Subtract thirty-two from August 1900 and what is your date? August 1868. When were the defendant and this victim married? In the fall of 1868. That birth was either before the marriage or right at the time. Gentlemen, there can be no question about this. The defense has placed it in our power to talk to you this way; they have introduced the evidence, and there can be no question but that the motive underlying this hatred, this malice on the part of the defendant was that she was compelled to marry this man; the man always had a loathing of her afterwards."

As Clammer spoke these last few sentences, a wild expression passed over the face of the defendant, but then she collected herself and her features regained their rigid look. Before Clammer had finished his words, William Berry was on his feet with an objection. There was no evidence, he said, to justify the claim that it had been a forced marriage. The assertion made by the county attorney was completely without support.

Clammer was ready with his response. He was making a simple point, based on sworn testimony from witnesses at the trial. Margaret Hossack had her first child in August 1868, and, according to the statement of her own brother, that was before her marriage to John Hossack. The conclusion was obvious and, based on these facts, irrefutable: The defendant had borne her first child out of wedlock.

In fact, Clammer was right about one thing. The Hossacks had lied about the date of their marriage, and Alex had been conceived prior to the wedding. But Clammer had apparently stumbled onto this fact. Only two people in the Indianola courtroom knew the true date of the Hossack wedding—Margaret Hossack and her brother, Donald Murchison, whose misstatement under oath provided Clammer with the opportunity to make his claim. Although the legal record of the date of the Hossacks' marriage was located less than two hundred miles away, in the Stark County courthouse in Toulon, Illinois, George Clammer never produced the marriage certificate as evidence. ☾

IT WAS LATE afternoon when Clammer suddenly stopped and rested his hand on the table beside him.

"Gentlemen, after all is there need that I should say more? Would it not be useless after all to stand here and talk to you of something that is so plain that it needs no talking about? And yet there may be one man among you who says he is not quite sure. There may be one who wants more evidence. He shall have it. And when I have shown you this I have shown you what weeks of eloquence cannot argue from the minds of honest men."

Clammer turned and asked that the bed in the far corner of the room be placed before the jury. The courtroom was very still while the bed, covered with bloody bedclothes, was carried into position. When it had been placed directly in front of the jury box, the county attorney began in a quiet tone:

"You see this bed. It is small, the furniture men call it a three-quarter bed. The evidence has shown you that John Hossack did not move after he was struck. We can see from the blood in what part of the bed he was lying."

With a dramatic gesture, Clammer then threw back the covers.

On the bottom sheet, almost in the center of the bed but inclining slightly to Mrs. Hossack's side, was the mass of blood showing where John Hossack's body had lain.

"This defendant, gentlemen, is a large woman. I will submit it to your good judgment whether she was lying in the space between the blood and this edge of the bed at the time her husband was murdered. I will leave it to you whether the murderer of John Hossack could stand at the side of the bed, as facts show he did stand, and raise this ax in the face of Mrs. Hossack, for she says she was lying with her face from her husband, and she be unconscious of the fact that he was standing there striking her husband in the head. I will leave it to you, for it tells its own story more plainly than I can attempt to tell it."

As she listened to Clammer's argument, the defendant looked horror-struck, and she seemed to shrink down in her chair. Clammer continued:

"They will talk to you about reasonable doubt. They will say that you must not convict this defendant if you are not satisfied beyond a reasonable doubt. Have you a bit of doubt? Is there any doubt in your minds? Is it not as clear as though you yourselves had seen that deed? Had seen those two blows struck? Had seen the woman walking from that house? The murderess of her own husband; washing the bloody ax, putting it away, walking back into the kitchen . . . carrying the light out into the kitchen perhaps, shutting the door leading from the bedroom into the sitting room, because Dr. Dale says there was some blood marks on the door knob next to the sitting room; walking out into the kitchen with her lamp and then after awhile she heard groaning; I must give the alarm, he don't know who did it, I can stand by the side of the bed, can talk to him; I will fix up my story; the story fixed up, he don't know who struck him; I am not in danger, he lay with his back to me, and she went and gave the alarm. Blew out the light, sitting perhaps in her underclothes. Gentlemen, she gave that alarm some half hour or more after John Hossack had been killed. The expert evidence shows it. Every reasonable supposition from the first of this case to the last shows the same thing. . . . Gentlemen, that this defendant is the guilty person, that malice, that hatred, that motive to get his property, and get rid of him, everything conspired together. Could you think that the God above could have placed such evidence against any person and that person not be guilty?

"There is not a shadow of a doubt in this case. It is all wiped away; every bit of investigation points in the same direction. Not one syllable is introduced by the defendant to show that any one else might have committed this crime. All points the same way. Not any doubt at all, gentlemen. Don't you worry about a reasonable doubt. The Court will tell you what it means. It means a reasonable, not a foolish fallacy, not mercy or pity on this defendant. Pity her as she pitied John Hossack. Pity her as she pitied him when she was creeping into that room. Pity her as she pitied him when she raised that ax, and twice brought it down upon his head. What pity does she deserve at the hands of this jury?

"Gentlemen, the manner in which she has done this, the dastardly nature of the crime, the cowardly nature of this crime, slipping as she did to the back of the sleeping man, unwilling to take even the chances of poison, that insidious method, any way to get rid of him, taking the hardest, the most difficult, most apt to be discovered method to commit this crime, taking the family ax, everything being foolish; gentlemen, what does this defendant deserve on account of that crime?

"Gentlemen, John Hossack is in his grave after life's fitful fever; he sleeps well. Domestic malice, hatred, poison, has done their worst, and John Hossack lies there at last at peace. How did he get there? The evidence shows so plainly, so absolutely, that I dare stand before you, as I would not dare to do if I had the shadow of a doubt, and ask you that your verdict shall condemn this defendant to death. She does not deserve to live, she has forfeited her right to.

"She did it, Gentlemen, and I ask you to return it to her in kind, that having considered all this case as honest, honorable men, knowing as you do your enormous responsibility that you will return to her a debt at the hands of the law. She has forfeited her right to live; she should be where John Hossack lies, rotting beneath the ground."

As Margaret Hossack listened to the closing sentences of Clammer's argument, her face was distorted with emotion. The reporter for the *Daily Capital* wrote that the words, vivid and terrible, were nearly beyond her endurance. And yet her obvious distress was evidence in her favor. According to the reporter, "Her whole attitude answered at last the question that has been asked so many times since the trial began: does she suffer as a woman on trial for murder would be supposed to suffer?" ☾

LATE ON MONDAY afternoon Judge Gamble allowed the defense to make a brief statement. Henderson rose from his seat and faced the jury. In angry words, he denounced the county attorney for his charge against the character of Margaret Hossack. The claim that Margaret Hossack had borne a child out of wedlock was not supported by the facts, but rested solely on a misstatement by Donald Murchison as to the marriage date. It was a contemptible accusation on the part of the county attorney, intended only to inflame and prejudice the members of the jury against the defendant.

Henderson finished, and court was adjourned.

16.

The stage, the arena, the court are alike in that each has its audience thirsting to drink deeply of the passing show. Those playing the parts vie for success and use whatever skill and talent they possess. An actor may fumble his lines, but a lawyer needs to be letter-perfect, at least, he has to use his wits, and he may forget himself, and often does, but never for a moment can he lose sight of his client.—CLARENCE DARROW, in "Attorney for the Defense"

After four months of association with Mrs. Hossack and her family, I can stand before this jury and before my God and say I believe her to be absolutely innocent of this crime.—WILLIAM BERRY, in his closing argument, April 9, 1901

AT TEN O'CLOCK the next morning, Senator Berry began his final appeal to the jury. He spoke until noon, when the proceedings stopped for lunch. Reporters rushed to make their deadlines for the afternoon newspapers. Susan Glaspell's story was published in the *Daily News* just a few hours after the morning session ended, reaching some readers before Berry had even finished the final stage of his argument later that day.

> INDIANOLA. April 9. (Special.)—Senator Berry is exhausting himself, his eloquence and oratory in the final effort of the defense to clear Margaret Hossack of the charge of murder. It is said to be the master effort of his life. . . . At times the jury without an exception was moved to tears. Strong men who had not shed a tear in

years sat in their seats mopping their eyes and compressing their lips in a vain effort to suppress the emotion caused by the senator's eloquent plea.

The theory of the defense, as it appeared from his argument, is that the insane man, William Haines, now confined in a mad house, is the man who, in a crazy moment, influenced by some fancied wrong, killed the best friend he had. . . .

Senator Berry commenced his argument by calling the attention of the jury to the Hossack family and impressing upon it the fact that it had their fate in its hands. He referred feelingly to the toddling grandchildren and told the jury that through all the time God spared them to live their future happiness was in its hands. . . .

While Senator Berry was speaking, the defendant, surrounded by her children, presented a most pathetic scene. For the first time since the trial began it would seem they appreciated the awful position in which their mother is placed and that the final effort of their lawyers is being made to show her innocence.

Time after time a tear stained face would be raised and an anxious gaze directed toward the jury. The boys of the family were even more affected than the girls. John Hossack, Jr. . . . sat with his head bowed while his gigantic frame shook with great sobs and he choked with emotion. At times when Senator Berry would pause, the sobbing of this man was audible throughout the room. Its effect upon the spectators can only be described by the word terrific.

Even the attorneys for the prosecution were seen to turn away their heads fearful lest the anguish of the family would unman them and the jury would have an impression which they could not afterwards remove.

At one time Attorney McNeil, the nestor of the Warren

> county bar, whose practice has extended over a half century, was so affected by the spectacle presented by the family group that he bowed his head and silently wept.
>
> When court adjourned at noon fully two thousand people went out in the sunshine, their faces stained by the tears which had coursed down their cheeks during the period when Senator Berry closed his most pathetic appeal. ☾

AT 1 P.M., COURT reconvened and Berry continued his argument, attempting to counter the powerful images from Clammer's description of the night of the murder. Berry's voice was usually loud and resonant, but now he spoke in low and somber tones.

"On the day before Thanksgiving, Willie went out and killed the turkey for the big family dinner there was to be on the day following. How little did the boy then dream that that which he was then doing in happy anticipation was to be taken and turned on his mother as proof that she killed his father. Well, they had the Thanksgiving reunion and the day after it and the Saturday which followed passed quietly and peaceably. On Saturday, Mr. Hossack went to the coal bank. Naturally enough for company he took with him his youngest son, that bright little fellow you saw on the stand. He got home at four o'clock and his wife and the girls got him supper at once, because he was hungry and did not want to wait until the time of the family meal. After night had fallen they sat around talking and then as is the custom in the country home, the younger children went to bed. The older ones, too, were tired, and at nine o'clock, they followed. Soon after ten the lights were out and the peace of the home had fallen on the prairie home.

"Margaret Hossack was born and reared in the Scottish highlands. All her life she has been a good mother. She has raised nine children and has helped her husband build up a home, with no criminal record behind her, with no criminal tendencies ever displayed. I want to ask you whether you would be justified in thinking that, with her husband sleeping by her side and her children asleep in the rooms above, with no provocation in all the world, she lay there and deliberately planned a brutal murder. It was a crime that only a few men could have done. Jesse James might have done it, but from what you know of her, do you think it was within the power of Margaret Hossack?"

As Berry spoke, he turned to the defendant. She was seated, her arms enclosing her three-year-old grandchild on her lap. Tears fell from her eyes as she listened to the words of her lawyer.

Berry turned back to the jury.

"If in the heat of sudden passion, she had committed this hideous crime, she would now be a broken woman. After she had taken that ax and thrown it under the granary she would never have returned to the house, to the husband she had murdered, and aroused her children to come and see her work. After she did it she would have been crazed. She would have wandered off in the night, anywhere, anywhere to get away. She could not have been guilty of that crime and contained herself all these months in the county jail, as she has done. In my heart of hearts I say I believe she is innocent of this crime and it is only the consciousness of that innocence which has so nobly sustained her."

Then Berry challenged the circumstantial evidence presented by the state. The experts, he reminded the jury, were not conclusive on the important points. They could not say that the blood or hairs on the ax were human, and without that evidence, there was nothing to prove that the family ax was the murder weapon. In fact, Berry argued, the evidence pointed against it: The family ax had a nick in its blade, and the wounds displayed no such mark. As for the scientific evidence that challenged the defendant's credibility—John Hossack's ability to speak, the appearance of the wounds—the experts were not in agreement.

Some of the medical evidence presented by the prosecution actually supported her story, whereas none of it conclusively proved that she was lying.

Berry stressed the testimony about the chemise worn by Margaret Hossack the night of the murder. The garment had been soaked in a pail of water, compromising its value as evidence. The state was to blame for its lack of care in maintaining the chemise in its original condition. But witnesses had seen the shirt while Mrs. Hossack was wearing it, and they remembered that the blood spots were only on the back; the front of the shirt was clean. Could that be possible, Berry asked, if she had struck two blows to her husband's head? Would not the front have been covered in blood if she had committed the murder? That fact alone, Berry declared, should support a reasonable doubt about the prosecution's story.

Berry spoke throughout the entire afternoon on Tuesday. He removed his jacket, loosened his tie, and pushed his rumpled shirtsleeves up to his elbows. His meaty hands gestured in the air. As he paced in front of the jury box, his boots thumped loudly against the wooden floor. His face reddened from the exertion; occasionally he paused to wipe the perspiration from his broad forehead.

During Berry's emotional closing argument, his co-counsel felt the strain of the proceedings to such an extent that he was unable to remain seated next to the defendant. Henderson paced in the hallway outside the courtroom, deep in thought, his hands clasped tight on his head as Berry's words echoed through the walls.

At 5:30 P.M., as the courtroom darkened with afternoon shadows, Berry approached the jury box and made one final plea for understanding and mercy in defense of his client.

"I have talked to you much longer than I had intended. Maybe I have wearied you, maybe in my zeal I have said too much. I know that may be true, and yet, though night has now fallen and though the day for us all has been one hard to endure, it seems that even now I cannot be content to say the final word. I have in my heart that fear that somewhere, sometime, in the course of these four months I have left undone something that might have aided the cause of Margaret Hossack. As I stand here now, with my work completed, I am oppressed with a terrible feeling that too late there will come to me something I might have done.

"But I have done all I could. The time has now come for me to stop. And in your hands I leave the results of my work, to you I must at last consign the fate of this defendant.

"Gentlemen, if any one of you is the only one upon this jury who entertains a reasonable doubt of the guilt of Margaret Hossack, I ask that you obey the law and refuse to vote for her conviction. I was surprised at the zeal with which the county attorney demanded not only the conviction but the life of this defendant. He went far beyond what the testimony warranted. After four months of association with Mrs. Hossack and her family, I can stand before this jury and before my God and say I believe her absolutely innocent of this crime. You are asked to hang her—oh, those bitter, those terrible words that were spoken in this courtroom.

"In conclusion, I only say to you this—when your verdict is found let it be such as that you standing beside of her on her gallows will have your conscience approve your decision when the rope is cut and she falls to the ground. Let your verdict be one that if you shall consign her to the felon cell for life you can say when the door has shut her out from the world forever, I have done right. Let it be one that whatever punishment you shall fix, when in the years that are to come you meet these daughters, these sons and these grandchildren you can say, I convicted your mother, but I did what I thought was right. And if your verdict cannot be such a verdict, follow the law as it will be given to you by this court. Do not condemn this woman unless you can stand in the presence of these generations yet unborn without one qualm of conscience.

"When you reach your jury room, consider the life of Margaret Hossack, its trials and burdens and those difficulties of wifehood and motherhood. Consider the tempests of unfortunate disagreements in the light of the reconciliation that followed. Find such a verdict as that when you meet her, as some day you will, in the presence of the judge who can judge, with all impartiality, you will have no regret for what you have here done. If you cannot say that you are convinced beyond a reasonable doubt, remember that as ye would have others do unto you, do ye also unto them. If there is a doubt, put yourself in her place and remember the rule that should govern us all. Mercy, mercy. Justice we cannot always do, we can but do the best we can. As you know that some day you will answer for what you have done, be sure that you do not commit to the hangman or to the cell an innocent woman. It is better even that the guilty should sometimes escape than that the innocent should ever be punished.

"Never in all my life have I felt the responsibility as I have in this case. I have never dreaded a responsibility as I have this, and I pray no such responsibility shall ever be cast upon me again. I am now leaving with you the fate of a woman who before high heaven I believe to be innocent."

Finally, Berry stopped speaking. He stood before the jury for a few moments, silent, with his head bowed. Then he raised his head, as if he intended to continue his plea but again he stopped himself. He looked directly at the twelve men in the jury box before turning and walking slowly back to the defense table, where he sat down next to his client.

The silence in the courtroom at the end of Senator Berry's address lasted for more than a minute before Judge Gamble declared the court adjourned for the day. The crowd filed from the courtroom, talking softly among themselves. Some congregated in the growing dusk on the lawn to continue their conversations; others ambled homeward in silence. Horses that had spent the day hitched outside stirred restlessly, anxious to be fed and watered.

The defendant followed the spectators out of the courthouse. Looking drained and aged, she was accompanied by the tall and slender figure of the deputy sheriff. The dispersing crowd moved aside to let her pass, watching her as she made her way. She walked slowly, holding a handkerchief to her face and keeping her eyes cast downward as Deputy Kimer escorted her back to the county jail.

17.

In arriving at your verdict, it is your duty to carefully and candidly consider the entire evidence in the case, and having thus examined and considered the whole case, you should convict the defendant if the proof should establish her guilt to such a certainty as fully and fairly satisfies you beyond a reasonable doubt, as above explained, that she is guilty, but if it does not so prove her guilt, you must acquit her.—from Instruction Number 8, as read to the jury by JUDGE GAMBLE, Wednesday, April 10, 1901

THE PROSECUTION WAS allowed a rebuttal argument, and Harry McNeil spent from 9 A.M. Wednesday until late that afternoon again making the case against the defendant to the jury. He carefully went over the state's evidence, focusing first on the defendant's motive and then on her lack of credibility. Standing next to the bed in which John Hossack was killed, McNeil demonstrated to the jury how, if she had been lying in bed next to her husband as she claimed, the weapon would have struck her. He spoke of the ax and of the testimony that she'd known where it could be found.

During most of his argument, McNeil's tone was detached and quietly analytical, with an air of impartiality rather than malice. Sometimes, though, when he repeated arguments made by the defense, his tone turned sarcastic and cynical. He gave a bitter laugh when he repeated the family's story that Shep had been drugged. At other times he spoke in a loud and angry voice. At one point he denounced the defense for insinuating that William Haines might be the guilty party, reminding the jury that Haines had been committed to the insane asylum only after William Berry had visited him. Shouldn't the defense bear the responsibility for his absence? Certainly, if the defense were going to finger Haines for the crime, it was convenient that Haines was not in the courtroom. Perhaps, McNeil suggested, the defense had arranged for that to happen.

Finally McNeil drew his argument to a close. He stood directly in front of the jury box, placing his foot on the platform on which the jury was seated. His voice was low, almost a whisper, and his words were audible only to the members of the jury and the spectators sitting within the bar:

"The eloquent attorney for the defense stands before you and asks for mercy. I say that in the light of all this evidence you have no right to return a verdict for acquittal. They talk to you of generations yet unborn and of how you will feel when you meet the defendant in the world that is to come. I say to you that there is a duty you owe the people of Warren County. I am tired of this county being known as Wicked Warren. I want some of the criminals punished.

"I have no more sympathy for this defendant because she is a woman than I would have for a man who murdered his wife. And you have no right to acquit her because she is a woman or even because she is an old woman. Never since the crucifixion of Christ has there been a crime of more hideous nature than this. If there are tears to shed, prepare to shed them for John Hossack. I have known John Hossack all my life. I can say of him as was said of Abraham Lincoln, 'God Almighty might have made a better man, but God Almighty never did.' Who in this county knows of any wrong John Hossack ever did? I have shed tears for him myself because there has been none shed for him by his family.

They have cried a little because they were afraid their mother was going to be hung, but they have not cried for their murdered father. If John Hossack's spirit is here today what must it think of this scene? What must it think of the hard, dogged face of the defendant? Gentlemen, Senator Berry has asked that you show mercy. I demand that you give justice.

"If you, Gentlemen of the Jury, as I believe you do, believe this woman guilty, let no technical error bias your judgment, and let no sympathy for an unborn generation, as appealed to you by Mr. Berry, lead you to a wrong verdict in this case, because the good citizens of Warren County demand of you and they expect from your hand . . . that you will render that verdict which justice demands, and that verdict will be guilty with the punishment of death, death."

When McNeil finished, Judge Gamble read the instructions to the jury. There were thirty-one different instructions, and the reading took slightly more than an hour. The jury was reminded that the defendant was charged with first-degree murder, and that she had pleaded not guilty. She was presumed to be innocent, and the prosecution must prove guilt beyond a reasonable doubt, meaning "a doubt that is real, not captious or imaginary, not forced or artificial, but one that without being sought after, fairly and naturally arises in your minds as reasonable men, after having carefully examined all the evidence." The jury must judge for itself the credibility of all witnesses, and jury members should keep in mind that testimony consisting of the repetition of oral statements is "subject to much imperfection and mistake," either because of misstatements by the speaker or miscomprehension by the listener.

Point by point, the judge explained the applicable criminal law to the jury, describing the weight to be given to different types of evidence. A conviction, he said, did not require direct proof of the defendant's guilt, such as testimony from an eyewitness. Circumstantial evidence—proof of facts and circumstances from which guilt may be inferred—was often stronger and more convincing, although the circumstances must not only clearly point to guilt, they must be incompatible with innocence. The jury could consider testimony from experts, although it should be cautious, the judge warned, in considering conclusions that were based upon hypothetical questions or upon less than personal observation.

The jury had several choices. If it was unable to conclude that the defendant had killed her husband, then she must be acquitted. If she had done the deed, then the verdict would depend upon a determination as to the defendant's state of mind at the time of the killing. If she had acted out of sudden passion, without the deliberate intent to kill or to harm, she was guilty of manslaughter. If she intended not to kill, but only to cause great bodily harm, then she was guilty of murder in the second degree. She could be convicted of first-degree murder only if the jury found, beyond a reasonable doubt, that she had acted with premeditation, requiring a deliberate intent to kill with malice aforethought, meaning that she acted with "a wicked and depraved heart." If she was guilty of first-degree murder, then the jury was asked to recommend the appropriate sentence: She could be imprisoned for life in the state penitentiary or she could be put to death.

The jury listened to Judge Gamble with rapt attention. Directly in front of them was the bed in which John Hossack had been murdered. The ax, claimed by the state to be the murder weapon, was resting against the bed. Other pieces of evidence, including several articles of clothing and the bloody square of carpet, were in view nearby. Prosecution and defense lawyers, exhausted after the long day, sat at the square table in the middle of the courtroom. Margaret Hossack and her family, none of them crying now, were just behind the lawyers, clearly visible to the jurors.

Finally, at 5:30 P.M., the judge came to the end of his task. The jury, he said, would be taken to dinner and would then begin its deliberations. The twelve men in the jury box, all unsmiling and serious, rose to their feet and, in single file, followed a bailiff out of the courtroom.

18.

> When the state rested in the Hossack trial, at 5 o'clock yesterday, the evidence might be characterized as sufficient to convict a nihilist in Moscow but not sufficient to convict an American citizen in Indianola.—DON BERRY, in the *Iowa State Register,* April 6, 1901

THE HOSSACK JURORS had listened to five days of testimony and two days of oral arguments. In all, the prosecution called forty witnesses to the stand; the defense called thirteen. Three people—Will and Cassie Hossack, as well as Fred Johnston—testified for both the prosecution and the defense. Of the fifty individuals to testify, thirteen were Hossack family members; nine were physicians or witnesses with scientific expertise; eight others were involved in various aspects of the official investigation of the crime; nearly twenty were neighbors who personally knew the Hossack family.

Ten women were called to the witness stand: five members of the Hossack family (the defendant herself and all four of her daughters) and five neighbors. The Hossack daughters were asked mainly about the events of the night of the murder; they were questioned only briefly about the relationship between their parents, and all reported that the family had lived together peacefully in the year after the reconciliation. Four of the neighbor women who testified—Mrs. George Grant, Nora Cart, Sue Himstreet, and Eleanor Keller—were on the stand for brief periods and were asked just a few questions about specific incidents. Only Rinda Haines, whose husband was unable to appear, was extensively quizzed by the attorneys.

Mary Nicholson, who was questioned closely at the coroner's inquest, did not testify. Nor did the wife of Will Conrad, who listened to Margaret Hossack's pleas at the Conrad farmhouse at Thanksgiving of 1899. Nancy Truitt, who knew the family well and attended the Thanksgiving party just days before the murder, was not called to the stand.

The unfurled narrative of the Hossacks' relationship and marriage was mostly told by the men who knew John Hossack best, the farmers Margaret Hossack turned to with her stories of family abuse. These witnesses offered the most detailed impressions of the defendant, recounting her complaints about her husband's behavior.

Throughout the trial, Susan Glaspell reported on the large number of women in attendance at the court sessions, noting their reactions as witnesses testified. In particular, Glaspell fixed her attention on the sheriff's wife, who sat next to Margaret Hossack in apparent sympathy with the defendant. To many in the courtroom, John Hossack's abusive behavior toward his family was less damning than his wife's conversations with the neighbors; but among some of the women who silently watched the legal proceedings there was subtle, perceptible support for the accused.

The fact that the stories of these women—neighbors who knew Margaret Hossack, as well as spectators who came to know her history at the trial—went largely untold in the courtroom was something that Susan Glaspell would not forget. ☾

AT THE COUNTY JAIL, Margaret Hossack spent the night in her cell, refusing to eat or to talk to anyone except her family. Sheriff Hodson told reporters that she was more distressed and broken down than at any time during the trial. Several of her sons visited that evening. Afterward they paced up and down the streets outside the jail. Cassie remained with her mother throughout the long night.

Two blocks away at the town square, small clusters of men congregated on the courthouse lawn. It was a mild spring evening, the temperature hovering in the low fifties, with a few stars piercing the darkness of the night sky. Occasionally a horse and buggy clattered past. The men in the square stared up at the lighted windows on the third floor of the courthouse, where the jury was deliberating. The fields were drying out, the men murmured, and it was warming up. It was time for farmers to get back to work. ☾

ON THE FIRST vote taken in the jury room, seven men voted in favor of conviction; five voted for acquittal. Debate continued throughout the night until all twelve jurors agreed on a verdict.

At ten o'clock the next morning, the jury sent a message to the judge that it had reached a decision. The news spread quickly, and within ten minutes, a large crowd was pushing through the doors of the courthouse, where Margaret Hossack's fate would be announced.

The defendant was brought in. Her family sat in a row behind her. Judge Gamble resumed his place on the bench.

After the crowd settled into their seats, Judge Gamble motioned to Deputy Kimer, who then stepped to the rear of the room and opened the door. Slowly and silently, the jury members filed in, many of them with their heads bowed and eyes averted. They looked pale and exhausted.

Judge Gamble soberly addressed the jurors: "Gentlemen, have you agreed upon a verdict?"

The foreman, J. P. Anderson, got to his feet and responded, "We have." He held up the verdict form signed by the twelve jurors.

The bailiff took the paper from the foreman and carried it to

Judge Gamble. All eyes were on the judge as he unfolded the sheet and, after silently reading the words, raised one hand to his forehead. Judge Gamble handed the verdict back to the clerk, who read it aloud:

"We, the jury, find Margaret Hossack guilty of murder in the first degree and recommend that she be sentenced for life to hard labor in the state penitentiary."

MRS. HOSSACK GUILTY OF MURDER IN FIRST DEGREE

TRAGIC SCENE IN THE COURTHOUSE IN INDIANOLA

Woman after the Jury Retires Breaks Down and Sobs—Her Children Join with Her and Still Believe Her Innocent

Special to the Capital. INDIANOLA, April 11—Without a tear or without a murmur [or] so much as the twitching of a finger Margaret Hossack this morning received a life sentence to the penitentiary. When the verdict of the jury was read she sat as though paralyzed and for a few minutes no member of her family shed a tear. It was not until the jury filed out and the time had come for Margaret Hossack and her children to leave the courtroom that they seemed to have recovered from the blow enough to let tears come. Then the scene was terrible. Mrs. Hossack gave way to feeling with utter abandonment. Her daughters clung to her hysterically and her oldest son leaning his head against the window sobbed as only a strong man can sob. Finally the woman found guilty of the murder of her husband was led back to the county jail and for hours she cried with a violence that brought at length relief in utter hysterical exhaustion. Mrs. Hossack has proven at least that she is a woman.

At the Warren county jail this afternoon her nine chil-

> dren are gathered around her and to them she is protesting her innocence. She is beseeching them to believe that she did not do it, that it is wrong, all wrong.—*Des Moines Daily Capital*, April 11, 1901

Susan Glaspell, in the last major story of her career at the *Daily News*, also reported on the jury's decision. Under the headline MRS. HOSSACK A MURDERESS, Glaspell's account was uncharacteristically matter-of-fact, reporting the verdict in short sentences and straightforward prose. A few paragraphs later, however, she depicted Margaret Hossack's reaction in more emotional language:

> The aged prisoner sat looking helpless and in a sort of dazed condition at the clerk. Then, suddenly seeming to realize the meaning of the verdict, she sank back in her chair and for the first time during the long and trying ordeal, gave completely away to her feelings.
>
> She was surrounded by her friends whose sobbing could be heard through the hall and into the open courtyard, continuing until Sheriff Hodson led the prisoner back to the jail awaiting final judgment. Senator Berry announced that he would move for a new trial. ☾

FIVE DAYS PASSED. Margaret Hossack next appeared in court at 8:30 A.M. on Tuesday, April 16, for formal sentencing by the judge. Once again she was surrounded by her children, sons-in-law, grandchildren, and lawyers.

First, Judge Gamble addressed a motion, made by Senator Berry and Judge Henderson, asking for a new trial. Stating that the defendant had been well represented by her attorneys and given a fair trial, he overruled the motion.

Then the judge turned in the direction of the Hossack family. "The jury has returned a verdict of guilty as charged in the indictment," he said, "and it now becomes my painful duty to pronounce sentence as provided by law." Speaking directly to Margaret Hossack, the judge asked, "Have you any reasons to offer why the sentence as fixed by the jury should not be pronounced?"

Margaret Hossack slowly rose and attempted to speak, but she was overcome by emotion and slumped back into her chair without uttering a word. While Judge Gamble waited, Senator Berry leaned down and spoke quietly to his client. Again she stood, this time leaning on Berry's arm for support. She raised her right hand, as if once again taking an oath to tell the truth, and spoke so softly that few in the audience could make out her words.

"Before my God," she said, "I am not guilty."

A moment passed as Judge Gamble gathered his thoughts. A veteran of the battle of Vicksburg, a man who in war had seen the most horrific events that history had to offer, Gamble responded in a voice that cracked with emotion. "Sometime and somewhere in the providence of God," he said, "it will be revealed whether or not you have spoken truly."

That afternoon, under the bold headline MARGARET HOSSACK GETS HER SENTENCE, the *Daily Capital* reported her final words to the judge and described the scene in the courtroom. Portraying the defendant as "a broken woman, looking nearer 70 than 57," the article noted that her neighbors had rallied to her support at the end of the trial: "The people from the vicinity of the Hossack home who were so constantly in attendance at the trial were present when the sentence was delivered this morning and they gathered around her in large numbers this afternoon, attempting to offer some words of consolation."

19.

Justice has demanded a heavy recompense and is satisfied. John Hossack's death has been avenged. But his must be a hard heart that has no pity or sympathy for her whose frail barque has been so long and fiercely tossed in life's tempestuous seas only to be engulfed in the wild maelstrom of crime at a time when she should almost have in sight the quiet waters of Jordan. Also that her sun should set in such unutterable darkness and that the resurrection morn must break to her through a prison's grated walls. What an awfully impressive verification of the truth of holy writ that says: "The way of the transgressor is hard."—*Indianola Advocate-Tribune*, April 18, 1901

Usually a woman convict is considered one of the lowest of God's creatures—if, in truth, she is supposed to belong to Him at all—for it is a well known fact that society always considers a fallen woman a thousand times more depraved and contemptible than the self-same character of the masculine gender.—MRS. A. M. WATERMAN, matron of the female department at Anamosa Penitentiary, in "Prison Work Among Women: Can They Be Reformed?" (1901)

ON APRIL 18, 1901, Sheriff Hodson, accompanied by his wife, arrived at the Anamosa State Penitentiary and relinquished custody of Margaret Hossack to William Hunter, the warden. Sheriff and Mrs. Hodson were assured by Warden Hunter that Margaret Hossack would be given a separate cell and the best of medical attention and care.

Before the Hodsons left, Margaret Hossack once again

pleaded her innocence. The *Daily News* reported that she said, "Sheriff Hodson, tell my children not to weep for me. I am innocent of the horrible murder of my husband. Some day people will know I am not guilty of that terrible crime."

Warden Hunter was fifty-five years old, a graduate of Grinnell College and a veteran of the Civil War, in which he had served as a drummer boy and a soldier. He'd been warden at Anamosa for a little over three years. He was a competent administrator, and he believed in the possibility of rehabilitation. He didn't have many female prisoners (fewer than twenty at the time of Margaret Hossack's arrival), and they caused him little trouble. He knew that the softspoken woman with gray hair who stood before him was a grandmother, and although she had been convicted of murdering her husband with an ax, she hardly seemed threatening. In fact, a few months after her arrival, Warden Hunter would become convinced of her innocence.

Margaret Hossack was escorted to a receiving room where she was examined and questioned. She was given a prisoner number—4654—and relevant information was recorded in the Female Convict Register. According to that document, the new prisoner was 57 years old, with blond complexion, blue eyes, and gray hair. She measured 5 feet 7 inches in height and weighed 162 pounds; her boot was size 7 ½. Her religion was Presbyterian. A housekeeper by occupation, she was a widow; her "conjugal relations" were recorded as "pleasant." The character of her associates, her moral susceptibility, and her financial condition were all noted to be good. Her crime was, of course, stated to be first-degree murder, with a prison term to last for the rest of her natural life.

Like all new prisoners, Margaret Hossack was next escorted to the bathhouse, where she was washed and disinfected. Then she was taken to her cell in the female department. ☾

ANAMOSA STATE PENITENTIARY, located in downtown Anamosa, Iowa, was an impressive sight. Built of high-quality dolomite limestone and nicknamed the "White Palace of the West," the Gothic structure had been authorized by the Fourteenth Iowa General Assembly in April of 1872 and constructed with inmate labor over a period of nearly thirty years. The walls of the rectangular building enclosed thirteen acres and were twenty-two feet high, six feet wide at the base, and four feet in width at the top, with guard towers strategically placed around the perimeter. The three-story building on the east side of the structure jutted out from the rectangular shape of the institution and contained the main entrance, the administration offices, and the warden's residence. Two enormous stone lions, each weighing five tons, stood watch outside the main entrance. The building resembled a European castle more than a prison.

A self-contained community existed inside the walls of the penitentiary. A power plant generated electricity, and four large boilers produced the steam necessary for heating the huge structure. A large vegetable garden grew next to a greenhouse and a newly built hog house with a feed lot. Inmates tended the plants and animals, producing most of their own food. The fortress also contained a stone shop and a tin shop, a carpentry shop, a machine shop, a foundry, a laundry and a clothing department, a barbershop, and a bathhouse. A well 2,000 feet deep provided fresh water; air compressors located in the power plant pumped water to a reservoir that could hold 45,000 gallons of water. The prison had its own hospital, chapel, and library.

The chapel and the library were particularly impressive. In 1896 a fire had destroyed them both, but they were soon rebuilt. The new library was housed in a second-floor room that was fireproof, well lighted, and ventilated. Five thousand books, most of them new, rested on the library shelves, and inmates could visit the library twice a week to read or check out materials. The spacious chapel encompassed more than 4,000 square feet and was furnished with a pulpit, a rostrum, and a pipe organ. More than ninety pews, each one supplied with hymnals, seated over 800 people. During services, the male inmates sat downstairs and the female inmates sat upstairs in the east balcony, facing the pulpit and a large stained-glass window on the west wall. A morning service was held every Sunday at 8:15 A.M., with Sunday school from 2:30 to 3:30 on Sunday afternoons. A full-time chaplain, E. G. Beyer, conducted the services and offered counseling to the convicts.

Approximately 400 men were detained as prisoners at Anamosa that spring. Most resided in the north and south cell houses, but a few were housed in the insane ward and prison hospital. A new section, located just south of the main entrance, was under construction and would house the women. The words FEMALE DEPT were engraved on its façade. ☾

THE ANAMOSA FEMALE DEPARTMENT was a community of young women. Only one was older than fifty-seven-year-old Margaret Hossack: a physician, seventy years old, who was serving a five-year sentence for performing an illegal abortion. During the two-year period between June 1, 1899, and June 1, 1901, fifteen of the twenty women admitted were younger than thirty years old. All but three of the female prisoners could read and write, and nineteen of the twenty declared their occupation as housekeeper. They'd been sentenced for a variety of crimes, the most common offenses being larceny, prostitution, and adultery. Margaret Hossack was not the only murderer; Sarah Kuhn, convicted of poisoning her husband, was also serving a life sentence at Anamosa.

Angie Waterman was in charge of the female department, having been hired as matron by Warden Hunter in 1898. Described in a prison publication as "a Christian lady" who took "great interest in the unfortunates in her department," Mrs. Waterman was an attractive young woman with previous experience as a nurse. Prior to working at the Anamosa Penitentiary, she'd been employed at the Hospital for the Insane, at Clarinda.

Mrs. Waterman was, at heart, a reformer and an optimist. She saw it as her duty to provide the women with practical and moral guidance, often referring to her charges as girls, and she wholeheartedly subscribed to the common notion of true womanhood. "That the standard of true womanhood should remain unalterably exalted cannot be questioned," she wrote. "There is no fairer sight, no godlier example, than a beautiful and noble woman." As Mrs. Waterman saw it, most of the women who passed into her care had suffered and fallen into a life of sin or lawlessness, but they were redeemable. They'd gone astray because they had miserable home lives or were unable to make an honest living in society. "Place within their hands the means of self-support," wrote Mrs. Waterman, "and they must be wanton indeed if they then deliberately choose a life of vice."

Mrs. Waterman agreed with the system, instituted by Warden Hunter a few years earlier, of evaluating prisoners based on their behavior and then dividing them into classes. The more privileged inmates, including Margaret Hossack, wore plain gray clothing (instead of the plaid worn by second-class prisoners or stripes by third-class) and were given better food than the lower classes. The differentiation of prisoners was said to encourage self-improvement and obedience.

In the 1901 report to the Iowa Board of Control, published after Margaret Hossack had been admitted to Anamosa, Mrs. Waterman urged that murderers not necessarily be judged more harshly than those who were convicted of lesser crimes but had more extensive histories of unacceptable behavior. She argued that even the grading system in place did not adequately segregate the women under her jurisdiction. "Take for instance,"

Waterman wrote, "women who are doing a life sentence, women who have murdered, but whose lives otherwise were honorable lives; it seems almost a wrong and it is obviously an injury, morally, to compel them to daily associate with the depraved and degenerate fruitage of the slums."

When Margaret Hossack came to Anamosa, female inmates had not yet been moved to the new section and were still housed on the first floor, occupying part of a wing designated as the insane ward. The cells, each occupied by one inmate, were small: approximately four and a half feet wide, eight feet long, and seven and a half feet high. Each cell was wired for electricity, lighted with a single bulb hanging from the ceiling. The building was kept warm in the winter with steam heat, and indoor plumbing provided hot and cold water in the bathrooms. Inmates were allowed one hot shower per week in a communal bathhouse.

That spring and summer Margaret Hossack adjusted to the routine of incarceration. After fifty years of grueling farmwork as the daughter and then the wife of ambitious farmers and as mother to nine children, she now settled into a community populated by women, with the responsibility of simple domestic chores. The female prisoners, who seldom saw or interacted with any of the male convicts, were expected to maintain their own living quarters and to follow a daily regimen of work dictated by the state prison system. They washed, they laundered and sewed clothes, they cleaned their cellblock. They didn't cook for themselves; hot meals were served to them three times a day in a dining facility separate from the male inmates'. The women were forbidden to talk during meals, but the food was good and well balanced: potato stew, roast beef, cod fish, pork, prunes and apricots, sweet corn and string beans, oatmeal, cheese, stewed peaches and apple pudding. Bread, sorghum, and coffee were provided at every meal.

When they weren't working, the female inmates remained in

their cells, often reading books borrowed from the prison library. They were allowed to write one letter a week. On Sundays they were taken to the chapel for church services and Sunday school. Chaplain Beyer regularly visited each woman in her cell. ☾

DESPITE ITS AUTHORITATIVE tone of finality, the legal verdict against Margaret Hossack and her sentence to the Anamosa State Penitentiary were only one chapter in a story that continued to evolve after the end of her trial.

Certainly, the verdict came as no great surprise to Mrs. Hossack's neighbors in Squaw Township. From the beginning, they'd predicted her guilt to reporters and to one another, many of them having served as witnesses against her. Yet almost immediately, those same people—some of whom had approached Margaret Hossack in the courtroom at the end of the trial to offer words of consolation—began to rethink the outcome of the judicial proceeding. They came to acknowledge their own role in what had happened: They had ignored or failed to act in regard to the dangerous situation that they knew had existed within the Hossack household.

The family's emotional reaction at the time of the verdict contributed to the concern about whether the defendant had been fairly judged. As one newspaper reported, "The children seem genuinely to believe in the innocence of their mother, and this, while without much value as legal evidence, sways the private judgment." There was some speculation that perhaps Margaret Hossack was protecting the real killer, an idea that framed her in a more sympathetic light. Writing a few days after the verdict, Susan Glaspell noted that it was "universally believed at Indianola that if Mrs. Hossack did not murder her husband, she knows who did." Was she lying out of a mother's impulse to protect one of her children? Given the early reports that the Hossack sons had quarreled with their father, the thought was a natural one, although investigators had never pursued any of the children as suspects. Maybe, too, Mrs. Hossack's own unwavering contention that she was innocent, expressed in her testimony as well as in her final words to Judge Gamble, caused her neighbors to wonder if justice had been done.

Several days after the trial ended, an editorial in the *Des Moines Daily Leader* criticized the verdict, highlighting Senator Berry's rebuke of the county attorney for telling the jury that its duty was to find and punish the guilty party rather than to focus on reasonable doubts that existed as to the guilt of the defendant. "Perhaps," the editorial stated, "the jurors unconsciously determined that, as a crime had been committed, it was their duty to fasten the commission of the same upon some one, and selected the only person it seemed possible to suspect." As the editorial noted, the evidence that pointed to Mrs. Hossack as the murderer was only circumstantial, leaving substantial room for doubt.

In June of 1901, just a little more than two months after her sentencing, the public feeling had shifted to such an extent that a headline in the *Daily Capital* declared MRS. JOHN HOSSACK MAY RECEIVE PARDON: FRIENDS OF NEW VIRGINIA MURDERESS ASK FOR PAROLE. The story reported:

> Ex-County Attorney Mosher of Warren County was in the city a short time today conferring with some of the political leaders concerning the coming primaries. Referring to the sensational trial which occupied the attention of Warren county courts recently, he said the bitter feeling entertained toward the alleged murderess had abated to a certain extent and that the aged woman was looked upon more in the light of pity. It is understood that at New Virginia, the scene of the crime, and where the Hossacks resided for so many years, agitation has begun looking toward a parole for Mrs. Hossack. Some of the prominent res-

> idents have signified their willingness to sign such a paper, and it is not unlikely that a move of that character will be made. It is realized that the woman has but a few years to live, and in view of the fact that guilt was not fully fastened upon her it is believed that a parole is due. ☾

In August, Will Hossack trudged up the wide stone steps of the Anamosa State Penitentiary. He was admitted through iron gates that clanked shut behind him. A guard took him to a small room where Will had a brief visit with his mother. He told her that people in the community were talking about the possibility of her release. He also explained that William Haines was no longer in the insane asylum. He'd been let out only a few weeks earlier and was once again living with his wife in the farmhouse a half mile north of the Hossack property.

As for Margaret Hossack's lawyers, Berry and Henderson had dissolved their law firm. Henderson was establishing a new one with his son, Frank, and Berry would practice alone, but the two men had agreed to work together on the appeal to the Iowa Supreme Court. The briefs would be filed in October, and the case would be set for oral argument later that month.

He also had news about the farm. Johnnie and Will had lived there in the spring after their father's death, doing what they could to maintain the property and the livestock, but the district court had ordered that the farm be sold to settle John Hossack's estate because, in the court's words, "the property cannot be equitably divided into the requisite number of shares." The Hossack farm—the pride of John Hossack's life—was to be sold at auction the following month. Fred Johnston, as executor of his friend's estate and one of the three referees responsible for the auction, was in charge of organizing the sale.

On September 18, six days after the assassination of President William McKinley, a crowd gathered once again at the Warren

County Courthouse. The previous day an announcement of the Hossack farm auction had appeared in the *Indianola Herald.* The sale was held at 11 A.M. on the south steps of the courthouse. C. C. Taggart, a landowner who lived near Medora, purchased Hossack's 200 acres and outbuildings for the sum of $6,840. Terms required Taggart to pay one third of the price in cash at the time of sale. Another third was due in one year, with the final payment due the following year.

Because John Hossack had died without a will, the proceeds from the sale were divided among his family according to the state law of intestacy. Despite her conviction for murder, Margaret Hossack was legally entitled to one third of the total amount. ☾

ALTHOUGH THE CASE of Margaret Hossack received statewide publicity during the weeks of the trial, she was not the best-known prisoner at Anamosa State Penitentiary. That honor belonged to a young man named John Wesley Elkins, who was also a convicted murderer. Just as in the case of Margaret Hossack, public sentiment for his release had been growing since his incarceration.

Elkins had confessed to the crime: the murder of his parents in 1889, when he was eleven years old. He'd lived with his father, his stepmother, and their infant child on an isolated farm in Clayton County. By most accounts, he was a normal, healthy young boy, but after the birth of his sibling, he'd been required to stay home and help with the baby's care. He resented this new obligation and ran away several times, only to be returned by neighbors to his home.

On the morning of July 16 he carried a rifle to his parents' bedroom and shot his father in the head as he slept. A few minutes later, unable to reload the weapon, he returned with a club and beat his stepmother to death with repeated blows. He picked up the baby, fed and dressed her, and then, carrying the infant, headed on foot toward his grandparents' house. On the way he stopped at a neighbor's farm and reported that his parents had been killed by an intruder.

Local authorities investigated the crime for several days. Young Elkins, who was supposed to be staying in town with an aunt, was seen running about his parents' farm and playing while the coroner conducted the inquest there. Gradually rumors started that the boy was the guilty party. Elkins eventually confessed, stating without remorse that he killed his father and stepmother because he no longer wanted to live with them or care for the baby. The community was shocked. Elkins was held in jail for four months before he was sentenced to life imprisonment at Anamosa.

At first Warden Marquis Barr didn't know what to do with the new prisoner. The boy was so young, and so slight, that it seemed impossible he would fit into the general prison population. Barr decided to make him his personal errand boy, working out of the warden's office. In time, impressed with the youngster's intelligence and character, Barr gave him more responsibilities, such as cleaning and doing small repair jobs in the chapel and helping in the library.

Elkins took advantage of the prison library to educate himself, and he began to communicate with supporters, arguing that he'd paid for his crime and deserved a chance at freedom. When he was eighteen, Elkins wrote a letter to Carl Snyder, an editor in New York, which was printed in the *Anamosa Eureka* and reprinted in the *Mt. Vernon Hawk-Eye.* The writing was praised by the newspaper for its "thoughtfulness and grace of expression, as well as beauty of penmanship and correctness of punctuation, very unusual in one of his age, for it must be remembered that he has been in prison over seven years and could have had only a very little schooling previous to his commitment to the Anamosa Penitentiary." It also caught the eye of Professor James

Harlan, vice president of Cornell College in Mount Vernon, Iowa. Harlan launched a public campaign for Elkins's release.

By 1901, after more than ten years in prison, John Wesley Elkins was about the same age as Margaret Hossack's daughter May, and he was considered a serious candidate for parole. After much public debate and despite the opposition of residents of Clayton County, where the crime was committed, Elkins was released from prison the following year. ☾

IN OCTOBER 1901 Senator Berry and Judge Henderson filed their appeal with the Iowa Supreme Court, arguing that the conviction of Margaret Hossack should be reversed and a new trial granted. In a lengthy brief, they claimed that various procedural errors had been made by Judge Gamble, mistakes in admitting certain evidence and in giving instructions to the jury. According to Berry and Henderson, the expert testimony about the hairs —the most important evidence connecting the ax to the murder—should have been inadmissible. They also argued that the instruction on the reconciliation was wrong—the jury hadn't understood or applied the proper rule of law—and that there were certain other legal points that had not been correctly explained by the judge to the jury.

Almost a third of the brief, however, was devoted to a broader claim: that the evidence, viewed in its entirety, did not support the guilty verdict. The lawyers asked that the court carefully consider a number of specific points, including the unusual behavior of the dog, testimony from the doctors that supported the defendant's story, evidence of the reconciliation, and the lack of blood spots on the front of the defendant's chemise—all of which, they claimed, proved her innocence.

The defense lawyers also asked the court to take into account Clammer's final presentation to the jury. It was, they claimed, unfairly prejudicial and injurious to the defendant: a "vituperative and inflammatory speech [that] abounded in invective suppositions." The county attorney had been overzealous, and his story, filled with vivid and horrific details, was based not on fact but rather on his "fertile imaginations," as he sought to "secure a verdict at all hazard." Many of his statements, including the unsupported charge of illicit relations between John and Margaret Hossack before their marriage, were intended to "arouse the passions" of the jury members instead of appealing to reason. Clammer was guilty of misconduct, claimed Berry and Henderson, for the way he had argued the case in the courtroom.

The lawyers cited earlier cases, in which the state Supreme Court had recognized an obligation to reverse a jury verdict that was based on popular opinion and local prejudice and that resulted from the "heat and excitement of the trial." According to Berry and Henderson, this was a case warranting judicial action. The conviction should be reversed and a new trial ordered.

The Attorney General for the State of Iowa filed the response, citing precedent to support Judge Gamble's rulings and his instructions and defending the jury's verdict.

The appellate brief echoed the legal points made in the oral argument prepared by Clammer and reiterated that it was not only the physical evidence that proved the defendant's guilt; her traits as a woman also incriminated her. She was large, broad-shouldered and "masculine in appearance." That she was "an inhuman wife and mother" was proved by her own admission that she had responded to a noise in the night by leaving her bedroom rather than by following the "natural impulse of a woman," which would have been to seek help from her husband. She was the mother of many children, and yet she claimed not to have awakened immediately when the alleged intruder entered her house. The implication was clear: Either she was lying or she was not a proper caretaker of her family. The guilty verdict, according to the lawyers for the state, was well justified.

Oral arguments were held in front of the Iowa Supreme Court in October 1901. Then it was up to the nine justices to make the next decision about Margaret Hossack's fate. ☾

SIX MONTHS LATER, on Wednesday, April 9, 1902, the Court rendered its decision in the case of *State of Iowa* v. *Margaret Hossack,* having unanimously voted to reverse the conviction and grant Margaret Hossack a new trial.

Without addressing the charge of prosecutorial misconduct, the court based its decision on two specific rulings made by Judge Gamble. First, he had erred in allowing the jury to consider Professor Tilton's testimony about the hairs. Since the chain of custody for the hairs had not been properly established, the hairs themselves could not be admitted; therefore, the analysis of those hairs should also have been inadmissible. The expert testimony had been an important element in showing that the Hossack family's ax was the murder weapon, and the ax was an important element in the state's case against the defendant. Since the defendant had been clearly prejudiced by the error, it was sufficient, by itself, to require a new trial.

Judge Gamble had made another mistake, this one in his instruction to the jury about the possible reconciliation between John and Margaret Hossack. Judge Gamble had correctly ruled that the jury had to decide whether or not the couple had reconciled in November 1899. But, according to the Supreme Court, he had not properly instructed the jury on the important ramifications of that decision in their subsequent deliberations. If jury members believed the prosecution—that the couple had *not* fully reconciled and that animosity had persisted during the year before John Hossack's death—then prior quarrels could be considered when judging the defendant's state of mind at the time of the murder. On the other hand, if jury members believed the defense—that the couple *had* fully reconciled and that ill feelings of the past had disappeared—then prior arguments between them could not be considered at all as evidence of malice on the part of the defendant. As the Supreme Court put it, "it is difficult to see why the law should resurrect troubles the parties had buried, and allow them any weight whatever." ☾

MARGARET HOSSACK WAS released from Anamosa State Penitentiary on April 18, 1902, exactly one year after her arrival. One newspaper reported that she "expressed her belief that a new trial would clear her." She was transferred back to the Warren County jail to await a new trial.

She was almost sixty years old, and her health had declined during the year she had spent at Anamosa. Dr. L. H. Surber, one of the physicians who had testified at the trial, examined her and stated in a deposition dated June 14, 1902, that she was "suffering from nervous prostration, disease of the spine and base of the brain." Her condition, he concluded, was dangerous and was worsened by her confinement. She would recover more quickly if she "were free to enjoy outdoor exercise and change of surroundings and especially such as riding and going to the homes of her children." Based on the deposition, a judge ruled that she could be released on bail if a $15,000 bond were posted, and a number of neighbors from Squaw Township came forward to sign as sureties for that amount.

A few days later, Margaret Hossack was released from the custody of Sheriff Hodson. She went to live with Annie and Ev Henry in Liberty, Iowa.

20.

> Mrs. Hossack was in court when the trial commenced. She seems aged and worn since her last trial. She has secured rooms at the home of Mr. and Mrs. George Lucas, and is constantly surrounded by her sons and daughters who loyally support their mother on trial for her life. Four or five sons, all men but one . . . good looking and intelligent farmers, watch the case with interest, and have never faltered in their allegiance to her. Her daughter, a young woman who greatly resembles her mother, is her constant attendant and sits by her side in the courtroom. Mrs. Hossack listens intently to every word of the attorneys.—*Indianola Herald*, February 19, 1903

IN LATE FALL of 1902, at the urging of Hossack family members, Senator Berry and Judge Henderson petitioned the court for a change of venue for Margaret Hossack's second trial. Citing the victim's favorable reputation in the community, the circumstances of his death, and the great publicity generated by the first trial, the lawyers claimed that it was impossible for the defendant to be fairly judged by residents of Warren County. The court agreed and ruled that Margaret Hossack's second trial would be conducted in Winterset, in Madison County, about twenty miles west of Indianola. The trial was scheduled for February 1903.

When his second term as county attorney expired in the fall of 1901, George Clammer did not run for reelection. He entered private practice and served on the local school board. But when it was clear that Margaret Hossack would be tried again, he was asked to join the prosecution team for the retrial, with the hope that he could repeat his success and convince another jury that she had murdered her husband.

It was Thursday, February 12, 1903, when George Clammer arrived at the Madison County courthouse for the first day of the trial. Although it was a crisp winter morning, a crowd was gathered in the town square, hoping to catch a glimpse of the defendant on her way to court.

The courthouse was a handsome building, designed by a French architect and situated in the exact geographic center of the county. It had been built in 1876 and was constructed of gray limestone in the shape of a Greek cross. It had a central dome, which towered more than 120 feet above the ground and contained a 1,500-pound bell. Inside, the woodwork was carved oak and black walnut.

The second-floor courtroom was a large, theaterlike space. Observers filled the seats in the balcony, which extended above the back half of the courtroom, and spectators downstairs crowded into rows behind the wooden railing that separated the audience from the legal participants. The entire courtroom had recently been refurbished and repainted; the wood paneling around the bench in the courtroom gleamed from the application of fresh coats of varnish.

The jurors had been selected the day before and were seated in the jury box. They were somewhat younger than the members of the first jury, although they had similar backgrounds. Eleven were farmers; one was a harness maker. The *Indianola Herald* declared the twelve men to be a "jury of more than average intelligence."

Circumstances surrounding the second trial were much different from those surrounding the first. Two years had passed since the murder, and the change of venue certainly had an impact. John Hossack had not been a resident of this county, and few, if any, of the jurors or spectators were personally acquainted with the man or aware of his good reputation; few knew of the family's domestic troubles.

Susan Glaspell was no longer working as a journalist, and she didn't attend the second trial, but the Des Moines daily newspapers as well as Warren County and Madison County weekly papers sent reporters to Winterset. This time the newspapers adopted a more neutral tone. Stories recounted the history of the case, but they included less speculation on possible motives or legal strategies. Readers were spared the gory details of the attack, and John Hossack, whose fine reputation had been so emphasized during the first trial, was rarely described except as victim of the crime.

Sentiment toward Margaret Hossack was also different. The mistrust and suspicion that had marked the newspaper portrayals of her two years earlier were now replaced with more compassionate portraits of an elderly and even pitiable woman. The *Winterset Madisonian*, for example, described her as "worn and fatigued, pale and sickly from the strain of the past two years." The damning evidence that had been used so successfully by the prosecution to prove motive in the first trial—the many stories from neighbors about John Hossack's treatment of his family—now seemed to arouse sympathy for his wife and children. Reports preceding the second trial focused on the defense more than on the prosecution, and the lawyers for Margaret Hosssack were quoted as being optimistic about the possibility of an acquittal. Community sentiment seemed to favor that result. Some residents of Madison County, especially the women, openly declared their hope that Mrs. Hossack would not be found guilty a second time. ☾

AT THE PROSECUTION TABLE, George Clammer was joined by Harry McNeil, his colleague from the first trial, and W. S. Cooper, the attorney for Madison County. Judge Edmond Nichols presided, and once court was officially convened, he invited Clammer to give his opening statement to the jury.

Clammer spoke for nearly two hours. Well aware that many in the audience favored the defense, he made a point of reminding the jurors of their duty under the law: to be objective and dispassionate in evaluating the facts of the prosecution's case against the defendant.

As in the first trial, Clammer exhibited a large diagram of the Hossack farm and outbuildings and a layout of the home's interior. He noted the history of the marriage, mentioning the couple's frequent quarrels over the years as evidence of the defendant's animosity toward her husband, and told the prosecution's version of what had happened that December night. When he reached the point when the victim's children first saw their wounded father in the bedroom, Margaret Hossack burst into tears and wept. Clammer paused for several minutes, allowing her to regain her composure before he finished his account.

The evidence was circumstantial, the prosecutor acknowledged, but the jury would recognize that it clearly pointed to Margaret Hossack as the murderer of her husband. They would see physical evidence that incriminated her: the bed in which John Hossack had died, the bloodied bedclothes and the ax, all preserved since the first trial. They would hear witnesses testify to her motive for murder. Throughout it all, the jury members must remember, he again stressed, that they were obligated to put aside their own sympathies and consider only the evidence and testimony presented to them.

When Clammer sat down, Judge Nichols adjourned for lunch. ℂ

In the afternoon, it was Senator Berry's turn. Madison County was part of the state senatorial district that he had represented during his four years in the state legislature, so Berry was known, at least by name and reputation, to most of the people in the courtroom. He'd campaigned in the district and been a vocal supporter of farmers' interests in the legislature.

Those in the audience who were seeing Berry in person for the first time would certainly have been struck by his confidence and ease in the courtroom. He spoke with conviction, but without the rhetorical flourishes and passion that had characterized his final plea to the jury on Margaret Hossack's behalf two years earlier. He would once again save that for the end.

At the first trial, the senator had begun with an appeal to the sympathies of the jury, relating the story of the defendant's life and stressing her years of hard work on the farm and her devotion to her family. This time, Berry tried a different tack. He began with a focus that he would continue throughout his questioning of witnesses and his closing argument: The evidence presented by the prosecution, he claimed, was simply insufficient to support a conviction. There was no witness to the murder; only circumstantial evidence could be produced as proof of guilt, and much of it, especially the testimony from the neighbors suggesting motive, was irrelevant and should be disregarded by the jury. As the cornerstone of his argument, Berry emphasized the couple's reconciliation in November 1899. Given the Supreme Court decision, this point was more important than it had been in the first trial. If Berry could persuade the jury members that husband and wife had put aside their differences and reconciled, then the jury would be bound to ignore all evidence of domestic quarrels in the years before. ☾

WHILE MARGARET HOSSACK was in prison, the farm had been sold and her children had dispersed. Johnnie had moved to Des Moines and taken a job with the gas company. May had married and now lived with her husband, Ira Coulter, in a house near New Virginia. Will and Jimmie were on their own: Will lived and worked at the Truitt farm, just as Johnnie had done before him, while Ivan, still in his early teens, had been sent by his older siblings to live with the family of George and Anna Van Patten on a nearby farm.

For the two weeks of the trial, the Hossack family reunited in Winterset. They rented rooms at a private home only a few blocks from the courthouse. Just as they had done during the first trial, the family—sons and daughters, in-laws and grandchildren—surrounded Margaret Hossack with their physical presence. In the mornings they walked together to the courthouse, usually arriving just a few minutes before the proceedings were to begin, and when court adjourned in the late afternoon, they retraced their steps. In the evenings they dined together at the boardinghouse and retired to their rooms.

The younger boys, however, sometimes ate their supper and then left the boardinghouse, venturing back to the town square. Ivan and Jimmie, and sometimes Will, stood together and talked about the trial with any of the townspeople who happened by. The boys said they were convinced that their mother was innocent, and they were unabashed about discussing the circumstances of the case. In the bitter frozen air, their lips numbed and their breath puffing out in plumes, Ivan and Jimmie recited the story as the members of the Hossack family told it, defending their mother and proclaiming her innocence.

In the courtroom, the family watched as Clammer presented the case, listening to the same chorus of voices—Conrad, Keller, Johnston, Morrison, Tilton, Hodson—they had heard in the first trial. For the most part, there were few surprises or even changes in the testimony of the neighbors, family members, or expert witnesses.

Margaret Hossack remained composed and stoic throughout the trial. She stayed with her family, walking to and from the courthouse with them and sitting quietly in the courtroom—an elderly woman surrounded by her children and grandchildren. She listened to the daily testimony but seldom turned to look at the large gallery that watched her. She kept her eyes cast downward or toward the witness box. She suffered from a bad chest cold, coughing frequently and holding a handkerchief to her mouth. A shawl was draped over her shoulders.

At breaks in the proceedings, women and young girls approached the defense table to speak to the defendant, "consoling her and expressing their sympathy." ☾

IVAN WAS NOW fifteen years old. The separation from his family had been bitter and sad. He had resisted the move to the Van Pattens', but his brothers and sisters all told him that there was nowhere else for him to go. None of his brothers except Alex had homes of his own, and Alex and his married sisters—Annie, Louie, and May—said they didn't have room for him. So Ivan had no choice but to accept the Van Pattens' offer. At least, their property was not far from the land where he'd grown up.

The Van Patten farm had turned out to be a comfortable place for Ivan. There was a large and well-maintained house on many acres of land, and Ivan was treated as one of the family. He helped with the chores and attended school with the Van Patten children, Loyd and Nina. Ivan and Loyd became close friends.

On Tuesday, February 17, Clammer called Ivan to testify. The boy took the oath, swearing to tell the truth, and sat down in the witness box next to the judge's bench. Ivan peered out at the great throng of strangers in the gallery. At the defense table, his mother sat quietly between her lawyers. He could see his brothers and sisters in the rows just behind her.

Clammer approached and began asking questions, taking Ivan through the events of that evening of more than two years ago. Yes, Ivan remembered Will's asking him to retrieve his coat from the woodpile on Saturday evening around dusk. And yes, he remembered that Will called to him to put the ax away, and that he then met his mother coming from the barn and told her that he was going to the granary with the ax.

Did he remember putting the ax inside the granary?

Ivan said he wasn't sure.

Clammer asked Ivan to refresh his memory by looking at the

transcript of his previous testimony. At the inquest, Clammer reminded Ivan, he had been positive that he put the ax inside the granary, and twenty-two months ago, when he testified at the trial, he had been fairly certain of the same thing. Ivan acknowledged that he remembered testifying at both proceedings. But now, he said, he couldn't be certain. He knew that sometimes he put the ax inside the granary and other times he simply threw it underneath. He didn't remember where he'd put the ax on the evening of December 1, 1900. ☾

As BEFORE, WOMEN made up more than half of the courtroom audience. Many of them attended each day of the trial, returning to the same seats they'd occupied the previous day, as if the spots were reserved for them. The newspapers poked good-natured fun at the phenomenon, suggesting that the women were neglecting their duties by spending their days at the trial, forcing the men "to go with a cold dinner and a late supper or go to the hotel or lunch counter."

The women listened attentively to the opening arguments and testimony as the prosecution's witnesses followed one another to the stand. The young prosecutor, with his spectacles and well-tailored suit, had an erudite presence and the wiry body of an athlete. With careful attention to detail, Clammer elicited testimony about the marriage of John and Margaret Hossack, with its long history of turmoil. Witnesses' accounts of the defendant's fears for the safety of her family were again presented as the strongest evidence of her motive for murder.

On Wednesday, February 18, William Haines took the witness stand. The Winterset newspapers had reported that this Hossack neighbor had been "violently insane," with a long commitment in the state mental institution. Although he had been unable to testify at the first trial, Haines was now ready to talk.

Under questioning from Clammer, Haines told his story, stating that Margaret Hossack had approached him several times with reports of her husband's mistreating his family. Haines remembered that she'd asked him to come to the house to "settle her husband," and once she'd said that she wished he would "finish" him. Haines explained, as he had at the inquest, that he had always refused her requests, saying he didn't want to get involved.

However, Haines's testimony raised questions about his own truthfulness. On the witness stand, he acknowledged that he'd lied to May and Jimmie when they came to his door early Sunday morning and asked him for help. Haines stated under oath that his wife hadn't wanted him to go out that night and so he'd invented the story that he had seen a stranger on his porch and was afraid to leave the house.

Then, under vigorous cross-examination from Senator Berry, Haines disclosed that he and John Hossack had a history of arguments. In fact, Haines admitted, they'd quarreled in public about their opposing political views just a few weeks before the murder. This admission contradicted the testimony that Haines had given a few days after the murder, when he had stated at the inquest, also under oath, that he had not argued with Hossack in nearly ten years. Now Haines remembered the date of their last reported dispute: It had been Election Day in early November 1900, less than five weeks before the murder.

The inconsistencies in Haines's statements brought his credibility into doubt, but with his long history of mental instability, it was certainly possible that he had imagined, or at least misinterpreted, the conversations he reported with Margaret Hossack. In any case, by the time Haines stepped down from the witness stand, it was clear that he was not the star witness for the prosecution that Clammer had anticipated.

That afternoon, George Clammer announced that the prosecution had no more witnesses to call. Margaret Hossack uttered an audible sigh of relief.

The trial had not yet concluded, but many in the audience had made up their minds. As court adjourned for the day, women from the galleries—the trial's most faithful followers—gathered and advanced to the front of the courtroom. They formed a line and stepped forward, in turn, to greet Margaret Hossack at the defense table, taking her rough hands in theirs and offering congratulations.

21.

Mrs. Hossack, as she sits within the enclosure, is the object of much interest and perhaps she and her actions are watched more closely than anything else connected with the trial. The terrible strain of the past two years is plainly visible on her pale and drawn face, furrowed with sorrow and care. Garbed in a plain, dark dress, she maintains a stolid indifference to everyone about her, yet at the same time she is awake to everything that is transpiring and watches in her keen perceiving way every witness who occupies the stand and listens attentively to every word uttered.—*Daily Leader,* February 17, 1903

Mrs. Hossack's attorneys are putting forth every effort in behalf of their client, and in the event that Mrs. Hossack is again found guilty, it will not be because any stone has been left unturned in their attempt to prove her innocence to the jury.—*Des Moines Register,* February 20, 1903

THE SECOND TRIAL of Margaret Hossack lasted four more days. The weather turned clear and mild, perhaps the harbinger of an early spring, which was a welcome sign for the eleven farmers on the jury.

Things also looked good for the defense team. The prosecution had concluded its case leaving the public unconvinced that a conviction would result. Under the headline HOSSACK CASE IS VERY WEAK, on Thursday, February 19, the *Daily News* reported:

The evidence, while it is accumulative, does not seem to have the force it carried when submitted at a

> time the incidents were fresh in the mind of everyone. The witnesses for the state do not seem to be so anxious to testify against Mrs. Hossack and the utmost skill on the part of the state's attorneys has been necessary to get at the seemingly unimportant and certainly now uninteresting details.

In order to refute claims made by the prosecution and raise doubts about the state's case, Senator Berry began his defense of Margaret Hossack by calling many of the same witnesses he'd questioned at the first trial: doctors, neighbors, and the Hossack children. In particular, Berry presented the jury with alternative suspects.

Haines was one possibility; his testimony about his strange behavior on the night of the murder made him appear suspicious. Berry also had a fact, which he had not brought out at the first trial, that suggested that Haines might be involved: The morning after the murder, Johnnie Hossack and Lewis Braucht had spotted footprints in the Hossack orchard, leading away from the house and heading north, directly toward the Haineses' farmhouse.

Berry produced an important new witness, a farmer named G. K. Burson, who lived three miles east of the Hossack farm. Burson told the jury of seeing a mysterious horseman on the night of the murder. The gallery paid particular attention to Burson, leaning forward to listen as he told his story. The man was passing Burson's house, riding away from the Hossack farm, just minutes after Margaret Hossack claimed her husband had been attacked. Burson said he was startled by a noise, which sounded like the "rapid clatter of a horse's hoofs" approaching from the west. Burson rushed out of his house and watched as the horseman crossed a forty-foot wooden bridge and headed up the hill. In the clear moonlight, he got a good look at the horse and rider as they raced past. The rider was a man, short and heavyset, wearing a dirty white hat pulled down over his eyes and a light drab coat. Burson noted that the horse was "blowing from the nostrils and the man was whipping him at every jump."

The prosecution subjected Burson to a spirited cross-examination, attempting to show inconsistencies in his statements while also suggesting that it was a common occurrence for country boys to run horses on that road when returning from town late at night. But the specific rider seen by Burson so soon after the Hossack murder was never identified, and the jury was left to ponder the possibility that the horseman, whoever he was, had been involved in the crime. ☾

ON FRIDAY AFTERNOON, the defense called Margaret Hossack to testify. The courtroom fell silent as she slowly rose from her chair at the defense table and walked haltingly to the witness box. She turned to Judge Nichols and raised her hand to be sworn. Then she sat down and faced the crowd.

Perhaps thinking that a local lawyer would be more persuasive to the jury, Berry had chosen John Guiher, the former Madison County attorney who was assisting with the defense, to question the defendant. The strategy of the questioning was clearly different from that of the first trial, where Margaret Hossack had been asked nothing about her relationship with her husband. She'd not talked about the difficulties of her marriage, or about the reconciliation. Now, given the decision of the Supreme Court, the existence of the reconciliation was much more critical. If the jury was persuaded that the couple had reconciled, then prior conflicts could not be considered as evidence of the defendant's motive. It was important to the defense that Margaret Hossack testify that animosity between her and her husband had ceased in November 1899.

Guiher asked whether she remembered when Fred Johnston and Frank Keller came to her home on the evening following Thanksgiving 1899. She said she did.

"State whether or not at that time it was agreed between you that you would let bygones be bygones; that you would forget the past, and all try to live without trouble in the future."

"Yes sir," she again responded.

Answering mostly in monosyllables and in a voice so low that both the court reporter and Judge Nichols frequently had to ask her to repeat herself, Margaret Hossack stated that there had been no trouble between herself and her husband from that time on. Her husband, she said, had been a good provider for the family, and he treated the children kindly. The family had lived in peace for the twelve months before his death.

Guiher asked her about the night her husband was killed, and Margaret Hossack answered the questions as she had before, at the coroner's inquest just days after the murder and then at the trial the following April. Her story had always been the same, and it was supported by the testimony of her children. Eventually, the lawyer came to his last four questions. To each of these, Margaret Hossack gave a clear and unequivocal response:

"Tell the jury, whether on the night of December 1, 1900, you struck John Hossack with that ax."

"I did not."

"Tell the jury whether you struck him with anything else."

"I did not."

"Tell that jury whether or not you know who struck him."

"I do not."

"Tell that jury whether or not you saw any person strike him."

"I did not."

That evening the headline in the *Daily News* proclaimed AN ACQUITTAL FOR MRS. HOSSACK QUITE LIKELY. Noting that the defendant's testimony was "convincing," the article concluded: "It is the general opinion here that the state has not produced sufficient evidence for conviction. Public sentiment is strong for the defendant and if she is convicted the community will be disappointed." ☾

On Monday afternoon, the lawyers began making their final presentations. Each of the six participating attorneys spoke, with the prosecution and defense taking turns. The final speeches were reserved for the lead attorneys, and it was late Wednesday morning when Senator Berry faced the jury to commence what would be a five-hour argument for acquittal.

As before, he stripped off his coat, loosened his tie, and rolled up his sleeves. Beads of sweat rolled down his cheeks as he strode from one side of the courtroom to the other. Refuting the evidence and conclusions of the prosecutors, he argued passionately for an acquittal as the only verdict that justice would allow. He had no doubts, he said; he believed in his heart—and would say before God—that Margaret Hossack was not guilty of the terrible crime with which she was charged. The jurors watched and listened intently. Many in the crowd wept as they listened to Berry plead for the defendant.

George Clammer's turn came the following day. Outfitted in his well-tailored suit, Clammer was thorough in his presentation, proceeding logically from point to point and buttressing his argument with references to the testimony. There was no other reasonable explanation, he argued, than the obvious one: that Margaret Hossack, after hating her husband for years, had killed him in his sleep.

As at the first trial, the former county attorney relied heavily on his props: the bed and the ax with the bruised handle and dented blade. Once again, Clammer painstakingly went through the evidence: the history of the troubled relations in the Hossacks' marriage, the pleas to the neighbors over the years, the family ax as the presumed murder weapon, the narrowness of the bed, and the defendant's incredible contention that she slept through the attack.

At the end of his argument, Clammer acted out the murder, playing the role of attacker himself. According to newspaper reports, the crowd "was still as death" as they watched his performance. Moving to the side of the bed, Clammer seized the ax. He raised it over his shoulder and brought the shaft down forcefully against the mattress and frame. The bed shuddered and the sound of the ax handle striking the wood echoed from the courtroom walls. Then he stepped back and waited, as if deliberating. Once again, he brought the ax up and struck a thundering blow against the bed frame.

The chief prosecutor then faced the jury and tersely concluded: "The defendant asks you to believe that she was not awakened by the sound of these blows."

When Clammer finished, Judge Nichols read his instructions to the jury. The thirty-three instructions were almost identical to the ones provided by Judge Gamble at the end of the first trial, with one significant difference. Judge Nichols told the jurors that they must decide whether they believed that a successful reconciliation between the Hossacks had been accomplished. If they were so persuaded, then they could not consider the previous quarrels between the defendant and her husband to have provided a motive for committing the crime.

With that point made clear, Judge Nichols turned the jurors over to the bailiff, who led the twelve men to a separate room in the courthouse to begin their deliberations.

Margaret Hossack and her children left the building.

MRS. HOSSACK BROKEN DOWN

Last evening at suppertime, Mrs. Hossack, the defendant, for the first time, broke down and gave way to her feelings. She has through all her terrible troubles maintained a stoic determination to allow nothing to break her down; but at the supper table at her boarding house last evening after she had spent the day listening to the arguments in the case, she burst into tears and was led away without being able to finish her supper. Her children remain with her and loyal to her to comfort her in her trying ordeal.—*Des Moines Daily News*, February 26, 1903

Downtown on the square a small crowd gathered, waiting for a sign that the jury had reached a verdict. Lights burned in the courthouse throughout the night.

The twelve jurors took a vote. Nine were in favor of conviction, with three for acquittal. The majority argued the case for the prosecution, trying to swing the three holdouts to their side. The debate, according to reports, was "long and heated."

After thirty hours of deliberation, the three jurors could not be persuaded to convict Margaret Hossack of murder. They never spoke publicly about their reasoning, but they stood in unwavering opposition to the majority.

On Friday evening, the jury returned to the courtroom, and the foreman informed the judge that it was impossible to reach a verdict. They were unanimous only in their conclusion that further discussion would not result in a decision. Judge Nichols questioned the men himself until he was certain that no agreement was possible. Then he thanked them for their time and discharged them, announcing to the assembled crowd that court was adjourned. ☾

A FEW HOURS LATER, Judge Nichols predicted that the case would not be retried. After two weeks, the Board of Supervisors of Warren County passed a resolution that it would not further aid in the prosecution of Margaret Hossack, stating its desire that the case be dismissed. W. S. Cooper, the Madison County attorney, wrote to the court that he believed Mrs. Hossack was guilty of the crime, but he knew of no person and no additional evidence that could be produced against her, so that the "result of another trial is very doubtful." A year later, Cooper amended that statement, strongly requesting that the case be dismissed, citing the lack of new evidence, the difficulty and cost of getting witnesses to testify yet another time, the publicity surrounding the two earlier trials, and the "advanced years and enfeebled condition and appearance" of Mrs. Hossack. According to his petition, the case against Mrs. Hossack should be dismissed "not because of the innocence of the defendant, but because it will be impossible to secure her conviction."

Margaret Hossack did not go back to court. Her legal ordeal was over. No one else was ever arrested or publicly named as a suspect in the murder of her husband.

The question of her guilt lingered in the community. Most people who believed she was innocent also thought she knew who killed her husband. The most likely theory seemed to be that she was covering up for one of her sons, who had attacked his father out of anger or, perhaps, to protect his mother. That possibility had been rejected or ignored by the investigators, who had never wavered from their view of Margaret Hossack as the main suspect. Over time, people in the community understood that neither she nor other members of her family would say anything more about the case in public, but many of those who thought she was guilty, or more knowledgeable than she would admit, did not view her with animosity. She was not a threat to the community, and she was perceived as a woman who had suffered greatly in her marriage.

A few days after the verdict, the *Daily Capital* published an editorial reflecting on the case, concluding with the words:

> There is a limit to the capabilities of all earthly courts. They may do what they can to bring the guilty to justice, but if the evidence is lacking to conclusively establish guilt, then there the matter must be dropped.

Margaret Hossack knows whether she is guilty of the crime charged against her, either as principal or accessory. Some day, and somewhere, her guilt or innocence will be established.

In the meantime the murder of John Hossack remains unavenged.

22.

"I might have known she needed help! I know how things can be—for women. I tell you, it's queer, Mrs. Peters. We live close together and we live far apart. We all go through the same things—it's all just a different kind of the same thing."—SUSAN GLASPELL, speaking in her role as Mrs. Hale, in the first production of *Trifles*, at the Wharf Theatre, August 8, 1916

IN AUGUST 1916, just seventeen days before the death of Margaret Hossack in Indianola, Iowa, the premiere of a one-act play was presented in a small theater at the end of a wharf in Provincetown, Massachusetts. The play was *Trifles*, and the playwright was Susan Glaspell.

Glaspell's last report on the Hossack case was published in the *Des Moines Daily News* in April 1901, just days after the jury returned its guilty verdict in the first trial. Shortly after Mrs. Hossack's imprisonment, Glaspell resigned her position at the *Daily News* and returned to her parents' house in Davenport. She began to write fiction, and over the next decade she established herself as a novelist and short-story writer. Her first book was a bestseller: *The Glory of the Conquered* told the story of a female artist's journey toward self-discovery through her work rather than through marriage or motherhood. A significant theme of the book, women and the obstacles to their success, was to recur in Glaspell's writing throughout her career.

Glaspell fell in love with George Cram Cook, a Davenport native from a wealthy and well-established family, who was divorced from his first wife and engaged to another woman. Cook, an idealist and intellectual, responded to Glaspell's quick mind and her capacity for serious conversation. Both were interested in liberal ideas: evolution, socialism, censorship, women's rights. Cook, called Jig by his friends, was loquacious and handsome, a dapper dresser who favored corduroy jackets and panama hats and smoked a corncob pipe. He was fond of alcohol and pretty women.

As rumors of a scandalous affair between the two spread through town, Glaspell moved to New York and Cook went ahead with his marriage. Glaspell immersed herself in the bohemian world of Greenwich Village, making friends with a collection of writers and social reformers who espoused progressive views and shared a commitment to social change. Her nascent feminism was awakened by philosophical talks with many of these friends—Ida Rauh, Neith Boyce, Jack Reed, Emma Goldman—on radical subjects such as the oppression of women and the importance of equal rights. A woman, they argued, should be able to vote and to hold public office. A woman should not be forced into the role of wife and mother and should be entitled to seek fulfillment in her work. These ideas were hardly new ones to Glaspell, but now, free from the conservative influences of her hometown, she embraced them openly and with great fervor.

Eventually Cook divorced his second wife and joined Glaspell in New York. On April 14, 1913, the two were married in a private ceremony in New Jersey. Glaspell, who was thirty-seven years old, kept her own name.

Soon after their marriage, the newlyweds retreated to a rented cottage in Provincetown, Massachusetts, to devote themselves to their reading and their work. Glaspell wrote, "Life is beauty and change and interest in a house by the sea." Their small one-story cottage in the old fishing village was near the water and next to a vacant lot overgrown with beach grass. In the mornings Glaspell wrote fiction. Jig converted the sandy lot into a small garden. In the afternoons, the two walked and played on the beach, mingling with fishermen and dogs. Many of their friends from New York visited them at the beach. For Glaspell, raised on the broad prairies of the Midwest, Provincetown seemed idyllic.

The couple continued to spend their summers in Provincetown, which had become a popular summer home for many artists and intellectuals from Greenwich Village. They bought an old clapboard house at 564 Commercial Street, which faced the water. Cook remodeled the house, knocking out downstairs partitions so the rooms would be larger. With dramatic flair, he painted inside and outside so that the house was ablaze in color: window casings were red, interior walls orange and yellow, one floor green, the woodwork black, and the doors purple and blue. Shelves went up to hold their large collection of books. "Two people do not really live together," wrote Glaspell, "until their books become one library." The largest of the upstairs rooms was converted to a bedroom that also served as a workplace for Glaspell. From her writing desk she could see the ocean waves pounding against the long wharves that jutted into the sea.

During the summer of 1916, Jig Cook launched an acting troupe that came to be called the Provincetown Players. The company was an outgrowth of one of Cook's grand ideas: a new kind of American theater, free from commercial restraints. He envisioned a community of like-minded writers and actors, working together to write and produce experimental plays with more meaningful messages than the trivial comedies so popular on Broadway stages. Glaspell supported Cook's endeavor, sharing his view that most contemporary plays were boring and insignificant.

Cook convinced the owner of an unused fish house, located at the end of a long wharf, to give him space to create a small theater. He and his friends set to work, cleaning out the building, constructing simple wooden benches for seating, installing electric lights, and building a small, movable stage that measured ten feet by twelve feet. The space was big enough to seat an audience of ninety. Cook planned to produce a summer season, which would include a short one-act play that he and Glaspell had written together, entitled *Suppressed Desires*—a repartee between a husband and wife on the subject of psychoanalysis. Promising that the season would feature other new and provocative plays, including one still to be written by his wife, Cook managed to sell enough subscriptions to finance the season. ☾

FOR GLASPELL, IT was a "great summer." She met a young aspiring playwright named Eugene O'Neill and introduced him to her circle of fellow artists. Glaspell and O'Neill became close friends, sitting together on the beach for hours and talking with excitement about their work. In the evenings she and Cook hosted dinners and parties, and their house hummed with animated conversation and political debate. Late into the nights, groups from the house wandered to the beach with bottles of wine, built huge bonfires, and continued to talk around the fire in the dark.

On July 13, 1916, the Provincetown Players opened their first official season by presenting three one-act plays, including *Suppressed Desires,* which was performed by Glaspell and Cook. The show was a success, and Cook was wild with enthusiasm and anticipation about the productions to come. The second bill of the summer featured a work written by O'Neill: *Bound East for Cardiff.* It was the first time one of his plays was presented on the American stage.

Now, less than two weeks before rehearsals were to begin, Cook needed the second play from his wife. In her memoir, *The Road to the Temple,* Glaspell recalled their exchange:

"Now, Susan," he said to me, briskly, "I have announced a play of yours for the next bill."

"But I have no play!"

"Then you will have to sit down to-morrow and begin one."

I protested. I did not know how to write a play. I had never "studied it."

"Nonsense," said Jig. "You've got a stage, haven't you?"

Glaspell was eager to please her husband, but she didn't consider herself a playwright. She was nervous about the project, especially knowing that she had to work quickly.

She left her house, crossed the street, and walked the length of the wharf until she got to the side door that opened into the theater. The tide churned noisily under the floorboards. Glaspell sat alone on one of the backless wooden benches and stared at the empty stage.

As she sat there, gazing at the small platform, an image came to her mind. She remembered a cold winter day in December 1900, when she was working as a reporter for the *Daily News* and had traveled from the county seat, Indianola, into the surrounding farmland. She had entered the kitchen of the Hossack farmhouse, a space similar in dimensions to the stage, and was struck by a sense of the woman's absence from the room where she had spent so many hours of her life.

Now, as Glaspell stared at the stage, she saw that dark and lonely place, and as she later said, she could see "where the stove was, the table, and the steps going upstairs." Then she envisioned people entering the room—not the accused woman, but several men, and then, following behind them, two women, hanging back and reluctant to enter.

Glaspell wrote *Trifles* over the next ten days, in the second-floor bedroom of her house on Commercial Street. Slowly the plot evolved. A man has been killed in his bed while he slept, and although no motive is apparent, his wife has been arrested and incarcerated. Three men have come to the woman's kitchen seeking evidence, and two of them have brought their wives to help collect personal items for the accused woman.

Gradually Glaspell began to invent the details of the scene: a soiled roller towel, an old rocking chair, jars of preserves frozen and burst by the winter cold, a half-finished quilt, a broken bird-cage, and a dead canary. When she had difficulty writing, she went back to the theater and sat on the bench, gazing at the small, dark space. All a playwright needs, Jig had told her, is a stage. ☾

TRIFLES FOLLOWS THE investigation of the murder of John Wright. Minnie, his wife of twenty years, has been arrested for the crime. The scene is the Wrights' kitchen, which, according to the stage notes, is a "gloomy" room in a state of disorder. "Unwashed pans under the sink, a loaf of bread outside the bread box, a dish towel on the table" are visible to the audience.

The play begins as a group of five people, the only characters in the drama, enter the room. The sheriff and the young county attorney are visiting the house in their official capacity to search for clues. Mr. Hale (played by Cook) is a neighboring farmer who has come along to tell how he discovered the murder the day before. Mrs. Peters, the sheriff's wife, is with the three men so that she can gather a few clothes for the accused woman, and she has asked Mrs. Hale (played by Glaspell) to accompany her. The women enter the room slowly and stand together near the fire, apart from the three men.

The sheriff and the county attorney take charge at once, and they ask for Mr. Hale's story. He tells them of going to the Wright home on an errand and finding Mrs. Wright in her kitchen, alone. She says that Mr. Wright is dead upstairs, having "died of a rope round his neck." She claims to have been sleeping next to her husband when he was killed. Mr. Hale expresses his doubt that she could have slept through the murder, a suspicion that is shared by the other men. At one point, Mr. Hale starts to talk of difficulties between Mr. and Mrs. Wright, but the county attorney cuts him off, stressing that he wants to focus only on the events of the day before.

The men linger just a few minutes in the kitchen, the place where Minnie Wright spent most of her waking hours. After only a quick look, they criticize her for what they see as deficiencies, with the county attorney noting the dirty towels and messy room as evidence that she lacked the "homemaking instinct." Mrs. Hale defends Minnie, noting how much work there is to be done on a farm, but her comments are ignored. Convinced of the insignificance of "kitchen things," the men laugh at their wives and Minnie for their concern over domestic matters and for their inability to understand anything important. As Mr. Hale says, "Women are used to worrying over trifles."

When the men leave the kitchen to search for clues upstairs, the women remain below and piece together the story behind the murder of John Wright. Evidence that means nothing to the men reveals to the women the hardship and loneliness of Minnie's life. Her old and much mended clothes and the sagging rocking chair remind them that her husband was stingy with money, perhaps the reason Minnie kept so much to herself in recent years. As Mrs. Hale says, "You don't enjoy things when you feel shabby." The house, down in a hollow out of sight of the road, has a desolate feel, and they imagine her passing her days there, without children or friends.

Mrs. Hale knows that John Wright, Minnie's one companion, was "a good man" in the eyes of the community: "He didn't drink and kept his word as well as most . . . and paid his debts." And yet, as Mrs. Hale remembers him, "Just to pass the time of day with him [was like] a raw wind that gets to the bone."

From the unfinished tasks in the kitchen and the irregular stitching on one piece of a quilt, the women understand that Minnie was in a state of particular distress. Then they discover the very evidence for which the men are searching—a clue to what could have triggered a violent reaction from Minnie. They find a broken birdcage that looks as if someone had been rough with it. In Minnie's sewing box, they find the dead body of a songbird, tenderly wrapped in a piece of silk as if in preparation for burial. The songbird's neck has been wrung, the life "choked out of him." Together, with few words spoken between them, the women deduce that John Wright strangled Minnie's bird, her one source of joy.

Throughout the play, Mrs. Hale and Mrs. Peters recognize their own lives in Minnie's. Her domestic world—cooking, sewing, canning fruit, laundering—is completely familiar to them. As they put themselves in her place, they empathize with the feelings of powerlessness and despair that might have led to her act of violence. Mrs. Hale blames herself for her own complicity in her friend's isolation: "Oh, I wish I'd come over here once in a while! That was a crime! Who's going to punish that?"

In the final moments, the voice of the county attorney is heard as the men come down the stairs: "It's all perfectly clear except a reason for doing it. But you know juries when it comes to women. If there was some definite thing. Something to show—something to make a story about—a thing that would connect up with this strange way of doing it. . . ."

At this point, according to the stage direction, "the women's eyes meet for an instant." They have decided to conceal the body of the songbird, knowing it is the evidence the men would use to convict Minnie of murder. Mrs. Peters tries to put the box in her handbag, but it won't fit. Mrs. Hale takes it from her, hiding it in her large coat pocket just as the men enter the room. The final words of the play are Mrs. Hale's. The county attorney asks facetiously how Mrs. Wright planned to finish her quilt: Would she quilt it or would she knot it? Mrs. Hale replies, "We call it—knot it." The line evokes the image of the knot around the dead man's neck, just as it also reinforces the silent but rebellious action of the two women in refusing to recognize the authority of the men. ☾

FIFTEEN YEARS EARLIER, during the course of the two-week murder trial, Susan Glaspell had watched as Margaret Hossack was judged in a courtroom dominated by men. Women were in the audience, though, and, every day, Mrs. Hodson, the sheriff's wife, was by the defendant's side. Mrs. Hodson had cared for Mrs. Hossack in her jail cell and had spent more time with the accused woman than anyone else in the months following her arrest. In court, Mrs. Hodson sat with the Hossack family, and sometimes, during emotional parts of the testimony, she cried.

But Mrs. Hodson's feelings weren't relevant to the case, and neither, it seemed, were the stories of many other women in the community. In both trials, the number of male witnesses, and the time they spent on the stand, was far disproportionate to the actual make-up of the community in which John and Margaret Hossack lived. In the years before the murder, Mrs. Hossack had talked to many of her women neighbors, and they remembered how she'd wept when she mentioned her family troubles and her fears for her children and herself. She had sometimes come to their houses looking for their husbands because it was the men, the friends and peers of John Hossack, whom she asked for help at the times when she was most desperate; they were ones who offered the possibility of coming to her assistance. The women had come to know Margaret Hossack in a different way, and perhaps they could have spoken to her character or shared their sense of the context of her life with her family. But these accounts weren't relevant in the courtrooms. It was the stories of the neighbor men—what they did, what they said, and what they heard—that most interested both the prosecutors and the defense attorneys, and that were heard by the other men, the judges and jury members, who decided Margaret Hossack's fate.

The lengthy testimony of several of the men reveals the frustration they had felt prior to the murder and, on the part of some, annoyance that they had been brought into a family conflict. The reactions from the women are more hidden, in part because they were asked fewer questions. At one point, Mrs. Keller was silenced by Judge Gamble when she haltingly began to speak of her own inaction and feelings of regret: "All you are asked for, Mrs. Keller, is the conversation between you and Mrs. Hossack, not what you thought."

Mrs. Hossack herself didn't have an opportunity to tell her whole story. Her lawyers never asked her about her marriage. Perhaps they expected that she would deny the abuse, as she had done at the inquest. And if she admitted her husband's cruelty? As the prosecution made clear, her suffering would only be used against her—as proof that she had a motive for murder. ☾

Trifles IS NOT A retelling of the story of Margaret Hossack. Many of the details are different, although the setting comes from Glaspell's recollection of the Hossack farm, and the small, dark kitchen is based on her memory of her visit there.

During the time of the trial, Susan Glaspell must have wondered whether Margaret Hossack had killed her husband, but the question of her guilt was not the one that interested Glaspell years later. In the play, Glaspell makes it clear that Minnie Wright committed the crime, and with the discovery of the strangled songbird, the audience learns why. The issues that remain are broader and more complex, and they reflect Glaspell's sense of what was missing in the courtroom in which Margaret Hossack was tried.

Trifles presents contrasting perspectives of the men and the women. The men are incapable of identifying with Minnie Wright. Their limited understanding, along with their preconceived notions about women and their concerns, suggests that the stories they would tell about the accused woman would be incomplete, ignoring the complexities of her life. The narrow focus of their investigation suggests that they will disregard the potential responsibility of others for the circumstances that led Minnie to her violent act.

The women offer a different way of judging. With the benefit of a shared context, they are able to imagine Minnie's experience, and they come to view her with empathy and compassion. Their understanding leads them to difficult questions of blame and culpability. They recognize how marriage to a cruel man eventually destroyed Minnie's spirit and vitality. As Mrs. Hale says after they discover the body of the bird, "No, Wright wouldn't like the bird—a thing that sang. She used to sing. He killed that too." In Mrs. Hale's eyes, the community must also bear some moral responsibility for its failure to come to the aid of Minnie Wright. "I might have known she needed help," she says. ☾

THE FIRST PRODUCTION of *Trifles* was a terrific success. Cook recognized the power of Glaspell's work. At the end of the summer, as he departed by train to return to New York ahead of his wife, he shouted to Glaspell, standing on the station platform, "Write—another—play."

Susan Glaspell took his words to heart. Over the next thirty years, she wrote twelve more plays, including a three-act drama, *Alison's House,* that won the Pulitzer Prize in 1931. She also visited the story of Margaret Hossack one more time, in 1917, when she reworked *Trifles* into a short story. Borrowing a phrase from an article by the early feminist Lucy Stone, who had strongly criticized the jury in the Lizzie Borden case on the basis that it was composed solely of men, Glaspell entitled the story "A Jury of Her Peers."

23.

Telling a story is like reaching into a granary full of wheat and drawing out a handful. There is always more to tell than can be told. As almost any barber can testify, there is also more than needs to be told, and more than anybody wants to hear.—WENDELL BERRY, in *Jayber Crow*

GEORGE CLAMMER NEVER ceased to believe that Margaret Hossack had killed her husband. His failure to secure a conviction in the second trial haunted him for the rest of his life. No one had been punished for the murder of John Hossack.

He gave up his political aspirations and the practice of criminal law. Although he had lived in Iowa all his life, he moved his family to Fort Collins, Colorado, in January 1904 and was admitted to the Colorado bar two months later.

The land around Fort Collins was as level and windswept as the prairies of Iowa; in the distance the peaks of the Rocky Mountains were visible, still snow-covered on summer days. But even in Colorado, George Clammer could not forget the murder of John Hossack. He remembered the violence of the crime, the damage rendered by those two powerful blows, and all the grisly evidence he had pondered for so many months. The memories, his wife confided to others, continued to upset him years after the case was closed.

Clammer built a successful civil law practice in Fort Collins, but after ten years, he moved his family again, this time to Manhattan, Kansas. He went into practice with a local firm. He earned respect as a civic leader, serving as president of the Rotary Club and Chamber of Commerce and on the boards of directors of several local businesses. Clammer devoted his private time to his church, writing, listening to music, and reading Shakespeare.

At his death in 1938 at the age of sixty-four, Clammer was praised as "a truly superior lawyer and a man of unimpeachable character." In his obituary, there was no mention of his early legal experience as a criminal prosecutor. ☾

WILLIAM BERRY FAILED to prove Margaret Hossack's innocence, but his defense and eloquent arguments won her freedom. Never again did Berry have a case that attracted such widespread news coverage, but he stood in the spotlight of public attention for another two decades. In 1907 the governor named Berry to the newly formed Board of Parole, where he was to serve as chairman for eight years. After the death of Justice Charles Bishop of the Supreme Court of Iowa in 1908, Berry was considered the front-runner to fill the seat. Both the Warren County and Madison County bar associations supported Berry's candidacy, though the seat was eventually offered to someone else. In 1912 he was prominently mentioned as a potential candidate for statewide office, and he told a reporter for the *Des Moines Register,* "I do not hesitate to say that I would like to be governor. I expect when the time comes to be in the field for the Republican nomination. . . ."

Despite initial interest in his candidacy, widespread support failed to materialize and Berry withdrew from the race. He never again ran for elective office. He continued his close ties with Simpson College, serving as a trustee until he resigned in 1917. In a private explanation of his resignation, Berry expressed his concern about the college's increasing emphasis on college athletics and fraternities, his fear that they were detrimental to the educational and intellectual goals that should be the school's highest priority. He poured tremendous energy into his work, and his law practice continued to thrive. He lived long enough to witness a landmark change in Warren County when, in September of 1921, Jennie Smith and Una Overton became the first women in the history of the county to be allowed to serve on a jury. They were seated as jurors in a civil case in the same courtroom where Margaret Hossack had been tried two decades earlier.

Berry remained intellectually vigorous and socially active until the end of his life, maintaining a full schedule of legal and political commitments. He went to work on the last day of his life, March 25, 1923, and suffered a major heart attack just as he arrived on the second floor of the Worth Savings Building. He died on the threshold of his office. ☾

NOT SURPRISINGLY, rumors continued to circulate in the county long after the trials of Margaret Hossack had ended. A few people whispered that members of the Hossack family had found a way to bribe enough jurors in Winterset to secure a hung jury. Most people assumed that family members knew more about the murder than they had admitted in court. A rumor started that May Hossack's young husband, Ira Coulter, might have been the one who assaulted John Hossack. William Haines, whose wife later sued him for divorce and charged him with cruelty, remained a suspect in the minds of some. No solid evidence ever surfaced to support any of these theories. The stories, though, passed down from generation to generation.

More than three decades after the crime, a new allegation arose. In 1935, Ray Dickinson, a rural mail carrier, ran an advertisement on the front page of the *New Virginian*, a weekly newspaper distributed in New Virginia and surrounding areas. Upset about a foreclosure hearing the previous year, Dickinson claimed that one of his neighbors, John J. McCuddin, had committed perjury during the proceedings. More provocatively, Dickinson alluded to the strange death of Ed Knotts. Several years before the Hossack murder, McCuddin and his brother, Charles, had twice been tried for killing Knotts, with the second trial ending in acquittal. The case had remained unsolved.

Dickinson's charges enraged McCuddin. A little over a year after the advertisement appeared, McCuddin allegedly threatened Dickinson with a scoop shovel in an alley behind the New Virginia post office. On December 24, 1936, Dickinson published a second advertisement, directly addressed to McCuddin and warning him that the "other ghost that had its head chopped open may wake up and talk to you if you keep on the way that you have been. I want to let you know that I mean business and I don't mean maybe." It was an unambiguous reference to the murder of John Hossack.

McCuddin had heard enough. He filed suit, charging Dickinson with libel and demanding damages. In a written interrogatory before trial, Dickinson was asked, "What did you mean by the statement in reference to a ghost that had its head chopped open?"

Dickinson replied: "By this statement is meant that the plaintiff J. J. McCuddin has knowledge of another homicide."

The case dragged on for several years. Eventually McCuddin was awarded damages of $100, although the decision was later overturned by the Iowa Supreme Court.

The legal authorities did nothing to reopen the Hossack case or formally question Dickinson about what he claimed to know. Most people in the community dismissed the charges as part of a longstanding family feud, but a few wondered whether there might be some truth to Dickinson's allegation.

At the time of the crime, the McCuddins lived just a few miles west of the Hossack farm, and both J. J. McCuddin and his father signed as sureties so that Margaret Hossack could be released from prison on bail in mid-December 1900. The families knew each other, and the McCuddin brothers were about the same age as the older Hossack boys. None of the McCuddins were ever called as witnesses in the legal proceedings relating to the murder of John Hossack. ☾

UPON HIS GRADUATION from Simpson College in June of 1903, Don Berry was hired by the *Des Moines Register.* A year later he left newspaper work to take up farming. His father helped him acquire land, and he farmed for nearly fifteen years. He married Bertha Sloan, a Simpson College classmate, and started a family. As he later wrote, however, "Printer's ink has a terrific pull, once a fellow gets it on his fingers." By 1919 he was back in the newspaper business. For most of the next forty years, he was editor-publisher of the *Indianola Record-Herald.* When his mother, Alice Berry, died in 1928, he and Bertha moved their family into the Berry residence on Ashland Avenue and continued to live there until 1966.

As time passed, Don Berry heard the stories that circulated in the county about the Hossack murder; fact and rumor were mixed, and the community continued to debate the guilt of Margaret Hossack and speculate about the possible involvement of others. Based on his own observations at the trial and a chance encounter with a stranger on a train in the summer of 1901, Don Berry developed a theory of his own.

Near the end of his newspaper career, Berry's interest in the county's history led him into a joint project with Gerald Schultz, the chairman of the sociology department at Simpson College. Together they wrote a history of Warren County, published in 1953. In a chapter titled "Crime and Other Social Problems," Professor Schultz recounted the history of the Hossack murder case, including Margaret Hossack's arrest at the New Virginia Cemetery and the results of the two trials. Don Berry added a footnote, signing it with his initials:

> *Editorial Note:* As a young newspaper reporter I covered the first trial of Margaret Hossack for the *Des Moines Regis-*

> *ter.* While the testimony did not prove her "not guilty," to my mind it fell short of proving her guilty. In the years passed since the trial, evidence has come to me still further casting doubt on her guilt; but I cannot repeat it here without casting a shadow on another party, now dead and against whom the evidence is not conclusive. However, I cannot allow this permanent record to go to press without saying more in defense of the name of Margaret Hossack than simply that the second jury disagreed. I do not believe she was guilty of the murder of her husband. D.L.B.

Interested readers knew that by the time Berry wrote the note, most of the witnesses in the case, including William Haines, and all of the Hossack children except for May Coulter had died. Berry never publicly disclosed the evidence he had received, nor did he indicate the name of the person he believed to be guilty of the murder, but near the end of his life he discussed the case.

In order to give a recounting of the significant events of his life and the history of the Berry family, Don Berry agreed to a series of taped interviews conducted by his son, Thomas. The stories were recorded on reel-to-reel tapes in several sessions. The last recording was made in 1970, when Mr. Berry was almost ninety years old. Near the end of the final audiotape, Thomas asked: "Got any other stories?"

Don replied:

> John Hossack and his wife and children lived about a mile north of the road running from Medora to New Virginia. And John Hossack was murdered one night. His wife woke up in the night and found that he had been hit in the head with an ax . . . and killed right there in bed beside her. The ax was found the next morning under the corncrib and still had some blood on it. The Grand Jury indicted her for murder. My father was the attorney for the defense, defended her.

John Hossack was a good, I guess, straight old chap but he was pretty strict with his children and pretty crochety with his children. . . . I think she could have cleared herself, but I think it would have involved testifying against her own son, and what would any mother do if she told what she knew and her son would hang by the neck until dead. She'd keep still. And Mrs. Hossack kept still. And the general feeling was that she either did it or knew who did it. Well, I think she knew who did it. I don't think there was any question about it. And father tried that case and I covered it. . . . That was the first big case I'd ever covered. I'd covered football before. . . .

She was convicted and sent to the penitentiary. One night I was coming down on the train from Des Moines to Indianola, and the conductor came to me and said there's a lady back here who would like to talk to you. Says she's a sister-in-law of the warden up at Anamosa.

I went back to talk to her and she says, "I'd like to talk to your father but I can't stop." She was going on south on the Q after she got to Indianola. She says, "The warden wants that woman out. He doesn't think she's guilty. He's never had another such a case in his life and he thinks she's absolutely innocent. And he wants your father to get her out of there." . . .

I don't remember just what the grounds of the appeal was. Something in the summation of the evidence. Then it came back and the prosecution asked for a change of venue and the case was taken to Winterset, tried over there, and it resulted in a hung jury. Now that was in 1903 because I remember that after the mail had come in we got a telephone call from Winterset there at the *Register* that said the jury had hung. And I wrote the story. . . .

The Board of Supervisors decided she'd taken a good

deal of punishment and they hadn't proved her guilty, and the county had spent all the money it was going to spend prosecuting her. I don't think the old lady was guilty. I think one of the sons did it.

And that night shortly after the murder—do you remember when you go down to Medora and turn east on the pavement you cross a hollow there in a little ways? Well, that hollow had a long wooden bridge over it and somebody heard a horse go across that bridge in about three jumps and that boy was apparently going back to the farm where he worked and I've heard the report—I don't know this for sure—that the man found his horse sweaty the next morning. So I think the boy killed him because he was a crusty old chap and wouldn't do what his children wanted and she kept still rather than send him to the gallows. Any woman, any mother, would have done the same thing. ☾

MARGARET HOSSACK'S BROTHER, Donald Murchison, died in 1910 in Elmira, Illinois. His obituary obliquely referred to a surviving sister who lived in Iowa, but in subsequent years the Murchison family attempted to expunge the name of Margaret Hossack from its history.

In 1938 a booklet entitled *Elmira Centennial and Scottish Pioneers 1838–1938* was published to celebrate the one-hundred-year anniversary of the founding of Elmira, Illinois. Frances Murchison, the daughter of Margaret Hossack's brother Alexander Jr., wrote the description of the Murchison family's emigration to America and omitted Margaret from the list of Alexander's children:

Alexander Murchison, Sr., who died in 1873 near Elmira, Illinois and Ann, his wife, who died in 1869, also near

> Elmira, came to America from New Kelso, Ross Shire, Loch Carron, Scotland in 1847. They sailed from Glasgow, were nine weeks in crossing, and landed in Quebec. They went up the St. Lawrence, through the Great Lakes to Chicago, by canal to Peru and by team to Elmira. Three children were born to them: Alexander, Jr., Jane (later Mrs. John McRae), and Donald.

Frances Murchison considered herself the keeper of the Murchison family history and took pride in relating anecdotes about her ancestors and their past to her own nieces and nephews. But she told them no stories about her Aunt Margaret, nothing about that aunt's marriage, nothing about the murder of John Hossack, nothing about the sensational trial at which her uncle Donald had testified. ☾

THE HOSSACK FARM, purchased at auction by C. C. Taggart on the steps of the Warren County Courthouse in September of 1901, remained in the Taggart family for more than half a century. Then, in 1953, in an odd twist of circumstance, ownership of the land, and the house in which John Hossack was murdered, returned to a descendant of the Hossacks.

That year LaVere Burchett took possession of the farm. LaVere, an ex-marine who'd just returned from service in the Korean War, was newly married to Marge Morris, whose uncle, Loyd Van Patten, was married to Ethel Henry, a granddaughter of John and Margaret Hossack.

The Burchetts moved into the big, drafty farmhouse. The dwelling had changed very little since the Hossacks first lived in it, and it still lacked modern conveniences: There was no electricity, no insulation, no running water, no indoor plumbing. In winter the house was heated only by an old coal stove.

The Burchetts made regular improvements to the property

over the next fifteen years. Their first renovation was to tear down the partition separating the two small bedrooms on the first floor and combine the spaces. They razed and replaced some of the older outbuildings, the barn and chicken house, and in 1967, tore down the original Hossack farmhouse. The carpenters who dismantled the old house claimed that they saw traces of John Hossack's blood on the bedroom walls and floor. On the site of the original house, the Burchetts built a modern one-story brick and clapboard house.

LaVere Burchett had heard the stories about the Hossack murder and knew that Hossack had been slain in the middle of the night by an unknown assailant. He knew the man's wife had been arrested and tried for the crime. After the Burchetts had lived in the new house for a few years, LaVere awoke in the night and saw the grayish shape of a man standing at the foot of his bed. He sensed that the figure was not human. Although it was silent, it was not threatening. The apparition startled Burchett. Then, a few moments later, it vanished.

Over the years, Burchett was to encounter the form more than a dozen times. He described it as the ghost of John Hossack, and it appeared to him in other parts of the house, including the hallway and the kitchen. Once, he saw it sitting on the edge of the bed. Burchett decided it was a protective presence watching over the household, a spirit that couldn't shake itself loose from the land. ☾

SOON AFTER THE second murder trial concluded, it was as if the strong bond that had been holding the nine Hossack children together finally snapped, freeing them to find their own lives. None of them, it seems, left a written record of their thoughts about the murder for future generations.

Two of the daughters, Cassie and Louie, left Iowa altogether. Cassie married Will Skelly and the couple moved to Utah. Louie and her husband, Joe Kemp, also moved west, choosing Colorado as the place to establish a new life for themselves and their young family. A few years later, in 1909, Louie died of complications of the birth of her fourth child. She was thirty-one years old. Joe Kemp had her body transported to Indianola so that she could be buried in Iowa, and he arranged for the infant, named Margaret Lucretia, after her mother and maternal grandmother, to be cared for by Cassie in Utah. Cassie raised the child and spent the rest of her life in the west, far away from her siblings.

Later Joe Kemp wrote an autobiography that was privately distributed to a few family members, but he had little to say about the murder of his father-in-law, noting only that a few days after Thanksgiving in 1900, his wife's father "was called to his home on High which was a severe and sudden shock to all of us." For Kemp, who had been instrumental in arguing for a change of venue for the second trial, the less said about the event, the better. When his eldest son, John Alger Kemp, who was born in the Hossack farmhouse six days after his grandfather's murder, moved to California as a young man, Joe Kemp advised him that he should never tell anyone that his grandmother had been tried for murder. Still, the story was passed down through the generations of the family. One of Kemp's granddaughters later referred to the murder as a "family secret" and admitted that she was "haunted by the thought of her tainted blood."

Annie Henry and May Coulter stayed in Iowa, close to the land where they'd been born, and both raised large families: seven children for Annie and six for May. Annie, who died in 1932, was plagued by depression and physical infirmities as she aged. Throughout her life, she insisted that her mother was falsely accused of murdering her father.

May suffered in an unhappy marriage. Ira Coulter, possessed of a temperament much like May's father's, was impatient and strict, an angry man with a sharp temper. Eventually, May suffered a nervous breakdown and left him. She lived the rest of her life in Indianola, bitter and unhappy. She was the last of the Hossack children to die, succumbing to heart disease in 1956, at the age of seventy-six.

Will and Johnnie Hossack, the two Hossack boys most often rumored to have been involved in the murder of their father, moved away from Iowa. Both lapsed into mental illness before their deaths.

After the second trial, Will Hossack roomed and worked at the Truitt farm, as his brother Johnnie had done before him. He shared a room with Harold Truitt, Ivan's friend. In an unpublished memoir, Truitt, as an adult, recorded his impression of Will:

> Will Hossack worked for us for two years after the murder, and I believe he was a nervous man after that for a long time. I had to sleep with him when he was with us, and I learned soon after his arrival to arouse him before I got into bed with him, because I almost caught his fist in the middle of my face. I surely hated to sleep with him, but I was afraid to tell the folks, so I lived with my cowardliness in silence.

Truitt later came to believe that Will was involved in the murder.

> Although I don't know about either Will or Mrs. Hossack's abilities to kill someone, I will say that I am pretty sure Mrs. Hossack swung the ax and Will held the lamp for her to swing it by.

By the time Truitt came to this conclusion, Will Hossack had moved to Colorado, where he found work in the mines and lost touch with his family. In his early thirties Will was hospitalized, as his brother John would be, in a mental institution, and in November of 1918, at the age of thirty-six and never having married, he died. The doctor, on the death certificate, noted the cause of his death as "general paralysis of the insane," the third and final stage of syphilis. Will was buried in a pauper's grave near Pueblo, Colorado.

Johnnie, too, moved away from Iowa and seldom communicated with his family. He left his job at the gas company in Des Moines and ventured to the west coast. He married a woman named Jessie and fathered two sons, eventually settling with his family in Rialto, California, and finding work in the oil fields.

Johnnie Hossack died at Patton State Hospital in 1936, a mental institution in San Bernardino, and his death certificate notes the cause of death as cerebral arteriosclerosis, accompanied by psychosis. He was fifty-eight years old, just about the age of his father when the elder Hossack was murdered.

After the second trial, Alex Hossack returned to Palo Alto County. His wife died several years later, leaving him with four young children. He lived an itinerant life, traveling alone across Iowa and into other parts of the Midwest, looking for work and never staying in one place for long. Unable to raise his children on his own, Alex finally left them with his wife's sister.

His wandering sometimes took him to Mitchell, South Dakota, where Ivan had settled. On occasion, Alex walked by his brother's house and talked to Ivan's young daughter when she played in the yard. He visited Ivan at his barbershop downtown, and sometimes Ivan opened the cash register and gave him money. Eventually Alex returned to Iowa, spending the last years of his life in Dubuque, where he died in poverty in 1939.

Jimmie, who had shared a room with Ivan in the old Hossack farmhouse, lived in Indianola for most of his life and worked for the railroad. For a while he lived with his mother in a boardinghouse. He never married or had children, and he had a tendency to be disagreeable and mean-spirited, as had his father. His younger relatives, nieces and nephews, disliked him. Jimmie, like

Alex, stayed in touch with Ivan. Occasionally he would send Ivan a postcard or letter, sometimes enclosing a photograph. Plagued by drinking problems throughout his adult life, Jimmie died in 1945 and was buried beside his sister Louie in the Indianola cemetery. ☾

It was Ivan, the youngest of the Hossack children, who was the most successful in attaining stability and happiness during his life.

A couple of years after the trial in Winterset, Ivan left the Van Pattens and joined the Ringling Brothers Circus, where he learned the trade of barbering. He later moved to Colorado and briefly lived near his brother Will. After serving in the military during World War I, Ivan settled permanently in Mitchell, South Dakota, a small town not unlike Indianola. The landscape of South Dakota was similar to what Ivan was used to in Iowa, the same flat fields and broad, endless prairie. Ivan opened his own barbershop and married. He and his wife, Myrtle, lived modestly, occasionally returning to Indianola to attend reunions at the Van Pattens' farm or to visit Annie, and May, and Jimmie. About his past and whatever painful memories he carried of the breakup of his family, Ivan had little to say. He held on to a few keepsakes, including the quilt his mother had made with his name stitched at the bottom, but he never talked about his youth.

In 1922 Ivan's only child was born, a daughter named Maxine. Ivan proved to be a devoted and protective father. One day, when Maxine was eight or nine years old, Ivan returned from the barbershop and saw her talking to a man outside their house. The man turned and Ivan recognized him at once as his eldest brother.

Alex had not identified himself to the child as her uncle. Ivan spoke angrily to his brother, telling him not to come to the house. It was all right for Alex to visit him at the barbershop, he said, but he didn't want him stopping at his home or talking to his daughter. Maxine didn't remember seeing her uncle again.

Ivan's pleasures were simple. He was well groomed and fastidious about his clothes, taking great pride in his appearance. He polished his shoes frequently and kept them lined up in an orderly row under the family's claw-foot bathtub. Around the time of his birthday in mid-September, he looked forward to the beginning of pheasant-hunting season. Alone or with a friend, Ivan would drive out of Mitchell, his guns loaded into the back of the car. He enjoyed the solitude of waiting in a field, the quiet broken only by the flutter of birds taking to the air and the sharp blasts from the guns that brought them down.

In his barbershop, Ivan got to know the local farmers and merchants, who weren't that much different from the people he had known in Iowa. They came into his shop smelling of sweat and smoke, sat in the elevated seat of the barber's chair, and talked about their lives. Ivan heard the stories of bad marriages and financial troubles and family disputes, and he sometimes interjected a few words here and there or related an anecdote of his own.

In the late 1930s, Ivan took Myrtle and Maxine with him to Iowa, and they visited the home of May and Ira Coulter. It was the first time Maxine, by then a teenager, had met her Coulter cousins. Away from the adults, Maxine sat outside with them and talked about the family. They told Maxine a story about her father's parents. Their grandfather had been killed, hit in the head with an ax in the middle of the night. Maxine's father and four of her aunts and uncles were living in the farmhouse on the night of the crime. A few days later, after the funeral, her grandmother had been arrested at the cemetery and charged with the murder. She was tried at the courthouse in Indianola and sent to prison. Later there was another trial, and then Grandmother Hossack was freed because the second jury couldn't decide on a verdict.

When Maxine asked her mother about the story, Myrtle confirmed that it was true, but said that Ivan had never told her any details. He hadn't wanted his daughter to find out about that time in his life, and it would be best if Maxine didn't let him know what she had heard.

Maxine never raised the subject with her mother again, nor did she tell her friends, but she longed to know more. She now understood that her grandfather's murder was the reason her father had gone to live with the Van Pattens as a young boy.

On only one occasion did Maxine ask her father anything about the murder. She phrased her question carefully so as not to reveal her knowledge: "What did my grandfather die of?"

For years, Ivan had borne the weight of his family's past by choosing to remain silent. Did he now think back to the last hours of John Hossack's life? That gray winter day when he had accompanied his father to the coal bank and the store in Medora? The way the head of the family sat at the kitchen table, eating his dinner and reading the newspaper to his family? Did he recall the game his father played with him and Jimmie before bed? That last evening, as his father read the newspaper, Ivan had gone outside to retrieve Will's coat and put the ax away in case it snowed. Did he remember now—four decades later—whether he'd put the ax in the granary or underneath it?

As a grown man who'd had a lifetime to reflect on it, surely Ivan knew that his testimony in the Winterset courtroom had helped save his mother from prison. In reply to his daughter's question, Ivan Hossack uttered just four words: "He died of meanness."

24.

She was a loving indulgent
mother, a faithful Christian woman . . .
—*Indianola Herald,* August 31, 1916

After the jury in the second trial failed to convict Margaret Hossack, she returned to Warren County and lived there quietly for the last thirteen years of her life.

Although the population of the county declined slightly over the next two decades, the number of people living in Indianola actually increased, reflecting the nationwide trend of migration from the farms to towns. Margaret Hossack and her bachelor son Jimmie resided in a rooming house at 400 Boston Street. Alger and Nancy Truitt, the Hossacks' neighbors from Squaw Township, also relocated to Indianola and lived just a few blocks away. The Truitts had taken in three of the Kemp children after Louie's untimely death, and Margaret sometimes visited her grandchildren. She was quiet as an older woman, neither cheerful nor outgoing; to her grandchildren she seemed cold and withdrawn.

Margaret Hossack witnessed progress and many changes during the years in Indianola. The Indianola Chautaugua Association formed to foster adult education, sponsoring lectures by William Jennings Bryan, Carry Nation, Billy Sunday, and Booker T. Washington. In 1904 a new public library was built with funds provided by Andrew Carnegie. The old courthouse began to deteriorate. The walls cracked and bowed out; keystones above the windows tumbled to the ground. Years later, when repair seemed too costly, the existing structure was demolished and a new one constructed on the same spot. The first motorcar, a Stanley Steamer, appeared on Indianola streets in the early 1900s, forcing horse-drawn vehicles to share the road. As more residents purchased cars, called "stink wagons" by some, citizens began to demand better roads. Telephone service also improved; by 1913 there were more than 1,000 phones in Indianola. With advances in transportation and communication, the rural areas of the county were more closely linked to the county seat.

None of the legal authorities most directly involved in Margaret Hossack's prosecution—George Clammer, Sheriff Lewis Hodson, Dr. Harry Dale—were reelected or served again in official capacities. Grant Kimer, Hodson's popular deputy, was elected sheriff in 1904, and he served ten years in that position. Sheriff Kimer was one of the first residents to buy a car and was often seen proudly riding around town in his Ford sedan. ☾

IN 1910 A CENSUS taker appeared at Margaret Hossack's door. He was taking a survey to determine the population and asked her a number of questions. She revealed little more than the basic facts of her life. She was sixty-seven years old, she said, and she could read and write. She was a renter rather than a homeowner, and her occupation was homemaker, just as it had been all of her life.

Was she married?

Margaret Hossack said only that she was a widow.

The rooming house on Boston Street was located within easy walking distance of downtown Indianola. On Sunday mornings, she passed by the town square and the old courthouse on her way to church. Perhaps she glimpsed the sheriff's residence, where Grant Kimer lived, or the barred windows of the county jail, from which she had peered out at the world on a beautiful Easter Sunday in April 1901.

There is no evidence that Margaret Hossack, at any time after the second trial, ever spoke of her husband's murder. No journals, letters, or diaries have been found in which she recorded her feelings about the trials or her knowledge of the crime.

Margaret Hossack died of natural causes on August 25, 1916, at the age of seventy-two. Dr. Surber, a witness at the inquest and for the prosecution at the first Hossack murder trial, and the doctor who attended her after her release from prison, signed the death certificate, recording the cause of death as "acute dilation of the heart."

Survived by eight of her children and nearly twenty grandchildren, Margaret Hossack outlived her parents, her in-laws, her siblings, her husband, and two of her children. The obituary that appeared in the *Indianola Herald* a week after her death did not mention a central fact of her life: that she had been accused and once convicted of her husband's murder. The short article focused instead on her qualities as a mother and her devotion to her church:

> OBITUARY—MRS. JOHN HOSSACK
>
> Margaret Murchison was born in Ross Shire, Scotland, November 19, 1843, and died at her home in Indianola, Iowa, August 25, 1916. . . .
>
> She was married in Stark County, Illinois, to John Hossack on November 19, 1867 and moved the following spring to a farm near Medora, Warren County, Iowa. Here they resided for many years.
>
> It was during this time she united with the Presbyterian Church in Medora, and in the faith and practices of this church reared her family, which consisted of ten children, eight of whom are living, the father and two children having preceded the mother. She was a loving, indulgent

mother, a faithful Christian woman, loving her church and attentive to its services so far as her health would permit.

The funeral services were held at the home on Sunday morning, conducted by Rev. Benj. F. Tilley, pastor of the First Baptist church, interment at New Virginia, in the family lot.

On a warm Sunday afternoon in late August 1916, Margaret Hossack was laid to rest in the northeast corner of the New Virginia Cemetery, only a short walk from the spot where Sheriff Hodson had arrested her more than fifteen years earlier. At the rise of a small hill, John and Margaret Hossack, husband and wife for thirty-two years, are buried side by side. A simple stone, engraved with their names, marks the site.

NOTES

WE HAVE TRIED to keep these notes informative and concise.

The reader will find that many of our primary sources, especially newspapers, are cited directly in the text. Other specific citations for many of the facts and quotations in this book may be found in Patricia L. Bryan's "Stories in Fiction and in Fact: Susan Glaspell's 'A Jury of Her Peers' and the 1901 Murder Trial of Margaret Hossack," the article from which this book evolved. That article was published at 49 *Stanford Law Review* 1293 (1997).

Chapters describing events at the Hossack farm, the coroner's inquest, and the trials of Margaret Hossack are based on contemporary newspaper accounts and legal documents, including the Transcript of the Coroner's Inquest into the Death of John Hossack, December 3–5, 1900; the Transcript of the Warren County Grand Jury Hearing, January 1901; the Briefs, Arguments and Abstracts of Record, *State* v. *Hossack*, 89 N.W. 1077 (Iowa 1902). Quotations from family members, neighbors, investigators, lawyers, and witnesses are taken from these documents or from quoted statements in newspaper reports. Many of the legal documents, including probate records, are located in the Warren County Courthouse in Indianola, Iowa, and the Madison County Clerk of Court's Office in Winterset, Iowa. Some anecdotal details were gleaned from interviews and unpublished memoirs or letters. An official description of the crime is included in the Iowa Supreme Court's decision ordering a new trial for Margaret Hossack: *State* v. *Hossack*, 89 N.W. 1077 (Iowa 1902).

The arrest of Margaret Hossack at the New Virginia Cemetery, depicted in chapter four, is based largely on an article in the *Des Moines Daily Capital* of December 6, 1900.

The most complete description of the murder of Augusta Cading and lynching of Reuben Proctor appears in *The History of Warren County, Iowa* (1879). Several Iowa newspapers covered the murder trial of Sarah Kuhn; we relied mostly on the stories in the *Des Moines Daily Capital* and the *Des Moines Daily News,* which appeared from December 7, 1900, through January 12, 1901. The Lizzie Borden case has been written about extensively; in particular, we recommend Robert Sullivan's fine account, *Goodbye Lizzie Borden.* Other references to incidents in Iowa history come from the published histories of Iowa, the local newspapers, or other sources listed below.

Information about the lives and careers of William H. Berry and George Clammer was drawn from a number of sources, including interviews with their descendants; Iowa State Bar Association publications; histories of Warren County; local newspapers, including the *Indianola Herald,* the *Indianola Advocate-Tribune,* and the *Simpsonian;* Simpson College yearbooks; articles in *The Palimpsest* and the *Annals of Iowa*; and the papers of Don L. Berry, which are archived at Simpson College. The obituary of George Clammer appeared in the *Manhattan Mercury* on August 15, 1938.

Chapter nine is based on interviews with descendants of the Murchison family, legal documents, and published works, listed below, describing rural life in the Midwest in the late 1800s. Readers who wish a more complete account of Emily Gillespie's life and diaries will be richly rewarded by reading *A Secret to be Burried: The Diary and Life of Emily Hawley Gillespie, 1858–1888,* by Judy Nolte Lensink. Entries from Gillespie's diaries that appear in our book have been excerpted from that excellent source. The quotation in chapter eight from *Godeys Lady's Book* comes from Lensink, and quotations relating to the experience of rural women in chapter nine are from Faragher, Hedges, Jeffrey, and Lensink. We found references to the Department of Agriculture Reports in

Lensink's book; our quotations, however, come from the reports themselves.

The Anamosa State Penitentiary deserves a book of its own. The facility is on the National Register of Historic Landmarks and operates today as Iowa's largest men's prison, housing over 1,200 convicted felons. The story of Margaret Hossack's year at the penitentiary is based on prison documents, newspaper articles, interviews with current employees, and a fascinating Web site maintained by Steve Wendl at www.asphistory.com. Various facts about the prison population appeared in the Third Biennial Report of the Board of Control of State Institutions of Iowa. Facts about John Wesley Ekins, his crime and his eventual parole and pardon, can be found in articles on the Anamosa Web site and in many newspaper articles from 1889 to 1902, including ones from the *Des Moines Daily Capital* and the *Des Moines Daily News.* Relics and exhibits from the prison's history are displayed in the Anamosa State Penitentiary Museum, located on the prison grounds.

Chapter twenty-two, recounting the story of Susan Glaspell in Provincetown, is drawn largely from Glaspell's book *The Road to the Temple.* Several biographies of Glaspell also helped us to reconstruct her life and her experiences. We read numerous scholarly articles on Glaspell and her work, and several of them were especially beneficial to us, including *A Jury of Her Peers: The Importance of* Trifles, by Karen Alkalay-Gut; *"Murder She Wrote": The Genesis of Susan Glaspell's* Trifles, by Linda Ben-Zvi; and *Small Things Reconsidered: Susan Glaspell's "A Jury of Her Peers,"* by Elaine Hedges.

To understand the history of Warren County and appreciate the social context in which these events took place, we have relied on several published histories of the region, especially *History of Warren County*, by Reverend W. C. Martin (1908); *History of Warren County, Iowa*, by Gerald Schultz and Don L. Berry (1953);

and Professor Joseph Walt's history of Simpson College, *Beneath the Whispering Maples.* In addition, we benefited from Professor Walt's series of articles on the history of the county, published in the *Record-Herald and Indianola Tribune* in 1999 prior to the town's sesquicentennial.

SELECTED BIBLIOGRAPHY

Newspaper Sources

We relied extensively on local newspapers for information about the crime and the proceedings that followed, as well as for descriptions of scenes, people, and events. These newspapers include the *Des Moines Daily News, Des Moines Daily Capital, Des Moines Daily Leader, Iowa State Register* (later renamed *Des Moines Register*), *Indianola Advocate-Tribune, Indianola Herald, Indianola Record, Winterset Madisonian,* and *Winterset Reporter* (later renamed *Madison County Reporter*).

Although none of the stories on the Hossack case published in the *Daily News* between December 1900 and April 1901 contains a byline, we have accepted, and agree with, the conclusion of Susan Glaspell's biographers that she is the author of these articles. The stories in the *Daily News* attributed to Glaspell include:

"Prominent Farmer Robbed and Killed," December 3, 1900
"Surrounded by Mystery," December 4, 1900
"Sheriff After Mrs. Hossack," December 5, 1900
"She Prepares to Fight," December 6, 1900
"Preliminary Hearing in the Hossack Case," December 8, 1900
"Goes to the Grand Jury," December 8, 1900
"It Is Still Unsettled," December 10, 1900
"Now Before Grand Jury," December 11, 1900
"Mrs. Hossack May Yet Be Proven Innocent," December 12, 1900
"Mrs. Hossack May Come Here," January 14, 1901
"Indicted Her for Murder," January 17, 1901
"Trial Comes in March," February 27, 1901
"Surprise Is Expected," March 23, 1901
"Hossack Trial on in Earnest," April 2, 1901
"Hossack Begged Wife to Aid Him," April 3, 1901
"Experts Say It Is Human Blood," April 4, 1901
"Looks Bad for Mrs. Hossack," April 5, 1901

"Testify for Mrs. Hossack," April 6, 1901
"Arguing the Hossack Case," April 8, 1901
"Allege Haines Was Murderer," April 9, 1901
"Her Dreary Easter Day," April 9, 1901
"Mrs. Hossack's Fearful Ordeal," April 10, 1901
"Mrs. Hossack a Murderess," April 11, 1901
"Mrs. Hossack's Parting Plea," April 19, 1901

Works by Susan Glaspell

Unfortunately, some of Glaspell's books and plays are out of print, although interest in her work has increased dramatically over the last twenty years. Glaspell's "A Jury of Her Peers" appears in both *Best American Short Stories of the Century* (2001), edited by John Updike, and *Best American Mystery Stories of the Century* (2001), edited by Tony Hillerman. It is the only story selected for inclusion in both volumes. The play *Trifles* can be found in many anthologies, as can *Alison's House*, for which Glaspell was awarded the Pulitzer Prize for Drama in 1931. Citations to these anthologies, as well as to Glaspell's works, productions and reviews of her plays, and many secondary sources (through 1993), may be found in Mary Papke's excellent reference book: *Susan Glaspell: A Research and Production Sourcebook* (1993). An outstanding film version of "A Jury of Her Peers," produced, directed, and edited by Sally Heckel (Texture Films), was nominated for an Academy Award in 1981.

Biographical Information about Susan Glaspell

Ben-Zvi, Linda. *Susan Glaspell: Her Life and Times.* New York and London: Oxford University Press, 2005.

Glaspell, Susan. *The Road to the Temple.* London: Ernest Benn, Limited, 1927; New York: Frederick A. Stokes Company, 1941 (republished with a new foreword).

Makowsky, Veronica. *Susan Glaspell's Century of American Women: A Critical Interpretation of Her Work.* New York and London: Oxford University Press, 1993.

Noe, Marsha. *Susan Glaspell: Voice from the Heartland.* Macomb: Western Illinois University Press, 1983.

Ozieblo, Barbara. *Susan Glaspell: A Critical Biography.* Chapel Hill: University of North Carolina Press, 2000.

Papke, Mary. *Susan Glaspell: A Research and Production Sourcebook.* Westport, Conn.: Greenwood Group, 1993.

Waterman, Arthur. *Susan Glaspell.* New York: Twayne Publishers, 1966.

Other Published Sources

Alkalay-Gut, Karen. "A Jury of Her Peers: The Importance of *Trifles.*" *Studies in Short Fiction* 21 (1984).

Ambrose, Stephen E. *Undaunted Courage: Merriwether Lewis, Thomas Jefferson and the Opening of the American West.* New York: Simon & Schuster, 1996.

Ben-Zvi, Linda. "'Murder, She Wrote': The Genesis of *Trifles.*" *Theatre Journal* 44 (1992).

———, ed. *Susan Glaspell: Essays on Her Theatre and Fiction.* Ann Arbor: University of Michigan Press, 1995.

Berry, Wendell. *Jayber Crow.* Washington, D.C.: Counterpoint Press, 2000.

Bogue, Allan G. *From Prairie to Corn Belt: Farming on the Illinois and Iowa Prairies in the Nineteenth Century.* Chicago and London: University of Chicago Press, 1963.

Bryan, Patricia L. "Stories in Fiction and in Fact: Susan Glaspell's 'A Jury of Her Peers' and the 1901 Murder Trial of Margaret Hossack." *Stanford Law Review* 49 (1997) 1293.

Darrow, Clarence. "Attorney for the Defense." *Esquire: The Best of Forty Years.* Compiled by the editors of *Esquire.* New York: David McKay Company, 1973.

Degler, Carl N. *At Odds: Women and the Family in America from the Revolution to the Present.* New York and Oxford: Oxford University Press, 1980.

Denno, Deborah W. "Gender, Crime, and the Criminal Law Defenses." *Journal of Criminal Law & Criminology* 85 (1994).

Faragher, John Mack. *Women and Men on the Overland Trail.* New Haven and London: Yale University Press, 1979.

Flexner, Eleanor. *Century of Struggle: The Women's Rights Movement in the United States.* New York: Atheneum, 1972.

Fox, Marie. "Crime and Punishment: Representations of Female Killers in Law and Literature." *Tall Stories? Reading Law and Literature.* John Morrison & Christine Bell, eds. Aldershot, England, and Brookfield, Vermont: Dartmouth Publishing, 1996.

Friedricks, William B. *Covering Iowa: The History of the Des Moines Register and Tribune Company, 1849–1985*. Ames: Iowa State University Press, 2000.

Hartog, Hendrick. *Man and Wife in America: A History*. Cambridge: Harvard University Press, 2000.

Hedges, Elaine. "Small Things Reconsidered: Susan Glaspell's 'A Jury of Her Peers.'" *Women's Studies* 12 (1986) 90.

The History of Warren County, Iowa. Des Moines, Iowa: Union Historical Company, 1879.

Jeffrey, Julie Roy. *Frontier Women: "Civilizing" the West? 1840–1880. (Revised Edition)*. New York: Hill and Wang, 1998.

Jones, Ann. *Women Who Kill*. New York: Random House, 1981.

Juster, Norton. *So Sweet to Labor: Rural Women in America, 1865–1895*. New York: Viking Press, 1979.

Kerber, Linda. *No Constitutional Right to Be Ladies: Women and the Obligations of Citizenship*. New York: Hill and Wang, 1998.

Lensink, Judy Nolte. *"A Secret to be Burried": The Diary and Life of Emily Hawley Gillespie, 1858–1888*. Iowa City: University of Iowa Press, 1989.

Martin, Reverend W. C. *History of Warren County: From Its Earliest Settlement to 1908*. Chicago: S. J. Clarke Publishing Company, 1908.

McDonald, Julie. *Ruth Buxton Sayre: First Lady of the Farms*. Ames: Iowa State University Press, 1980.

Mintz, Steven, and Susan Kellogg. *Domestic Revolutions: A Social History of American Family Life*. New York: Free Press, 1988.

Motz, Marilyn Ferris. *True Sisterhood: Michigan Women and Their Kin, 1820–1920*. Albany: State University of New York Press, 1983.

Myres, Sandra L. *Westering Women and the Frontier Experience, 1800–1915*. Albuquerque: University of New Mexico Press, 1982.

Norris, Kathleen. *Dakota: A Spiritual Geography*. New York: Houghton-Mifflin Company, 1993.

Noun, Louise R. *Strong-Minded Women*. Ames: Iowa State University Press, 1969.

The Palimpsest. Iowa City: State Historical Society of Iowa, November 1963.

Pleck, Elizabeth. *Domestic Tyranny: The Making of Social Policy Against*

Family Violence From Colonial Times to the Present. New York and Oxford: Oxford University Press, 1987.

Report of the Commissioner of Agriculture for the Year 1862. Washington, D.C.: U.S. Government Printing Office, 1863.

Riley, Glenda. *Frontierswomen: The Iowa Experience.* Ames: Iowa State University Press, 1981.

———. *Prairie Voices: Iowa's Pioneering Women.* Ames: Iowa State University Press, 1996.

Robertson, Cara W. "Representing 'Miss Lizzie': Cultural Convictions in the Trial of Lizzie Borden." *Yale Journal of Law & the Humanities* (1996) 351.

Royce, Sarah. *A Frontier Lady: Recollections of the Gold Rush and Early California.* Lincoln: University of Nebraska Press, 1977.

Rutland, Robert A. *The Newsmongers: Journalism in the Life of the Nation, 1690–1972.* New York: Dial Press, 1973.

Schultz, Gerald, and Don L. Berry. *History of Warren County, Iowa.* Indianola, Iowa: Record and Tribune Company, 1953.

Schweider, Dorothy. *Iowa: The Middle Land.* Ames: Iowa State University Press, 1996.

———. *Patterns and Perspectives in Iowa History.* Ames: Iowa State University Press, 1973.

Schweider, Dorothy, Thomas Morain, and Lynn Nielsen. *Iowa Past to Present: The People and the Prairie.* Third Ed. Ames: Iowa State University, 2002.

Stone, Lucy. "A Flaw in the Legal System." *The Women's Journal,* June 17, 1893.

Strasser, Susan. *Never Done: A History of American Housework.* New York: Pantheon Books, 1982.

Stratton, Joanna L. *Pioneer Women: Voices from the Kansas Frontier.* New York: Simon & Schuster, 1981.

Sullivan, Robert. *Goodbye Lizzie Borden.* Brattleboro, Vermont: Stephen Greene Press, 1974.

Third Biennial Report of the Board of Control of State Institutions of Iowa. Des Moines: Bernard Murphy, State Printer, 1903.

Trillin, Calvin. *Killings.* New York: Ticknor and Fields, 1984.

Trueblood, Elton. *While It Is Day: An Autobiography.* New York: Harper and Row, 1974.

Tucher, Andie. *Froth and Scum: Truth, Beauty, Goodness, and the Ax Murder in America's First Mass Medium.* Chapel Hill: University of North Carolina Press, 1994.

Wall, Joseph Frazier. *Iowa: A Bicentennial History.* New York: W. W. Norton & Company, 1978.

Walt, Joseph W. *Beneath the Whispering Maples: The History of Simpson College.* Indianola, Iowa: Simpson College Press, 1995.

Ward, Geoffrey C., and Ken Burns. *Not for Ourselves Alone: The Story of Elizabeth Cady Stanton and Susan B. Anthony.* New York: Alfred A. Knopf, 1999.

Waterman, Angie G. "Prison Work Among Women: Can They Be Reformed?" *Bulletin of Iowa Institutions,* vol. 3. Des Moines: Welch Printing Company, 1901, pages 290–293.

Unpublished Sources

Berry, Don L. Interview conducted by Thomas Sloan Berry. Audiotape. Circa 1970.

———. Papers. [Series 8/6/0/6] Simpson College: Indianola, Iowa. Archives.

D'Amico, Diane. "Susan Glaspell's *Trifles* and the Hossack Murder Trial." Manuscript in the authors' collection. 1992.

Kemp, Joseph L. "Summary or Resume of the Checkered Career of Joe L. Kemp." Memoir.

Truitt, A. Harold. "Iowa and Wisconsin by Way of Prairie Schooner from Kansas." Indianola, Iowa, Public Library.

Tupper, Kari Lynn. "Alternative Justice: Susan Glaspell's Literary Reconstruction of Confession, Motivation and Causation." In "Women and Crime: Desire, Transgression and Confession in American Law and Literature," Ph.D. diss., University of Michigan, 1997.

Walt, Joseph W. "How to Become a Patriarch Without Really Trying: The Story of Don Berry, Iowan." Paper delivered before the Prairie Club, Des Moines, Iowa, November 1970.

ACKNOWLEDGMENTS

WE OWE SINCERE thanks to Judith Wegner, professor and former dean at the University of North Carolina School of Law, who encouraged the idea of this book from the beginning; Gene Nichol, professor and current dean at the University of North Carolina School of Law, who has been steadfast in his support; and the North Carolina Law Center Foundation, which provided a part of the funding for Patricia's work. We are also particularly grateful to Duncan Murrell, former editor at Algonquin Books, for his confidence in the material and his many suggestions that set us in the right direction; Don Knefel and Walter Bennett, for helping us figure out the best way to tell this story; Milton Clark, for his perceptive comments on the penultimate draft of this book; and N. William Hines, professor and former dean at the University of Iowa College of Law, for providing us with the opportunity to return to Iowa to live and work for a semester.

For assistance in our research into local history, we are indebted to the Warren County Historical Society and its many devoted volunteers, especially Edith Conn and Thelma Pehrson. Our understanding of Warren County, past and present, was enriched by the work of Professor Joseph Walt and Marty Ford. Thanks also to Suzanne Null of the Madison County Clerk's Office, who led us to the most significant legal records; Jason Clayworth, who helped publicize our search; James Fowler, Robert Leudeman, and Rod Powell, who answered questions about Iowa law and lawyers; and Stephen Hall, who was knowledgeable on every subject we discussed with him.

We appreciated stories and information from past and present residents of Warren and Madison Counties, including those who responded to our advertisement, "Who Killed John Hossack?" that appeared in the *Record-Herald and Indianola Tribune* in 1998. Robert Moore was especially helpful to us, as was Lonnie Baughman, who put us in contact with his mother, Rosa Baughman. Born in 1905, Rosa Baughman had heard about the murder from her father, George McIntosh, one of the first neighbors to arrive at the Hossack farm on the night of the assault. She later took her own children to the New Virginia Cemetery to see the Hossack graves, and she recalled for us what her parents had told her about the bloody scene in the farmhouse on the night of the murder and the discovery of the ax under the granary.

For research related to Anamosa State Penitentiary, we are deeply grateful to Richard Snavely and Steve Wendl, who have organized an incredible collection of information and artifacts relating to the Penitentiary, and who led us on an eye-opening tour of the inside of the facility.

We received invaluable assistance from many librarians in Iowa and elsewhere, including Cynthia Dyer at Dunn Library, Simpson College; Robyn Copeland, also at Dunn Library; Linda Brown-Link and Nancy Kraft at the State Historical Society of Iowa in Iowa City; Sharon Avery at the State Historical Society of Iowa in Des Moines; Linda Robertson at the State Library of Iowa; Mary Anne Knefel at the University of Dubuque; and staff members at the Indianola and New Virginia Public Libraries as well as at the libraries of the University of Iowa and the University of North Carolina.

A number of talented researchers, most of them law students, have helped us immensely over the years, including Lance Koonce, who undertook a thousand-mile journey to Iowa in the summer of 1994 to search for legal records; and Ann Hopkins Avery, David Bright, Susan Campbell, Suzanne Collins, Laura Devan, Todd Eveson, Eric Gordon, Jennifer Green, Heather

Lindamood, Beverly Pearman, Chad Peterson, Jennifer Williston, and David Winchell. We appreciated the technical assistance of Andy Church, who transferred the Don Berry interview from audiotape to compact disc.

For more than a decade, students in Patricia's seminars on Law and Literature have discussed the Hossack case in relation to "A Jury of Her Peers," and their spirited debates have made this a better book.

Many scholars and colleagues contributed to this project, and we are especially grateful to Linda Kerber, who first mentioned the Hossack case in connection with Susan Glaspell's work. We benefited from the work and collegiality of numerous Glaspell scholars, particularly Marina Angel, Linda Ben-Zvi, Diane D'Amico, Marcia Noe, and Kari Lynn Tupper. Others who commented on early drafts or supported us with their friendship include Barbara Babcock, Ted Ballou, Jack Boger, Lissa Broome, Deidre Barnes, Ken Broun, Todd Canon, Marion Crain, Glenn George, Elizabeth Gibson, Brian Ingram, Joe Kennedy, Sherryl Kleinman, Eric Muller, Sid Nathans, John Orth, Rich Rosen, Des Runyan, Nick Sexton, Dave Shaw, Ross Terman, Susan Tifft, Deborah Weissman, Sharon Williams, and Larry Zelenak. We owe special thanks to Carol Ballou, Julie Bosworth, John Bryan, and Carol Runyan, who offered valuable reactions and constant encouragement; and to Doris Bryan, who also tendered many excellent copyediting suggestions that improved every draft of this book.

We were fortunate to have the assistance of two fine editors after Duncan Murrell left Algonquin Books. We are grateful to Greg Michalson, whose sound judgment and sensitivity to the time and place of the story contributed greatly to the manuscript, and to Andra Olenik, who guided us through the final stages with her thoughtful and perceptive advice. We appreciate the assistance and support of our agent, Gary Morris at the David

Black Agency, who saw the potential in this story while we were still grappling with the best way to write it. It was a pleasure to work with Judit Bodnar, who did a meticulous job as our copy-editor.

We owe an immeasurable debt of gratitude to members of the Hossack, Murchison, Berry, and Clammer families, whose ancestors are at the heart of our work. Many of them invited us into their homes and shared their memories, ideas, and research. We especially appreciated the help of Bill Berry, who sent us photographs as well as the audiotape of his grandfather, Don Berry, talking about the Hossack case.

And finally, we wish to acknowledge our three sons, John, Michael, and David, who have grown up knowing about our work on this book, and who have always taken an unabashed interest in the story. We've valued their thoughtful, and often unique, opinions and theories about who killed John Hossack and why.